The Curse of Agade

Jerrold S. Cooper is professor of Near Eastern studies at The Johns Hopkins University and associate editor of the *Journal of Cuneiform Studies.* He is also author of *The Return of Ninurta to Nippur: an-gim dím-ma* and *Reconstructing History from Ancient Inscriptions: The Lagash-Umma Border Conflict.*

THE JOHNS HOPKINS NEAR EASTERN STUDIES

Hans Goedicke, General Editor

Hans Goedicke, *The Report about the Dispute of a Man with His* Ba
J.J.M. Roberts, *The Earliest Semitic Pantheon*
John D. Schmidt, *Ramesses II: A Chronological Structure for His Reign*
David Lorton, *The Juridical Terminology of International Relations in Egyptian Texts through Dyn. XVIII*
Bernard Frank Batto, *Studies on Women at Mari*
Hans Goedicke, *The Report of Wenamun*
Hans Goedicke and J.J.M. Roberts (eds.), *Unity and Diversity: Essays in the History, Literature, and Religion of the Ancient Near East*
Patrick Miller, Jr., and J.J.M. Roberts, *The Hand of the Lord: A Reassessment of the "Ark Narrative" of 1 Samuel*
Thomas W. Mann, *Divine Presence and Guidance in Israelite Traditions: The Typology of Exaltation*
Hans Goedicke, *The Protocol of Neferyt*
Jack M. Sasson, *Ruth: A New Translation with a Philological Commentary and a Formalist-Folklorist Interpretation*
Michael Barré, *The God-List in the Treaty between Hannibal and Philip V of Macedonia: A Study in Light of the Ancient Near Eastern Treaty Tradition*
Jerrold S. Cooper, *The Curse of Agade*
James M. Lindenberger, *The Aramaic Proverbs of Ahiqar*

The Curse of Agade

Jerrold S. Cooper

The Johns Hopkins University Press
Baltimore and London

The Johns Hopkins University Press, Baltimore, Maryland 21218
The Johns Hopkins Press Ltd, London

Library of Congress Cataloging in Publication Data

Cooper, Jerrold S.
The Curse of Agade.

(The Johns Hopkins Near Eastern studies)
Includes bibliographical references and indexes.
1. Curse of Agade. 2. Babylonia—History—Poetry.
I. Title. II. Series.
PJ4065.C6 1983 899′.95 82-14885
ISBN 0-8018-2846-5

To the scholars whose fundamental studies made this edition possible

S. N. Kramer
for his eighty-fifth birthday

H. G. Güterbock
for his seventy-fifth birthday

A. Falkenstein
in memoriam

CONTENTS

PREFACE

When studying the *Curse of Agade* during the writing of "Sumerian and Akkadian in Sumer and Akkad" (Or 42, 239ff.), it became clear to me that despite Falkenstein's masterly edition in ZA 57, the large number of unpublished manuscripts of that composition made a new edition imperative. I began collecting the manuscripts in 1974 and began work in earnest on the composition two years later. The final version of this manuscript was completed by the end of 1980, and very little has been added since then.

Among the many colleagues who encouraged and supported me in this work, two must be singled out for special thanks. Miguel Civil supplied me with his preliminary catalogue of Sumerian literary texts, and this formed the basis of my list of manuscripts. The great majority of these manuscripts are in the University Museum, and there Åke Sjöberg was an unending source of hospitality and logistical support and, in addition, made available to me the files and manuscripts of the Pennsylvania Sumerian Dictionary. Others who provided texts, collations, photos, comments, suggestions, and hospitality are B. Alster, J. Bottéro, J. Van Dijk, V. Donbaz, J.-M. Durand, R. Falkowitz, P. Gerardi, J.-J. Glassner, W. Hallo, J. Heimerdinger, T. Jacobsen, D. Kennedy, S. N. Kramer, M. Lambert, B. Leicknam, P. Michalowski, J. Oelsner, A. Shaffer, H. Vanstiphout, C. Walker, A. Westenholz, and C. Wilcke. I am grateful to them all.

The authorities of the following institutions and expeditions have kindly given permission to publish material from their collections: Andrews University Museum, Baghdad School Committee of the American Schools of Oriental Research, British Museum, Deutsche Forschungsgemeinschaft and Bavarian Academy of Sciences Expedition to Isin, Istanbul Archaeological Museum, Musée du Louvre, Oriental Institute, University Museum and the Yale Babylonian Collection.

Collation of tablets in museums abroad was made possible by a grant from the American Philosophical Society. The Johns Hopkins University has supplied both travel funds and clerical assistance, as well as a superb research environment. The university's Department of Near Eastern Studies and Faculty of Arts and Sciences made a generous subsidy available to offset publication costs.

A final word of thanks to Hans Goedicke, for offering to include my work in the Johns Hopkins Near Eastern Studies series; to Jane Dreyer, for her assistance in manuscript preparation, to John Mitchell for help correcting proofs and indexing; to David Lorton and Joanne Hildebrandt for their typographic skills; and to Bill Sisler, Jane Warth, and Jim Johnston of The Johns Hopkins University Press.

The Curse of Agade

BIBLIOGRAPHIC ABBREVIATIONS

All abbreviations used are those of the *Chicago Assyrian Dictionary*, with the following exceptions and additions:

Alster Shuruppak	B. Alster, *The Instructions of Šuruppak*
Alster Studies	B. Alster, *Studies in Sumerian Proverbs*
ANET[3]	J. Pritchard, *Ancient Near Eastern Texts* (3rd edition)
ASJ	*Acta Sumerologica*
Bauer Wirtschaftsurkunden	J. Bauer, *Altsumerische Wirtschaftsurkunden aus Lagasch* (St Po 9)
Bi Mes	*Bibliotheca Mesopotamica*
Buccellati Amorites	G. Buccellati, *The Amorites of the Ur III Period*
BWL	W. Lambert, *Babylonian Wisdom Literature*
CAH	*The Cambridge Ancient History*
Castellino Shulgi	G. Castellino, *Two Šulgi Hymns*
Cohen Enmerkar	S. Cohen, *Enmerkar and the Lord of Aratta* (Univ. of Pennsylvania diss.)
Deimel SF	A. Deimel, *Ṣchultexte aus Fara* (WVDOG 43)
Durand	J.-M. Durand, report in *Annuaire de l'école pratique des hautes études,* IVe section, 1974/75
Edzard Rechtsurkunden	D. Edzard, *Sumerische Rechtsurkunden des III. Jahrtausends*
ELA	*Enmerkar and the Lord of Aratta* (see Cohen Enmerkar)
Erra	L. Cagni, *L'epopea di Erra*
Essays Finkelstein	*Essays on the Ancient Near East in Memory of J. J. Finkelstein*
EWO	*Enki and the World Order* (line numbering as C. Benito, *"Enki and Ninmaḫ"* and *"Enki and the World Order"* [Univ. of Pennsylvania diss.])
Falkenstein	A. Falkenstein, "Fluch über Agade" (ZA 57 43ff.)
Farber-Flügge Inanna	G. Farber-Flügge, *Der Mythos "Inanna und Enki"* (St Po 10)
GEN	A. Shaffer, *Gilgamesh, Enkidu and the Netherworld* (Univ. of Pennsylvania diss.)

Grayson ABC	A. K. Grayson, *Assyrian and Babylonian Chronicles* (TCS 5)
Green Eridu	M. Green *Eridu in Sumerian Literature* (Univ. of Chicago diss.)
Inanna and Šukalletuda	PSD ms. (to be published by S. Cohen)
InEb	*Inana and Ebiḫ*, PSD manuscript (to be published by B. Eichler)
Inninšagura	A. Sjöberg, ZA 65 161ff.
Klein Shulgi	J. Klein, *Šulgi D* (Univ. of Pennsylvania diss.)
LEr	*Lamentation over Eridu* = M. Green, JCS 30 127ff.
Letter (followed by number)	from Michalowski Royal Correspondence
LN	*Lamentation over Nippur*, PSD ms. (to be published by H. Vanstiphout)
LSU	*Lamentation over Sumer and Ur*, PSD ms. (to be published by P. Michalowski)
LU	*Lamentation over Ur* = S. Kramer, *Assyriological Studies* 12
Lugale	lugal(-e) ud me-lám-bi nir-gál, ms. of edition to be published by J. Van Dijk
LW	*Lamentation over Uruk* (ms. to be published by M. Green)
Michalowski Royal Correspondence	P. Michalowski, *Royal Correspondence of The Ur III Period* (Yale University diss.)
Ninmešara	W. Hallo and J. Van Dijk, *The Exaltation of Inanna* (YNER 3)
OLA	*Orientalia Lovaniensia Analecta*
OPBF	*Occasional Publications of the Babylonian Fund*
Or An	*Oriens Antiquus*
PSD	*Pennsylvania Sumerian Dictionary*
RAI	*Compte rendu, Rencontre Assyriologique Internationale*
Reisman Royal Hymns	D. Reisman, *Two Neo-Sumerian Royal Hymns* (Univ. of Pennsylvania diss.)
RGTC	*Répertoire géographique des textes cunéiformes*
SAHG	A. Falkenstein and W. von Soden, *Sumerische und akkadische Hymnen und Gebete*
SANE	*Sources from the Ancient Near East*
Shulgi D	see Klein Shulgi
Steible Haja	H. Steible, *Ein Lied an den Gott Haja*
Steible Rimsin	H. Steible, *Rīmsîn, mein König*
St Po	*Studia Pohl*
Syncrétisme	J. Van Dijk, contribution to S. Hartman, *Syncretism*
TRS	Textes religieux sumériens (= TCL 15-16)
Voix de l'opposition	A. Finet (ed.), *La voix de l'opposition en Mésopotamie*

CHAPTER I

INTRODUCTION

The *Curse of Agade,* one of the most popular compositions in the Old Babylonian scribal curriculum, is the story of the rise and fall of the first great Mesopotamian empire. It begins[1] with a brief historical *mise en scène*: Enlil, chief of the Sumerian pantheon, has brought defeat to the warring cities of Kish and Uruk and has bestowed sovereignty over all of Mesopotamia on Sargon of Agade. In consequence of this shift in authority, the great goddess Inanna (who had been the patron deity of both Kish and Uruk) installed herself in Agade and worked incessantly to secure power and prosperity for the city. A new king, Naramsin—in reality, Sargon's grandson and third successor—appears in l. 40, followed by an enumeration of the geographical areas and officials, both Sumerian and foreign, sending their goods and offerings to Inanna at Agade.

In lines 55ff., Inanna suddenly turns against her protégés, seemingly because Enlil has refused permission for a proper temple to be built for her. The crucial lines 56f. are, unfortunately, enigmatic. She abandons Agade, the gods withdraw their favor, the city is in the throes of agony. Naramsin foresees the finality of the city's misfortune in a dream so dreadful that he is unable to talk about it, and he sinks into a seven-year depression.

The king then performed extispicy (94ff.), hoping that Enlil would at last permit "the temple" to be built. This must be the temple of Inanna at Agade, the lack of which had earlier precipitated the goddess's abandonment of the city. When the omens were unfavorable, Naramsin lost patience, and in an extraordinarily outrageous act for a Mesopotamian ruler, he attacked and plundered Enlil's sanctuary Ekur, in the holy city of Nippur, hoping to force a change in Enlil's negative posture (98ff.). Extensive descriptions of the destruction of Ekur culminate in the collective mental breakdown of the city Agade, whose king had perpetrated the sacrilege (148f.). Enlil avenges his temple (151) by unleashing the barbarian Guti on Babylonia (152ff.). The resulting havoc affected even Enlil, who reduced the size of his religious establishments and their stores (194f.). Those who survived the Gutian rampage performed a lament (196ff.), hoping to soothe the angry god, but he simply retreated into his inner chambers. Then the great gods of Babylonia themselves try to pacify their angry leader, resorting not to the traditional pleas known from the city-laments (see Chap. III), but to a long, unique, and terrible curse directed at Agade (210ff.), whose ruler, Naramsin, through his violence against Ekur and Enlil, was the cause of the land's misfortune. The curse becomes reality (272ff.), and the composition ends by proclaiming Agade's destruction and praising Inanna.

History of Scholarship[2]

In 1934 H. G. Güterbock reconstructed and edited as much as was possible of the *Curse of Agade* based on texts published up to that time.[3] The composition was used by him to illustrate his thesis that Mesopotamian historiography interpreted the past in terms of alternating periods of fortune and misfortune (see Chap. II). On the basis of evidence then available, he understood the composition to end with Naramsin victorious once again, bringing booty to Nippur,[4] but the passage in question is now known to describe an angry Naramsin carrying booty away *from* Nippur (lines 143f.). His edition was to remain indispensable for thirty years, although as early as 1940, S. N. Kramer was able to make considerable progress in reconstructing the composition, during his study of the unpublished Sumerian literary texts in Philadelphia and Istanbul. Writing that it "laments a calamity that befell Agade during the reign of Naramsin,"[5] Kramer recognized that the composition does not end well for the city and its king. Falkenstein, in 1953, entitled the composition the "Lament over the Destruction of Agade."[6] Both scholars, in characterizing the composition as a lament, were responding to the numerous similarities and parallels between the *Curse of Agade* and the Sumerian city-laments, discussed in Chapter III, below.[7] But it was only when the last half of the composition could be fully restored, using the tablets studied by Kramer at Jena, that the real character of the text could be discerned.[8] In 1955 Kramer announced his results, dubbing the composition "The Curse of Agade: The Ekur Avenged."[9] He saw the work as a Sumerian historiographer's attempt to explain the fall of Agade as the result of the sacrilegious behavior of Naramsin toward the Sumerian cult center at Nippur. Falkenstein was quick to point out the relationship between this understanding of historical events and the *Weidner Chronicle*.[10]

Following the publication of the copies of the Jena tablets,[11] A. Falkenstein produced his masterly edition of the entire composition, based on all texts published up to that time.[12] A translation only, utilizing many unpublished texts in a reconstruction by A. Berlin (Feigenbaum), was subsequently brought out by Kramer.[13] Falkenstein rightly saw that the key difficulty in interpreting the composition lay in lines 55ff.: Why do Enlil and Inanna suddenly turn against Agade? Despite a quadrupling of the number of manuscripts now available for reconstructing the text, these lines remain problematic, and still cannot be translated satisfactorily.

It was Van Dijk who first suggested a solution.[14] The offerings brought to Inanna at Agade in lines 44-53 are the offerings that customarily went to Enlil at Nippur, the Sumerian cult center. The hostility of Enlil and Inanna, whom Van Dijk equates with the Nippur clergy and a Sumerian priestess stationed at Agade respectively, is thus caused by Naramsin's insensitivity to Sumerian religious tradition. He was followed in this interpretation by Edzard,[15] Kienast,[16] Wilcke,[17] and Durand.[18] The last three understood the composition to reflect contemporary hostility from the Sumerian south against the centralization of religious and economic authority by the Agade dynasty, where Falkenstein has seen the composition as a later expression of Sumerian nationalism under the Third Dynasty of Ur.[19]

A new, annotated translation was presented by Durand in 1975,[20] by which time many more mss. beyond those available to Falkenstein had been published. He made substantial progress in the interpretation of the composition by understanding lines 55-57 to mean that Inanna could not accept offerings in Agade because she lacked a proper sanctuary in which to do so. The silence from Enlil's temple in l. 57 would then be an allusion to a refusal of Enlil to grant permission for Inanna's temple to be built, and the negative oracles in 94ff. would likewise refer to a temple at Agade. Nippur, whence the oracles come, is then attacked by Naramsin because Enlil's continued hostility prevents him from building the sanctuary and securing Inanna's return.

In 1976 C. Wilcke published his much needed collations of the Jena tablets, together with a list of fifteen manuscripts published since Falkenstein's edition, and numerous suggestions for reading and interpreting individual lines.[21]

Two recent studies have considered the *Curse of Agade* at length, offering both general interpretations of the overall meaning and impact of the composition, and specific discussions of individual lines and passages. T. Jacobsen, AfO 26 7ff. (1979), situates the *Curse of Agade* within a historical framework reconstructed from literary-historical texts (see Chap. III below) and fragments of copies of Naramsin's own inscriptions. These texts portray the rebellion of Babylonian cities against Naramsin at the beginning of his reign. Since Nippur was one of these cities, Naramsin's attacking Nippur in the *Curse of Agade* can be seen as a reflection of his suppression of the rebellion. The entire conflict is understood by Jacobsen in geopolitical, not ethno-linguistic terms. For Westenholz, Mesopotamia (Copenhagen) 7 110ff. (1979), the conflict was very much ethno-linguistic: the Sumerian south's resentment of the religious and political innovations of Naramsin and his predecessors led to a widespread uprising. The *Curse of Agade* would describe Naramsin's razing of the Ekur prior to a delayed rebuilding begun late in his reign and concluded under his son Sharkalisharri. The razing of the temple and the sight of it in ruins for so many years would have provoked the anger of Sumerian traditionalists, an anger reflected in our composition.[22]

Classification and Function

The composition has no native genre subscript or subdivisions,[23] and, in Edzard's words, "Die literarische Gattung des Textes . . . lässt sich nur schwer definieren."[24] The work's affinities both to the Sumerian city-laments, and to a diverse group of Sumerian historiographic compositions are demonstrated in Chapter III. For the modern reader, it is a historiographic composition, interpreting a specific historical event—the fall of the Akkadian Empire—that employs heavy doses of the poetic imagery characteristic of the city-laments. The ancients' classification of the composition is not discernible from its position in ancient literary catalogues (for which see the Commentary to line 1), nor from any internal characteristics.[25]

All of the scholars cited in the preceding paragraphs agree that the *Curse of Agade* is a tendentious composition, written from the viewpoint of Sumer or Nippur, and both Falkenstein and Van Dijk assert, without doubt correctly, that it was composed at Nippur.[26] Falkenstein attributed its popularity at Nippur to its theme, that a mighty empire fell because its ruler profaned Nippur's main sanctuary. But, although there are possibly more surviving manuscripts of the *Curse of Agade* than of any other Sumerian composition, with the exception of *Lugale,* and the vast majority of these tablets come from Nippur, the vast majority of *all* extant Sumerian literary texts have been found at Nippur, and the *Curse of Agade* is comparatively well-represented in the much smaller groups of Sumerian texts found at other sites, and of unknown provenience in the collections of museums (see the List of

Manuscripts in Chap. VII). It is quite possible, then, that the composition was a popular text throughout Babylonia, not for the specific lesson it teaches about respecting Nippur, but because of the hold the Dynasty of Agade had on the imagination of succeeding generations of Mesopotamians for nearly two millennia (see Chapter II), and because the text explained that dynasty's history within the parameters of the dominant centralist political ideology of the period (see below).

Four scholars speculate on a specific function that the composition may have filled. M. Lambert, in an intriguing note,[27] suggests that it was written in order to show that the fall of Agade was attributable to an avoidable error of Naramsin, and was not the inevitable result of an imperial strategy. The acceptance of this explanation by the ancients would have contributed to the reconstitution of the empire around the city of Ur. Krecher, similarly, ascribes a political role to the *Curse of Agade.* It served to provide a demarcation between a recent period of great Mesopotamian power when the government seat was in the north (Agade), and the present period of great power when the government seat is in the south (Third Dynasty of Ur). By providing a religious justification for the north's loss of sovereignty, the composition sought to deter any doubts, raised by memories of Sargonic glory, about the legitimacy of Ur's sovereignty.[28] Both suggestions are possible, but would be difficult to prove. According to Durand,[29] the absence of any mention in the composition of an attack by the Guti on Agade itself, or of the death of Naramsin, could mean that the text was composed for the reconsecration of the Ekur, after the Sumerian south broke with the Semitic north, but before the end of the Gutian invasions. This hypothesis was suggested, no doubt, by the *Curse of Agade*'s close relationship to the city-laments, but is based on highly speculative chronological arguments (see below). The absence of the liturgical rubrics found in the laments[30] argues against any cultic use for the composition. Westenholz suggests that the *Curse of Agade* may have been composed to coincide with the razing and reconstruction of the Naramsin-Sharkalisharri Ekur by Urnammu. By pointing to the old structure's unholy origins, the king of Ur could justify destroying a still serviceable structure.[31] But the *Curse of Agade* nowhere speaks of *building* the Ekur, and it is difficult to imagine Urnammu having any necessity to justify his lavish rebuilding plans.

The origin and function of Sumerian literary texts that are not clearly intended for use in the cult or court ceremonial remain central problems of Sumerian literary history.[32] Solutions will not be ventured here, but the impetus for the composition of the *Curse of Agade* and the reason for its propagation may be sought in a political and religious ideology that held there to be only one legitimate divinely sanctioned king of Babylonia at any given moment. This ideology, which can be traced back to the great Lugalzagesi inscription, permeates the *Sumerian King List,* the Ur laments, the so-called royal hymns, and much else.[33] In the *Curse of Agade,* the history of Agade was told in terms of the granting and withdrawing of divine favor. The special circumstance that distinguished Agade's fall from that of other defeated dynasties of the Babylonian past was that the city was indeed destroyed and abandoned forever, except, probably, for a small religious settlement around the Inanna temple of E'ulmaš.[34] A city-lament for Agade, similar to those composed for Ur, Nippur, Uruk, Eridu, and other cities, would have been an impossibility, if those laments were, as has been suggested, composed on the occasion of a destroyed city's restoration.[35] Agade's unprecedented fate was accounted for by Naramsin's hubris and sacrilege, which elicited the eternal enmity of the gods, rather than the reconciliation and pleas by the gods for restoration typical of the city-laments (see Chap. III).

Is the Curse of Agade *anti-Akkadian?*

This has been a much discussed question ever since Falkenstein's characterization of the composition as "anti-akkadisch."[36] If, by anti-Akkadian, one means anti-Agade, then the text, with its unambiguous doxology glorifying the destruction of Agade (l. 281), leaves no doubt in the reader's mind that it is very anti-Akkadian indeed. The failure of the ruler of Agade to submit to divine will led to the ruin of Ekur, the devastation of Babylonia, and the destruction and curse of Agade itself. But, when anti-Akkadian is extended to mean sentiment against an Akkadian-speaking, mainly north Babylonian ethno-linguistic group—sentiment emanating from the Sumerian-speaking inhabitants of southern Babylonia—then there is precious little evidence to support the assertion. Leaving aside the question of the extent of spoken Sumerian and Akkadian in Babylonia in the late third millennium,[37] and the cultural differences thereby implied, the fact remains that there is no explicit statement of anti-Akkadian (in the ethno-linguistic sense) sentiment anywhere in Sumerian literature. Nor is there any evidence for Falkenstein's "Wiederaufstieg des Sumerertums" and resentment of Akkadians under the Third Dynasty of Ur.[38]

Wilcke has reinterpreted all Sumerian myths in which Inanna is a major actor as either pro- or anti-Akkadian,[39] but his interpretation becomes especially complicated with regard to the *Curse of Agade.* For Wilcke, Inanna is always Ištar of Agade in Sumerian guise, and so the myth of *Inanna and Ebiḫ* is pro-Akkadian, because it is really about victorious Agade's conquests in eastern Assyria, whereas *Inanna and Šukalletuda* is anti-Akkadian, because the Akkadian goddess is humiliated by a gardener. In the *Curse of Agade,* according to Wilcke, when Inanna abandons Agade and is praised for its destruction, "Die Sumerer haben . . . ihren Konflikt mit der Göttin überwunden, indem sie ihr die Vernichtung ihres Feindes zuschrieben, der ihre Göttin Inanna usurpiert hat."[40] But the texts nowhere speak of two Inannas, or of usurpation; the *Curse of Agade* is very clear, in lines 7ff., that Inanna settled in Agade as a direct consequence of that city's selection by Enlil, a Sumerian god if there ever was one, to exercise hegemony over Babylonia.[41]

Kienast and Durand both stress this legitimacy, in orthodox Sumerian terms, of Agade's hegemony, and see the hostility in the composition directed at political and religious policies developed under Naramsin, and not against Akkadians.[42] Van Dijk would have those policies begin already with Sargon, and feels that the hostility thereby generated, and expressed in the *Curse of Agade,* created a Sumerian-Semitic conflict where before there had been none.[43] Similar sentiments are expressed by Westenholz.[44] However, the only possible place in the entire composition where one could find hostility expressed toward a people, and not just toward Naramsin and his capital, Agade, is in lines 129f.:[45]

> The people saw the bedchamber, its room which knows no daylight,
> Akkad (uri^{ki}) saw the holy vessels of the gods

If any deeply felt hostility is intended here, it is understated to the point of impotence. In a long note devoted to this question, Jacobsen rejects the arguments of those who would see the composition as an expression of ethno-linguistic hostility, and rightly concludes that any attempt to impose a matrix of Sumero-Akkadian conflict onto the text is an anachronistic projection of contemporary concerns: "Looking at isolated passages and expecting them to testify yes or no within a 'Fragestellung' already presupposing the ethnic distinction that is to be proved, can only warp them out of shape for us and mislead us."[47] In the words of

M. Lambert, the *Curse of Agade* is "un exposé théologique, nullement un pamphlet Suméro-accadien."[48]

The Curse of Agade *as a Historical Source*

Although Kramer, in his pioneering exposition of the *Curse of Agade,* never explicitly affirms or denies the historicity of the events portrayed in the composition, his use of it to sketch the history of the Agade period suggests that he accepted it as a valid historical source.[49] Falkenstein rejected this implicit judgment for three reasons: it is known from inscriptions found there that Naramsin actually rebuilt Ekur;[50] statues of the Sargonic kings were honored at Ekur in the Ur III period; and Agade could not have been destroyed forever in the time of Naramsin, because there were kings who reigned there after him.[51] The first argument is irrelevant, since Naramsin could have destroyed Ekur sometime before or after he built there, but it is hard to imagine that a king who destroyed Ekur would be worshipped there only two hundred years later; and certainly Agade survived Naramsin.

For Van Dijk, however, the composition is a faithful reflection of religious and political tensions of the period, and Naramsin's attack on Nippur could not have been invented. He deals with one of Falkenstein's objections by suggesting that the veneration of the Sargonic kings in the Ekur could be the result of their rehabilitation by the Ur III rulers, who followed the same centralist ideology. But he does not explain how the destruction of Agade can be placed in the reign of Naramsin, a destruction which he understands the composition to ascribe to an alliance of Sumerians (symbolized by the gods in lines 210 and 222)[52] and the Guti.[53] Durand also accepts the *Curse of Agade* as historically accurate, and does away with Falkenstein's chronological objections by insisting "que nulle part il n'est parlé d'une attaque Guti contre Agadé, de la chute de la ville ou de la mort de son roi impie."[54] This statement is impossible to reconcile with the poem's final line, which states explicitly that Agade is destroyed, implying, it seems, that its ruler, too, has suffered a similar fate. Nor is there any reason to assume that the attack of the Guti, which is portrayed as country-wide, was considered by the text to have bypassed Agade.

Both Westenholz and Jacobsen, in the recent studies mentioned above, embed the text within a historical reconstruction of the reign of Naramsin that derives mainly, though not entirely, from the literary-historical compositions discussed in Chap. II. The attack of Naramsin on Nippur is a literary reflection of the suppression by Naramsin of a southern Babylonian uprising against his rule. That uprising, unfortunately, is known almost exclusively from such reflections in literary-historical texts. In copies of Naramsin's own inscriptions, its very existence can be deduced only from a few fragmentary passages.[55] The military action of Naramsin in the south, then, can be affirmed, but the *Curse of Agade* reflects only the fact and not the actual circumstances of this action. The primary sources can be used to show what elements in the composition's narrative have some historical foundation, but the composition cannot be used to flesh out or complete the primary sources.

When the image of Naramsin's reign that emerges in the *Curse of Agade* is compared with information derived from primary historical sources (royal inscriptions and year names, economic and administrative documents), "the actual course of events was considerably more complex,"[56] and the studies of both Hallo[57] and M. Lambert[58] show that the composition is far from an accurate historical narrative. It belongs to the traditional historical literature discussed in the following chapter, and for reasons given there, literature of this sort cannot be used for historical reconstruction. This text, like the city-laments dealing with the fall of Ur (LU, LSU), and many other texts of the traditional historical literature, was composed in a priestly milieu, and explains the fall of a great empire in religious terms.[59] There is just no way to ascertain whether the religious conflict depicted in the composition reflects any real conflict of the Agade period or is simply an explanation, made up after the fact, in Kramer's words, "to interpret a historical event in the framework of a currently held world view."[60] To accept its interpretation in the reconstruction of history is to don the blinders of the ancient clerics and to underestimate the multiplicity of forces that were vastly more important than theological disputes in shaping the history of ancient Mesopotamia.[61]

Date of Composition

The *terminus post quem* is the reign of Naramsin (ca. 2200 B.C.) or better, ca. 2150, after kings ceased to reign at Agade. Three manuscripts of the Ur III period (R_3, S_3, K_4) provide a *terminus ante quem* of ca. 2000. The problems in dating Sumerian literature can be demonstrated by the twice repeated assertion of Falkenstein that the text could only have been written after the Ur III period, since during that period Naramsin was honored in Ekur, and it was, according to him, inconceivable that during this same period a text would be composed and transmitted that vilified him as the destroyer of Ekur.[62] When he edited the text a few years later, he had already been told of (but had not seen) the Ur III fragments,[63] and assigns the composition to that period, as the work of Sumerian nationalist sentiment.[64] In Falkenstein's opinion, the period between Naramsin and Ur III was, at Nippur, where the text must have been composed, too confused and depressed for literary activity to have taken place.[65] This is the same kind of "logical" reasoning that led him earlier to dismiss the Ur III period as a possible time of composition. Cannot texts be composed in times of adversity? And the contradiction that he indicated, in his earlier statements, between an Ur III date of composition and the worship of Naramsin in Ekur in that period remains.[66] For Hallo, the composition seems "most at home in a neo-Sumerian milieu," but he does not elaborate.[67]

M. Lambert dated the *Curse of Agade* to a period before the beginning of the Third Dynasty of Ur, so that it contributed to an ideological climate that made that dynasty's empire possible (see above). Van Dijk's interpretation of the composition (see above) implies that it was written soon after the events portrayed, and Durand would date it to the reign of Naramsin himself,[68] but this must be rejected for reasons already given. The grounds for Westenholz's suggested dating of the composition to the reign of Urnammu have similarly been judged unlikely.

Very little is known about the development of Sumerian literature between the time of the Fara and Abu Salabikh texts (ca. 2500) and Ur III, and we are even poorly informed about the Sumerian literary corpus in circulation during the Ur III period itself. The large number of often verbatim parallels between the *Curse of Agade,* attested in the Ur III period, and city-laments (see Chap. III) that commemorate the end of that period or even later calamities, suggest that a whole repertoire of such topoi, and a literature employing them, existed then, but all that survives is the few Ur III fragments of the *Curse of Agade.* The discovery of Abu Salabikh versions of compositions otherwise attested only in manuscripts written 700 years later, in the Old Babylonian period, has shaken the confidence of scholars in the common-sense approach to Sumerian literary history that for so long dominated Assyriological studies:[69]

> Die archaische Fassung . . . zeigt überdies, dass gerade ein Passus, der zunächst einen terminus post quem für die Datierung zu bieten schien, entweder selbst eine Modernisierung und also für die Datierung unerheblich sein kann, oder dass vielmehr eine Wendung, die erstmalig in einem Überlieferungsbereich der Periode X bezeugt und da offenbar beliebt ist, sehr wohl schon vor der Periode X, nur eben in einem anderen Überlieferungsbereich, existiert haben kann.[70]

No doubt the Ebla material, when known, will add to those insecurities, at least temporarily. At present, there is no sound basis for assigning the *Curse of Agade* to a specific moment in the 150 years between the destruction of Agade and the later part of Ibbisin's reign.

Notes

1. Cf. the outline in Chap. IV. For a justification of the controversial portions of this resumé, see Chapters II, III, and VIII.

2. This section is not written to weary the reader with a point-by-point exposition and evaluation of the works that have dealt with the *Curse of Agade,* but rather to acknowledge the more important treatments of the text and their theses.

3. ZA 42 25ff.

4. Ibid. 34f.

5. JAOS 60 235.

6. SAHG.

7. This relationship had already been indicated by Güterbock, op. cit. 12.

8. The crucial lines are 224, 269, 271, 278, 280f.

9. WZJ 5 759ff., repeated in *The Sumerians* (1963), 62ff.

10. OLZ 1958 142f.; see below, Chap. II.

11. TuM NF 3 (1961).

12. ZA 57 (1965) 43ff.; see the List of Manuscripts in Chap. VII for Falkenstein's texts.

13. ANET^3 (1969) 204ff.

14. OLZ 62 (1967), 234f.; Syncrétisme (1969) 191f. and 204.

15. *Kindlers Literaturlexikon* 6(1971) 2121f.

16. Or 42 (1973) 498.

17. RAI 19 (1974) 231.

18. Durand (1975) 180.

19. ZA 57 50. M. Lambert also connects it with the Ur III empire, but in a quite different way (see below).

20. Durand.

21. Wilcke Kollationen 28ff.

22. Mesopotamia 7 122 n. 32. The same point is made by Jacobsen, op. cit. p. 14. The discussion of the composition by Finkelstein in H. Lasswell, *Propaganda and Communication in World History* I 77ff., came to my attention after this manuscript was completed.

23. For these, see Wilcke, AS 20 252ff.; Krecher, in Röllig, *Altorientalische Literaturen* 116f.

24. Op. cit. 2122.

25. Hallo says the composition is "formally a hymn" (AS 20 188) because of its doxology, but that doxology (DN zà-mí) is in no way characteristic of hymns alone. See An Or 52 4; Krecher, op. cit. 117.

26. ZA 57 45; Syncrétisme 191.

27. Or An 13 19f. n. 85.

28. Saeculum 26 27.

29. Durand 181.

30. Green Eridu 283ff.

31. Mesopotamia 7 122f. n. 36.

32. Cf. An Or 52 8f.

33. See, e.g., Hallo, *The Ancient Near East* 38ff.; Grayson, *Papyrus and Tablet* 92ff.; and the references cited by each.

34. Cf. RGTC I & II s.v. Akkade; RLA s.v. Akkad and Eulmaš; Sjöberg, TCS 3 147ff.

35. Green Eridu 310ff.

36. ZA 57 49.

37. Or42 239 ff.; Wilcke, Voix de l'opposition 42f.; Lieberman, HSS 22 20; Heimpel, AfO 25 171ff.

38. ZA 57 50. This is a strange statement, since he points out two pages earlier that the deified Akkadian kings were offered sacrifices at Nippur in the Ur III period. Wilcke, RAI 19 23ff., would see this respect for the kings of Agade as a possible reflection of a policy of reconciliation between Sumerians and Akkadians, pursued by Shulgi, as symbolized by a presumed replacement by Shulgi of the title "King of Sumer and Akkad" with "King of the World", i.e., abolishing any distinction between the two parts (and peoples) of Babylonia.

39. Voix de l'opposition 54ff. On p. 37, he defines "Akkadian" as referring either to the Akkadian language or to the political system of the Agade period.

40. Ibid. 64.

41. The highly speculative nature of Wilcke's interpretations can be illustrated by two examples. With reference to *Gilgamesh and the Bull of Heaven,* he says that Inanna, who is refusing Gilgamesh the right to render judgment in Eanna, must be the Akkadian Inanna, because it is inconceivable that the Sumerian goddess would deprive the ruler of her own city of his sovereign powers (op. cit. 58; see now W. G. Lambert, 19.DOT 72 n. 4. Interestingly, in the Iddindagan sacred marriage ceremony, it is Inanna, not the king, who renders judgment in the temple [JCS 25 189:116ff.]). But that is what the story is about! If, as in the Akkadian version, Gilgamesh had refused to do *his* duty to Inanna, then she had every right to keep him out of her temple. And how would the goddess of Agade be in a position to prevent Gilgamesh from exercising functions in a temple in Uruk? In *Inanna's Descent,* according to Wilcke, the Akkadian Inanna causes the death of Dumuzi, who represents Sumer and whose resurrection symbolizes the hope of Sumer for a restoration of its autonomy (op. cit. 62). But why would Inanna of Agade begin her journey to the netherworld from Uruk? The pitfalls in trying to interpret myth as a reflection of specific historical events or conditions can be seen by comparing Wilcke's equation of Dumuzi and Sumer, with Durand's suggestion that in the story *Dumuzi and Enkimdu,* the shepherd Dumuzi represents the nomadic (!) Akkadians, and the farmer Enkimdu the sedentary Sumerians (Durand 179).

42. Or 42 498; Durand 178.

43. Syncrétisme 181f.

44. Mesopotamia 7 110ff.

45. Cf. Jacobsen's discussion of these lines, AfO 26 9f. n. 36. Van Dijk's interpretation of dumu-gi$_7$ in l. 56 as indicating Inanna's Sumerian (as opposed to Akkadian) identity (OLZ 62 234f.; Syncrétisme 194 and 204), can no longer be maintained (see the comm. to lines 55f. and 129f.)

46. For uri^{ki}, see Wilcke, RAI 19 202ff.

47. AfO 26 10 n. 36.

48. Or An 13 20 n. 85.

49. WZJ 5 759ff; The Sumerians 62ff.

50. Note also the year-name AfO 20 22 C.1, reporting that Naramsin built the Ekur.

51. ZA 57 47f.; cf. already OLZ 1958 142f., and OLZ 1962 370.

52. Cf. also Durand 181.

53. Syncrétisme 206.

54. Durand 181.

55. PBS 5 36 vif., 4 iii′ (for maintaining Poebel's obv. and rev., see Michalowski JCS 32 328 n. 17); HS 1955 obv.? iif. (AfO 20 20).

56. Hallo, *The Ancient Near East* 66.

57. Ibid.; RLA s.v. Gutium.

58. Or An 13 1ff.

59. Cf. Chap. III, Excursus A.

60. *The Sumerians* 62; cf. M. Lambert, Or An 13 20 n. 85 "mais que cette explication ait été donnée, qu'elle ait été admise, n'eu fait pas pour autant une vérité historique."

61. Cf. M. Lambert, op. cit. An illustration of the problems created by taking the theological interpretation of the historical-literary texts too seriously is Van Dijk's assertion that the collapse of Ur's empire can also be traced to that city's reigning dynasty falling afoul of the Nippur clergy (Syncrétisme 204 n. 1). Enlil's withdrawal of favor from Naramsin in the *Curse of Agade* was, according to Van Dijk, actually the alienation of the Nippur priesthood, as was An and Enlil's withdrawal of favor from Ibbisin in LU and LSU. But if the hostility of the Nippur clergy toward Naramsin derived from his diversion of offerings from Nippur to Agade, what could have prompted the hostility of that clergy toward the Third Dynasty of Ur, whose massive support of the religious establishment at Nippur is documented by scores of thousands of tablets? Wilcke's interpretation of passages in the historical literature that speak of Enlil and the gods withdrawing their support from Ibbisin as reflections of an actual Sumerian Assembly meeing at Nippur (Voix de l'opposition 49ff.), is no more convincing than Van Dijk's as an attempt to demythologize the texts and use them as historical sources.

62. OLZ 1958 142f.; OLZ 1962 370.

63. ZA 57 44.

64. Ibid. 49f.

65. Ibid.

66. Even accepting Wilcke's hypothesis of a rehabilitation of Naramsin and Agade by Shulgi (see n. 34), would one not also then expect the suppression of a composition so pronouncedly anti-Agade as the *Curse of Agade*?

67. AS 20 188.

68. See above.

69. Perhaps best exemplified by Falkenstein, RAI 2 12ff. and MDOG 85 1ff.

70. Krecher, in Röllig, *Altorientalische Literaturen* 109.

CHAPTER II

NARAMSIN AND THE TRADITION OF BABYLONIAN HISTORICAL LITERATURE

Historical events in Babylonia through the mid-second millennium found written expression either in the inscriptions and year names of royal participants in those events, or in a very diverse body of literature that has been dubbed the "historical tradition," or "historical-literary texts."[1] Both categories of texts are tendentious, and neither can be used with the same confidence as can the objective, if parochial, astronomical diaries and Babylonian Chronicle Series of the first millennium.[2]

The biases of royal inscriptions are theoretically rather simple: the king is being glorified, and the historian expects that defeats or stalemates may be turned into victories, actual victories exaggerated, and disasters unmentioned. In practice, it is usually impossible to pinpoint these inaccuracies (which victories were defeats? etc.) without the supplementary data culled from administrative and economic records, correspondence, and, at times, the inscriptions of contemporary dynasts.[3] But even without this supplementary data, we do not expect a king to claim conquest of a distant place with which he actually had no contact whatsoever,[4] or to have built a temple that he did not, at least, refurbish. The parameters of royal testimony tend to be accurate, even if the activity within those parameters may be distorted.[5]

Historical *literature* is rife with methodological problems of a different order. When dealing with events of even the relatively recent past, authors are less constrained by historical reality,[6] more susceptible to the use of literary topoi rather than accurate description, and unabashedly distort the past—consciously or not—to support the thesis underlying their composition, or simply to make a better story. The "historical kernel" frequently assumed to underlie, for example, the epics of the early rulers of Uruk, or the Sargon romances, or even the city-laments, is completely elusive without corroborating evidence.[7] We can only speak of probabilities. Did Enmerkar really campaign against distant Aratta?[8] Perhaps. Did Sargon really rescue the merchants of Purušḫanda? Probably not.[9] Do the regnal years of the later Pre-Sargonic kings in the *Sumerian King List* represent authentic and accurate local traditions? Who knows?[10] The practice commonly used in historical reconstruction, especially for the Sargonic period, of weaving together evidence from contemporary documents with plausible episodes in the historical-literary tradition, is not methodologically sound.

What can be done, however, is to compare assessments drawn on the one hand from contemporary sources and, on the other, from the historical tradition relating to a particular period or personality, and then evaluate the accuracy of the tradition, observing the ways in which it distorts historical events as known from the contemporary sources, and molds them into literary patterns.[11] Unfortunately, especially for earlier historical periods, there is rarely enough contemporary evidence to do this, which is why so many reputable scholars have felt justified in using materials from the historical tradition to write history.[12]

The paradigmatic role of the Agade dynasty for future generations of Mesopotamians was demonstrated by Güterbock, and more recently was given a more nuanced characterization by Finkelstein.[13] Only the two greatest kings, Sargon and Naramsin, were remembered in the tradition, and the rise of the dynasty was associated with the former and its fall with the latter.[14] Only the historical episodes preserved in omen collections mention other kings of the Sargonic dynasty, and only the omens, according to Finkelstein, who is arguing for their historicity, present a positive, and thus historically more accurate, image of Naramsin.[15] Otherwise, "Naramsin is cast in this tradition in the role of the near tragic 'Unheilsherrscher'. The blame for the downfall of the empire is placed on his shoulders. . . ."[16]

But this assessment of Naramsin's place in the historical tradition is not entirely correct, given the tradition as we now have it. The texts in question, beside the *Curse of Agade*, are:[17]

1. *The Naramsin Epic* (Güterbock, AfO 13 46ff.)
2. *The Cuthean Legend* (Gurney, AnSt 5 93ff. [NA]; Finkelstein, JCS 11 83ff. [OB]; Otten, KBO 19 98 and 99 (?) [Bogh. Akkadian]; Güterbock, ZA 44 49ff., and Hoffner, JCS 23 17ff. [Hittite])
3. *The Great Rebellion* (Grayson and Sollberger, RA 70 103ff., texts G and M)[18]
4. Grayson and Sollberger, RA 70 103 ff., text L
5. Van Dijk, VAS NF 1 42
6. *Naramsin and Erra* (Lambert, BiOr 30 357 ff.)
7. The Hittite Naramsin Inscription (Güterbock, ZA 44 67 ff.)
8. *The Sumerian King List* (Jacobsen, AS 11)
9. *The Weidner Chronicle* (Grayson ABC, Chronicle 19)
10. *The Chronicle of Early Kings* (Grayson ABC, Chronicle 20)

The fragmentary OB epic (No. 1) tells of Naramsin's well-known conquest of Apišal[19] and undoubtedly had a positive outcome. Texts Nos. 2 through 7 are pseudepigraphal inscriptions,[20] all but No. 6 written in the first person, and all but No. 7 OB in date, or with an OB version (No. 2). Of these, the *Cuthean Legend* (No. 2) is the best preserved and has the widest geographic and chronological distribution. In it Naramsin—here the son of Sargon—relates, as a lesson to future generations, how his armies were decimated by the barbarian Umman-Manda because he failed to heed omens warning him not to do battle. He finally obeys the omens, and the Umman-Manda are scattered as Naramsin remains safely locked within his city. The conclusion is far from disastrous (unlike the *Curse of Agade*).

The *Cuthean Legend* purports to be the text of a stele left in Emeslam, the temple of Nergal at Cutha, and text No. 6 tells how Erra (= Nergal) helped Naramsin in battle, and Naramsin gratefully built a temple for him, possibly the very same Emeslam.[21] The tenor of text No. 6 is completely positive, as is No. 5, possibly a copy of a genuine inscription, reporting Naramsin's final defeat of a rebel coalition after nine previous encounters. This text must be connected with genuine Naramsin inscriptions that tell of his defeat of nine armies in one year,[22] and with the reverse of No. 3, text M. The *Great Rebellion* (No. 3) lists a large coalition of Babylonian and foreign rulers allied against Naramsin, then breaks off.[23] Text No. 4 begins with an enumeration of foreign enemies, and after a break reports Naramsin's defeat by the Guti in language strikingly similar to the *Cuthean Legend*,[24] but the end is broken. Parallels with other texts suggest that Naramsin was ultimately victorious in both texts 3 and 4; indeed, the form of the fictitious royal inscription presumes that the protagonist at least survived to tell his story. The Hittite fictional inscription (No. 7) is an account of Naramsin's victory over seventeen rulers, nearly all foreign, as in No. 4.

Three chronographic texts preserve traditions about Naramsin. The *Sumerian King List* (No. 8) presents what has become the accepted outline of the period's history:[25] Naramsin is the son of Maništušu (hence the grandson of Sargon), and was succeeded by his son, Šarkališarri. There followed three years of chaos, then two long-reigning kings.[26] Between the end of Agade and the Guti, the *King List* inserts the Uruk IV dynasty, which was contemporary with the last Agade rulers and the Gutian "dynasty."[27] The *Weidner Chronicle* (No. 9) anachronistically portrays the depredations of the Guti as Marduk's retribution for Naramsin's destruction (?) of Babylon. The *Chronicle of Early Kings* (No. 10), however, has only positive things to say: Naramsin, the son of Sargon (as in text No. 2),[28] conquers Apišal[29] and Magan.[30]

Three themes predominate in the Naramsin traditions. One is his defeat of large coalitions of Babylonian and foreign armies, reminiscent of the heterogeneous coalitions that we know actually existed in later periods from the Mari correspondence. Some of his opponents in these texts are attested as such in contemporary inscriptions, while others are obvious anachronisms.[31] One of his own inscriptions mentioning nine victorious battles in one year, which has been connected above with texts 3 and 5, claims that he captured only three kings, so if the traditions of these grand coalitions were originally inspired by that year of nine battles, the scope of Naramsin's victories has been greatly expanded. Conflation, too, has probably occurred, with campaigns of many years combined into a mammoth confrontation, similar to that known from the fictional Sumerian inscription of Lugalannemundu.[32]

A second theme is the conquest of Apišal, an event not mentioned in contemporary records. The city occurs as one of the coalition members in text No. 3.[33] Its conquest is the central concern of the epic fragment No. 1, and it is one of two episodes in the Naramsin sections of the fictional *Chronicle of Early Kings* (No. 10), and the historical omen collection that duplicates portions of that chronicle.[34] It is also the only concrete event associated with Naramsin in the historical apodoses that are found in other omen collections.[35]

The third theme is confrontation with an other-than-human barbarian enemy,[36] the Guti in texts 4 and 9, and the Umman-Manda in text 2. In the ten texts under discussion, it is this theme alone, found in Nos. 2, 4, and 9, that generates a less than happy ending for Naramsin. In No. 2, and most probably in No. 4, he survives despite severe setbacks. Only No. 9 (The *Weidner Chronicle*) ends in unqualified disaster for him, and it is this fictional chronicle, among all the preserved Naramsin traditions, that presents an historical tradition of Naramsin as the king under whom Agade was destroyed, which is the tradition, in far more lavish form, of the *Curse of Agade*. The cause of Agade's destruction is also similar in both the *Curse of Agade* and the *Weidner Chronicle*: Naramsin destroys Ekur/Babylon, and Enlil/Marduk sends the Guti against Agade to avenge Naramsin's sacrilege.[37] But the tradition of the *Cuthean Legend* (No. 2), in which Naramsin's impiety lies not in the destruction of a sacred place, but in his frustration at and disrespect for omens, is also present in the *Curse of Agade*, which ascribes Naramsin's attack on Ekur to just such frustration and disrespect.

The image of Naramsin in the *Curse of Agade* as an overly proud, impatient monarch who will not submit to divine will is found then in only two of the later Akkadian literary-historical compositions in which that monarch figures, and only one associates him with the fall of his dynasty, a flagrant historical error that perhaps originated with the *Curse of Agade.* Other literary-historical compositions portray him as a valiant warrior, defeating his numerous enemies with the help of the gods. The complex and sometimes contradictory web of traditions surrounding this ruler, which mingles fact and fiction, often inextricably, demonstrates the difficulties, mentioned at this chapter's beginning, that face the historian who wants to use these traditions to reconstruct the past.

Notes

1. Güterbock, ZA 42 1ff.; Grayson BHLT Chap I and Or 49 182ff.; Green Eridu 321ff. A few texts of questioned authenticity are classified by some scholars as genuine royal testimony and by others as historical literature (e.g., the Utuḫegal and Lugalannemundu inscriptions, the Ur III Royal Correspondence, or the Naramsin text published by Lambert, Bi Or 30 357ff.)

2. For which, see Grayson ABC 8ff.

3. E.g., Grayson, AS 16 340ff.; Edzard Zwischenzeit 157. Cf. the general discussion by Grayson, Or 49 170f.

4. There is, however, the interesting accusation in the *Nabonidus Verse Account* that Nabonidus claimed, in his inscriptions, hegemony over areas controlled by Cyrus. Such claims, based on a tradition of NB hegemony, are reminiscent of the claims of Isin rulers to Babylonian cities that had long since passed under the control of others.

5. Laudatory hymns and epics composed during a king's lifetime would also fall into this category of historical evidence, although the poetic medium tends to favor hyperbole and stereotype to an ever greater extent than the inscriptions.

6. The scribes did have access to actual historical records, as we know from the Old Babylonian copies of the inscriptions of Sargonic and Ur III rulers.

7. Cf. Green Eridu 325, and for an even more extreme statement, Alster, RA 68 49ff. Alster's citation on p. 49 of my statement in Or 42 246 on the historical memory of the Mesopotamians is inappropriate. I was not arguing for the historicity of the Uruk epics, but suggesting that the Mesopotamian penchant for preserving traditions about their early history would lead us to expect some reference, somewhere, to ethno-linguistic rivalry, if such rivalry had been at all significant.

8. Wilcke Lugalbanda 3 implies that these campaigns reflect more the realities of the Ur III period, without ruling out similar conflicts in earlier periods.

9. E.g., Bottéro, *Fischer Weltgeschichte* 2 103. Preliminary reports on Ebla tablets mentioning Kaneš (RLA 4 12; *Biblical Archaeologist,* May 1976, 48) may revise the tendency to dismiss the Sargon story out-of-hand.

10. For a more skeptical attitude than Jacobsen, AS 11 166, see, e.g., Nissen Friedhof 128f.

11. In the study cited in n. 13, Finkelstein attempted this, but, as will be shown below, was not entirely successful (cf. RAI 26 99ff.) The treatments of the reign of Naramsin and decline of Agade by M. Lambert, Or An 13 1ff., and Hallo, *The Ancient Near East* 60ff., keep the primary sources and later tradition apart, and both adopt critical stances toward the *Curse of Agade.*

12. See, e.g., Jacobsen's epigraph to his study in ZA 52 91ff. and his masterly reconstruction of Naramsin's reign in AfO 26 1ff. A characteristic expression of scholarly ambivalence toward the traditional historical literature can be found in Bottéro's discussion of the Sargonic period in *The Near*

East: The Early Civilizations 92ff., where his very sensible caveat regarding this literature on pp. 93ff. is frequently disregarded by his own use of the material on subsequent pages.

13. PAPS 107 466ff., and in H. Lasswell, *Propaganda and Communication in World History* I, 77ff.

14. There are parallels for tradition ascribing the fall of a dynasty not to the ruler who was actually the last to reign, but to the last great ruler of the dynasty. Güterbock, ZA 42 74f., and Drew, JNES 33 390 n. 31, cite Sardanapalus (= Ashurbanipal), and Hallo, *The Ancient Near East* 63, cites the later ascription of Nabonidus's bizarre behavior to his illustrious predecessor, Nebuchadnezzar. See also Michalowski, Essays Finkelstein 156f.

15. PAPS 107 468f.

16. Ibid. 467.

17. Add perhaps the Old Akkadian excerpt MAD 1 172 studied by Jacobsen, AfO 26 1ff., which does not by itself mention Naramsin, but seems to refer to traditions about his reign.

18. See the extensive comments by Jacobsen, op. cit., and cf. Michalowski, JCS 32 235 ff.

19. See RAI 26 99ff.

20. Grayson BHLT 7.

21. Note that in the Naramsin inscription b 5:12ff. (AfO 20 74), Nergal clears Naramsin's way to Syria.

22. Naramsin a2 and 3 (AfO 20 17); Sumer 32 63ff.

23. A rebellion in Babylonia is probably the subject of Naramsin b2 (AfO 20 19f.)

24. Cf. Grayson and Sollberger, RA 70 106.

25. E.g., Hallo, RLA 3 710.

26. But note the recensional variants suggesting, according to Hallo, loc. cit., a tradition of virtual Akkadian collapse after Šarkališarri.

27. Cf. Hallo, RLA 3 714f.

28. This same tradition of Naramsin being Sargon's son was reported by Nabonidus (AfO 20 26).

29. See RAI 26 99ff.

30. Known from the Naramsin inscription a2 (Hirsch, AfO 20 17).

31. Cf., e.g., RA 70 108.

32. Ed. Güterbock ZA 42 40ff. An unpublished tablet, identified by M. Civil, duplicates PBS 5 75 rev., but is very poorly preserved. The inscription has been judged fictional by nearly everybody, but the elaborate background for the fiction concocted by Curchin, RA 71 95, is very unconvincing.

33. RA 70 112:31.

34. AfO 20 24, and cf. RAI 26 99ff.

35. AfO 20 26, and cf. RAI 26 99ff., and J.-J. Glassner, *La chute d'Akkad* (diss. Paris, 1980).

36. See Chap. III Excursus B for a discussion of this topos.

37. Cf. Falkenstein, OLZ 1958 142f. Hallo's view, AS 20 188, that the *Weidner Chronicle* is an Akkadian adaptation of the *Curse of Agade*, exaggerates the relationship.

CHAPTER III

THE CURSE OF AGADE IN THE CONTEXT OF SUMERIAN LITERATURE

The *Curse of Agade* is unique in its subject matter: the destruction of a Babylonian city, which is never again to be rebuilt. The uniqueness lies in the permanence of the destruction; the theme of the destruction of cities, however, is a commonplace, and forms the subject matter of both the OB city-laments, which commemorate specific historical disasters,[1] and the OB and first millennium *balag* compositions, which lament the destruction of cities and temples in more general terms.[2] It is not surprising then, that when the *Curse of Agade* was only partially reconstructed, it was classed with the city-laments, with which it shares so much phraseology.[3] But the city-laments are usually quite vague about mundane political circumstances. Only once is a ruler named,[4] and enemies are referred to in general terms more often than by ethnic designation; destroyed cities are listed, but there is no historical depth. The focus of the laments is on the divine decisions, actions, and responses surrounding the destruction (and restoration) of the city or cities in question. In contrast, the *Curse of Agade* speaks of the earlier hegemonies of Kish and Uruk (2f.), the selection of Sargon as the new world ruler (4ff.), and the rise and fall of Naramsin (40, 86, 92, 133), who is a prime actor in the composition. The *Curse of Agade's* willingness to name names, and its treatment of the rise and fall of a specific dynasty, approaches the character of the tradition of literary-historical texts discussed in the preceding chapter. In order to elucidate the special relationship between the *Curse of Agade* and both the city-laments and literary-historical texts, parallel passages will be juxtaposed on the following pages, rather than buried in the Commentary.

The **Curse of Agade** *and the City-Laments*[5]

Enlil's frown, which so ominously opens the *Curse of Agade,* is, in the beginning, directed not at Agade, but at the two earlier hegemonies which Agade is to replace. A similar frown heralds the divine decision to destroy Ur in LSU 22 u_4 an-né kur-kur-ra sag-ki ba-da-an-gíd-da-ba "When An frowned over all the lands. . . ."[6] Except for a brief historical introduction, the *Curse of Agade* is concerned in its first 54 lines with the strength and splendor of the new capital. The laments, on the other hand, always begin with portraits of destruction or divine decisions to destroy. In the *Curse of Agade,* the initial prosperity serves as a foil for the subsequent destruction;[7] in the laments, the initial destruction is juxtaposed with a concluding restoration, or hoped-for restoration. The divine and human supplication for restoration in the laments is in direct contrast to the destructive curse that the gods utter in the *Curse of Agade,* a curse designed precisely to prevent the restoration known from the laments. It is this curse, the finality of the destruction, that makes the text unique.

Green has stressed the imporance of divine abandonment in the laments: a city can be destroyed only when its god has left.[8] In the laments, this is usually preceded by a decision of An, Enlil, and the divine assembly. In the *Curse of Agade,* a mysterious pronouncement from Enlil's temple Ekur (57), leads Inanna to abandon Agade (60ff.):

> uru^{ki}-ta dúr-ra-ni ba-ra-gub
> ki-sikil ama$_5$-na šub-bu-gim
> kù ^{d}inanna-ke$_5$ èš a-ga-dè^{ki} mu-un-šub
> She withdrew her dwelling from the city,
> Like a young woman abandoning her woman's domain,
> Holy Inanna abandoned the sanctuary Agade.

Compare LSU 375f. ^{d}nanna . . . uru^{ki}-ni ba-ra-è ^{d}suen-e . . . é-a-ni ba-ra-an-tuš "Nanna . . . left his city, Suen . . . dwelt away from his temple", and LEr 1:11ff.:

> lugal-bi uru-ni . . . bar-ta ba-ra-gub . . .
> a-a ^{d}en-ki uru-ni . . . bar-ta ba-ra-gub . . .
> nin-bi mušen dal-a-gim uru-ni ba-ra-è
> ama é-mah-a kù ^{d}dam-gal-nun-na uru-ni ba-ra-è
> Its master moved outside his city . . .
> Father Enki moved outside his city . . .
> Its mistress like a flying bird, left her city,
> The mother of the lofty temply, holy Damgalnuna, left her city

The abandonment by the city-god leads to the withdrawal of divine support by other deities (67ff.):

> sa nam-en-na aga nam-lugal-la
> ma-an-si-um ^{giš}gu-za nam-lugal-la sum-ma
> ^{d}ninurta-ke$_4$ é-šu-me-ša$_4$-na ba-ni-in-ku$_4$
> uru^{ki} inim-inim-ma-bi ^{d}utu ba-an-túm
> geštu$_2$-bi ^{d}en-ki-ke$_4$ ba-an-túm
> me-lám an-né im-ús-sa-a-bi/an-né an-šà-ga ba-e-e$_{11}$
> ^{giš}targul kù im-dù-dù-a-bi/^{d}en-ki-ke$_4$ abzu-a mi-ni-in-bu
> ^{giš}tukul-bi ^{d}inanna-ke$_4$ ba-an-túm
> Ninurta brought (back) into his (temple) Ešumeša
> The sovereign insignia, the royal crown,
> The . . . and the royal throne which had been bestowed,
> Utu took away the city's counsel,
> Enki took away its wisdom,
> An took up into heaven's midst its radiant aura that reached heaven,
> Enki tore down into Abzu its well anchored holy mooring pole,
> Inanna took away its weapons

Similarly LSU 58ff.:[9]

an-né ke-en-gi ki-tuš-ba bí-in-ḫu-luḫ un-e ní bí-in-te
^{d}en-líl-le u$_4$ gig-ga mu-un-zal uru-a me bí-ib-gar
^{d}nin-tu-re arḫuš kalam-ma-ke$_4$ ^{giš}ig-šu-úr im-mi-in-gub
^{d}en-ki-ke$_4$ ^{íd}idigna ^{íd}buranun-na a im-ma-da-an-kéš
^{d}utu níg-si-sá inim gi-na ka-ta ba-da-an-kar
^{d}inanna-ke$_4$ mè-šen-šen-na ki-bal-e ba-an-sum
^{d}nin-gír-su-ke$_4$ ke-en-gi ga-gim téš-e ba-an-dé
An frightened Sumer in its dwellings, the people are afraid,
Enlil brought to pass a miserable day, he silenced the city,
Nintu put door-locks on the wombs of the land,[10]
Enki dammed up the water of the Tigris and Euphrates,
Utu withdrew truth and justice from (people's) mouths,
Inanna bestowed battle and combat on a rebellious land,
Ningirsu spilled out all of Sumer like milk

The withdrawal of divine favor is final in the laments, and the city's impending doom cannot be averted.[11] In the *Curse of Agade,* Agade and Naramsin anticipate the worst (77-93), but Naramsin looks for a change in fortune by performing extispicy, which, predictably, gives negative results (94-101). At this juncture, the desperate king tries to force Enlil to change his mind by attacking Enlil's temple, Ekur. Naramsin's motives are expressed in precisely the same terms that LSU and LU use to express the futility of such an attempt (98f.):

ì-sì-ga-na šu-a bal-e-dè
^{d}en-líl níg du$_{11}$-ga-ni ba-en-dè-kúr
In order to effect a change in his situation,
He tried to alter Enlil's pronouncement.

nam-tar-ra-bi níg nu-kúr-ru-dam a-ba šu mi-ni-íb-bal-e
Their (An, Enlil, Enki, Ninhursag) determination cannot be altered; who would try to change it? (LSU 56)

an-né du$_{11}$-ga-ni ur$_5$ nu-kúr-ru-dam
^{d}mu-ul-líl-le ka-ta è-a-ni šu nu-bal-e-dam
An never alters his pronouncement,
Enlil does not change that which issues from his mouth (LU 168f.)

After Naramsin plunders Ekur, however, and the Guti are ravaging the land, Enlil does not abandon Nippur, but simply consolidates and reduces his establishments (193ff.). The survivors then perform a lament, in which they utter cries (a uru$_2$-mu . . . a lú-bi . . . a é-kur "Alas my city! . . . Alas its people! . . . Alas the temple Ekur!") which are typical of both the city-laments and balag laments (e.g. LU 247f. a uru$_2$-mu . . . a é-mu). Immediately thereafter, nam-bé-éš ^{d}en-líl itima kù ba-an-ku$_4$ šà ka tab-ba ba-an-nú "Because of this, Enlil entered his holy bedchamber, and lay down fasting." This passive retreat in the face of a lamenting populace is mirrored by Enki's reaction—he has already abandoned his city—to his wife's lament over the destruction of Eridu and other Sumerian cities (LEr 7:5ff.):

^{d}en-ki lugal abzu-ke$_4$
šà ba-an-sìg u[r$_5$-r]a-ni ba-bad . . .
ní-te-a-ni i-si-iš mi-ni-ib-lá šà ka tab-ba ba-an-nú

Enki, king of the Abzu,
Grew depressed and anxious . . .
He moaned to himself, and lay down fasting.

The destruction of Sumer and its cities is accomplished, in the laments, by enemies that are sometimes named, and frequently referred to metaphorically as raging storms.[12] Curiously, the storm metaphor is absent in the *Curse of Agade,* except where applied to the angry god Enlil (149f.). The descent of the Guti into the alluvial plain is treated similarly in the *Curse of Agade*—gu-ti-um^{ki} . . . ^{d}en-líl-le kur-ta nam-ta-an-è "Enlil brought the Guti . . . out of the mountains" (155 ff.)—and in LSU 75, where they are but one of several named foes: u$_4$-ba ^{d}en-líl-le gu-ti-um^{ki} kur-ta im-ta-an-e$_{11}$ "Then Enlil brought the Guti down from the mountains."[13] The largest part of the city-laments comprises detailed description of the destruction itself, as does over half of the *Curse of Agade.* It is here that the bulk of the close parallels between the laments and the *Curse of Agade* are to be found. In the latter, these descriptions occur in four different contexts: Agade's reaction to Inanna's abandonment (77-82), Naramsin's destruction of Ekur (102-45), the ravages of the Guti (158-92) and the curse of the gods (214-21, 227-71). A complete discussion of the themes of destruction[14] in all their permutations is beyond the scope of this monograph, but an extensive account of the most similar treatments of these themes in the city-laments and the *Curse of Agade* is necessary to underscore the close relationship between the former and the latter.

Reaction of the City

èš a-ga-dè^{ki} zi-bi suḫur^{ku_6} tur-ra-gim engur-ra ba-an-til
Sanctuary Agade's life, like a tiny carp, was brought to an end in the watery depths (77)
un-bi ku$_6$ šu-dab$_5$-ba-gim zi-bi mi-ni-ib-túm-túm-mu
Its people, like fish being caught, tried to save their lives (LSU 302)
ku$_6$ a nigin$_2$-na lu-ga-gim zi-bi in-tùm-tùm-mu-dè
Like fish swarming in a pond, they tried to save their lives (LSU 407a)

am-si mah-gim gú ki-šè mi-ni-ib-gar
As a giant elephant, it bent its neck to the ground (79)
gud-gim saṃan ul$_4$-la-bi šub-bu-dè gú ki-šè lá-a-dè
That it be tethered quickly like a bull, neck bent to the ground (LSU 54)
urí^{ki}-ma am gal ù-na-gub-ba gú ki-[šè]
In Ur, the great triumphant wild bull [bends] its neck to the ground (LSU 262)

bàd kù-zu en-na sukud-rá-bi a-nir ḫé-em-da-sá
May your holy walls resound with mourning to their highest points! (227)
bàd-bi en-na nigin$_2$-na-a-bi-da a-nir ba-da-sá
Its walls resound with mourning around their entire perimeter (LSU 380)
še-eb sag-a na-ám-tar-zu gig-ga-àm íb-ši-šìr-šìr
On top of the masonry (walls), they sing of your bitter fate (LN 141)

Wrecking, Profanation, and Pillage

gi-gun$_4$-na-aš eše gín ba-ši-in-ak
He treated the *giguna* as a thirty shekel (prize) (105)
lú su^{ki} elam^{ki} lú ḫa-lam-ma eše gín ba-an-ak

The Su-people and the Elamites, vandals, treated it (the temple) as (worth only) thirty shekels (LU 244)

é-e . . . ^{urudu}ḫa-zi-in gal-gal ba-ši-in-dé-dé
^{urudu}aga-silig-ga á min-na-bi-da u_4-sar ba-an-ak
For the temple . . . he had large axes cast,
He had double-edged *agasilig*-axes sharpened (112ff.)
é zi-ba ^{urudu}ḫa-zi-in gal-gal-e téš-bi ì-kú-e
In its fine temple, large axes consume everything (LU 243)
uri^{ki}-ma ^{urudu}ḫa-zi-in gal-gal-e igi-bi-šè ù-sar ì-ak-e
In Ur, large axes are sharpened before them (LSU 382)

ká silim-ma-bé ^{giš}al-e bí-in-ra
At its "Gate of Well-Being," the pickax struck (125)
úr-bi in-bu-ra-àm al-e bí-in-ra
Their foundations are ripped up, the pickax struck them (LN 98)

^{giš}ká-na-bi ba-ra-an-si-ig téš kalam-ma ba-kúr
He removed its door frames, and the land's vigor was subverted (122)
^{giš}ká-na-bi ba-ra-an-si-ig (var. BU) é-e igi ba-ab-kúr
It (the storm) removed its door frames, and the temple's appearance was distorted (LEr 2:18f.)

itima é u_4 nu-zu-ba un-e igi i-ni-in-bar
^{urudu}šen kù dingir-re-e-ne-ke_4 uri^{ki} igi i-ni-in-bar
The people saw the bedchamber, its room which knows no daylight,
Akkad saw the holy vessels of the gods (129f.)
á-ná-da kù ^{d}nanna-ka gìr ki mu-u[n-]
^{urudu}šen kù lú igi nu-bar-re-dam $erim_2$-e igi i-ni-in-bar
In Nanna's holy bedroom [he s]et foot,
The enemy saw the holy vessels, which no one should see (LSU 449f.)
^{urudu}šen kù lú igi nu-b[ar-r]e-da/lú su^{ki} elam^{ki} lú ḫa-l[am-ma igi in-ni]-in-bar
The Su-people and Elamites, vandals, saw the holy vessels, which no one should see (LEr 4:9f.)
⌈itima⌉ kù u_4 nu-zu-ba un-e igi hé-ni-in-bar
The people saw the holy bedchamber which knows no daylight (LEr 6:12)

é-e ^{giš}má gal-gal kar-ra ba-an-ús
Large ships were docked at the temple (143)
kù ^{na_4}za-gìn-bi má gal-gal-e bal-še ì-ak-e
He loaded its (the city's) silver and lapis onto large ships (LSU 172)

Disruption of Husbandry and Agriculture

ùz gi ^{d}en-líl-lá amaš-ta ba-ra-ra-aš na-gada-bi bí-in-ús-ú-ús
šilam tùr-bi-ta ba-ra-ra-aš unu_3-bi bí-in-ús-ú-ús

They drive the trusty goats of Enlil from the fold,
and make their herdsmen follow,
They drive the cows from the pens, and make their cowherds follow (164f.)
tùr gul-gul-lu-dè amaš tab-tab-bé-dè
gud-bi tùr-bi-a nu-gub-bu-dè
udu-bi amaš-bi-a nu-dagal-e-dè
That the pens be destroyed, the folds decimated,
So that its bulls do not stay in their pens,
So that its sheep do not expand in their folds (LSU 6ff.)
gud-mu tùr-bi-a ba-ra-an-šub mu-lu-bi ba-ra-gub
e-zé-mu amaš-bi-a ba-ra-an-šub na-gada-bi ba-ra-gub
My bulls are cast out of their pens, their (herds)men moved out,
My sheep are cast out of their folds, their herders moved out (LU 267f.)
amaš [lú]sipa zi-da dù-dù-a-ri ní-bi-a ba-an-sù-sù
tùr utul gal-e dù-a-ri ní-bi-a ba-an-x
The fold built by the trusty shepherd has gone off of its own accord,
The pen built by the great cowherd has . . . of its own accord (LW 2:14f.)

a-gàr gal-gal-e še nu-um-túm . . .
pú-[giš]kiri$_6$ làl geštin nu-um-túm
The great agricultural tracts produced no grain . . .
The irrigated orchards produced neither syrup nor wine (172, 174)
gán uru$_2$-gá-ka še ba-ra-ma-al . . .
pú-[giš]kiri$_6$ làl geštin si-a-mu giš-gír kur-ra ḫa-ba-mú
In my city's fields there is no grain . . .
My irrigated orchards which overflowed with syrup and wine, grow mountain thorn bushes (LU 271, 273)

Slaughter and Starvation

KA ba-dub-dub sag ba-dab$_5$-dab$_5$
KA ba-dub sag numun-e-eš ba-ab-gar
Mouths were crushed, heads were crashed,
Mouths were crushed, heads sown as seeds (188f.)
u$_4$ mud-e KA ì dub-dub sag ì-dab$_5$-dab$_5$
On that bloody day, *mouths* were crushed, heads were crashed (LSU 81)

sag zi sag lul-la šu-bal ba-ni-ib-ak
mes mes-e an-ta i-im-nú
úš lú lul-e úš lú zi-da-ke$_4$ an-ta na-mu-un-DU
Honest people were confounded with liars,
Young men lay upon young men,
The blood of liars ran upon the blood of honest men (190ff.)
lú lul lú zi-ra an-ta nú-ù-dè
uri$_3$ lú lul-e lú zi-ra ugu-a-na DU-šè
So that liars lay upon honest men,
The blood of liars ran upon (the blood of) honest men (LSU 114f.)

numun zi sag lul-la sag zi-da šu-bal mi-ni-ib-ak-a-a-aš
They confounded good offspring, liars and honest people (LW 3:21)

uru^{ki}-bi šà-gar-ra ḫé-ni-ib-ug$_7$-e
May that city die of hunger! (248)
urí^{ki}-ma si-ga kal-ga-bi šà-gar-ra im-ug$_7$
In Ur, the weak and strong died of hunger (LU 227)

dumu-gi$_7$ ninda ša$_6$-ga kú-kú-zu ú-šim-e ḫa-ba-nú
May your aristocrats, who eat fine food, lie (hungry) in the grass! (249)
lugal ninda ša$_6$-ga kú-kú-a kur$_6$-re im-ma-an-dab$_5$
The king, who always ate fine food, receives (common) rations (LSU 305)
gír PA-a gu$_4$ kú udu kú-ra ú-šim-e ba-[da]-nú
The . . . who ate bulls and sheep, lies (hungry) in the grass (LSU 313)

Disruption of Transportation Network

lú-kin-gi$_4$-a ḫar-ra-an-na nu-mu-un-gin
Messengers no longer travel the highways (162)
kaskal-la gìr nu-gá-gá-dè ḫar-ra-an nu-kin-kin-dè
So that no feet would be set on the roads, no journeys undertaken (LSU 39)

gú ^{giš}má-gíd-da íd-da-zu ú gíd-da ḫé-em-mú
ḫar-ra-an ^{giš}gigir-ra ba-gar-ra-zu ú a-nir ḫé-em-mú
May long grass grow along your canal bank tow-paths!
May mourning grass grow on your highways laid for coaches (264f.)
íd má-gur$_8$-re ba-ab-du$_7$-a-za šà-ba ú-ú^{sar} ba-an-mú
ḫar-ra-an ^{giš}gigir-e ba-ab-gar-ra-za šà-ba
giš-gír kur-ra ba-an-mú
Grasses grow in your canals that could accommodate cargo ships,
Mountain thornbushes grow on your highways laid for coaches (LU 367f.)
(íd-bi . . .) gú-dù-a-bé gìr nu-gál ú gíd-da ba-an-mú
There are no feet on their (the canals') built-up banks, long grass grows there (LSU 329)
^{íd}idigna ^{íd}buranun-na gú SI.A-a-bé ú ḫul mú-mú-dè
That evil grass should grow on the . . . banks of the Tigris and Euphrates (LSU 38)

Alteration of Landscape and Water Supply

eden šà ú ša$_6$-ga mú-a-zu gi ír-ra ḫé-em-mú
May "lamentation reeds" grow upon your plains, where fine grass grows! (268)
eden-e ú a-nir mú-mú-dè
That mourning grass should grow on the plains (LSU 11)

a-ga-dè^{ki} a du$_{10}$-ga dé-a-zu a mun-na ḫé-em-dé
Agade, may your flowing sweet-water flow as brackish water! (269)
íd-bi a uri$_3$-na tùm-ù-dè
That its rivers should carry bitter water (LSU 9)

Other parallels between the Curse of Agade and the city-laments, as well as the balag laments, will be found in Chapter VII.

In the previous chapter, a disparate group of texts that treat historical events, but are not contemporary with those events, was analyzed to elucidate its image of Naramsin. With the sole exception of the *Sumerian King List,* all of the texts were in Akkadian, because the *Curse of Agade* is the only other such text in Sumerian to mention Naramsin. But there *is* a corpus of such texts in Sumerian, a rather large one if one includes the city-laments[15] and certain royal hymns.[16] Only one of these compositions deals with the Agade dynasty, and a tiny piece of it (TRS 73) was already known to Güterbock, who noted its affinity to the *Curse of Agade,* but correctly emphasized the differences in style between the two texts.[17] TRS 73 can now be augmented by 3NT 296, a 57-line single-column tablet from Nippur to be edited by the author and W. Heimpel.[18] Although the two tablets do not overlap, they are clearly part of the same composition, beginning with Urzababa on the throne of Kish, and ending (as preserved) with an imminent victory of Sargon over Lugalzagesi. The middle of the composition, on the unpublished Nippur tablet, tells, in very difficult terms, how Sargon came to replace Urzababa. The style of the composition as known from TRS 73 is maintained in the unpublished tablet: concise narrative and dialogue, without the expansive poetic rhetoric that characterizes the *Curse of Agade.*[19] It is in its narrative portions that the *Curse of Agade* parallels and even duplicates phrases in the Sargon story.

The relatively rare KI.UD-ba/bi is used by both texts to introduce Sargon, on TRS 73:10 after Enlil has decided to remove sovereignty from Kish, and in almost the very same context in *Curse of Agade* 4. The climax of dynastic prosperity is portrayed in nearly the same language by both texts:

lugal-bi sipa ^{d}na-ra-am-^{d}sin-e
bara$_2$ kù a-ga-dè^{ki}-šè u$_4$-dè-éš im-è (40f.)
Its king, the shepherd Naramsin,
Rose like the sun on the holy throne of Agade

lugal-bi sipa ur-^{d}za-ba$_4$-ba$_4$
é kiš^{ki}-a-ka ^{d}utu-gim àm-è
Its king, the shepherd Urzababa,
Rose like the sun in the house of Kish (TRS 73:6f.)

When the reality of divine displeasure and his own imminent fall become clear to Naramsin, he is unable to articulate or discuss the unpleasant realization (87): šà-ga-ni-šè mu-un-zu eme-na nu-um-gá-gá lú-da nu-mu-un-da-ab-bé "He knew it deep in his heart, but would not articulate it with his tongue, nor discuss it with anyone." Precisely the same sentence occurs three times in the Sargon story (3NT 296 4, r.23, 25) also in contexts of foreboding.[20] A final point of comparison in the language of the two texts is the parallels to the difficult l. 128 discussed in the commentary thereto.

In the preceding chapter, the tradition in the *Curse of Agade* regarding Naramsin's anger at unfavorable omens (94-101) was compared to a similar tradition in the Akkadian *Cuthean Legend.* Whereas Naramsin's anger in the *Curse of Agade* leads to complete disaster, in the Cuthean Legend, after several devastating setbacks resulting from his disregard of the omens, he finally obeys the divine will and survives. A similar tradition is preserved about Amarsin, who ruled at Ur nearly two centuries after Naramsin.[21] Two poorly preserved

Sumerian fragments tell, among other things, of an initially negative oracle when the king wanted to build the temple of Enki, followed by an anxious eight year wait for a propitious sign.[22] The negative omens are expressed very similarly in Curse of Agade and the Amarsin text:

é-šè máš-àm šu-gíd-dè
é dù-a máš-a nu-mu-un-dè-gál
Performing extispicy with regard to the temple,
The (omen for) building the temple was not present in the extispicy (94f.)
é-^{d}en-ki-ga-šè dù-ù-dè máš-e šu mu-un-gíd-da-a
máš-bi-ta é dù-a nu-mu-un-na-ab-bé
When he performed extispicy about the building of Enki's temple,
The result of that extispicy did not tell him to build the temple (UET 8 32 r.2′f.)

The ensuing depression of Amarsin during his eight-year wait has striking parallels in the description of Naramsin's seven-year depression following his foreboding dream, but prior to the unsuccessful extispicy:

nam-é-kur-ra-šè ^{túg}mu-sír-ra ba-an-mu$_4$ . . .
á-ŠITA$_4$-a nam-lugal-la-ka-ni im-ma-ra-an-ba-ba
Because of (the negative decision from) Ekur, he donned mourning garb . . .
He gave away his royal paraphernalia (88, 91)
^{d}amar-^{d}sin-na me nam-lugal-la-na [ ]
^{d}amar-^{d}sin-na lu-bu-uš-tum nam-l[ugal-la-ka]-ni ^{túg}mu-sír-ra ba-an-[ku$_4$]
Amarsin . . . his powers of kingship . . .
Amarsin changed his kingly garments for mourning garb (UET 8: 33:9′, 11′)

Similar instances of royal depression can be found in Ibbisin's reaction to his land's devastation and his own imminent fall in LSU 108ff., and Naramsin's unhappiness after his military defeats in the *Cuthean Legend.*

A long and poorly preserved pseudepigraphic inscription of Lugalannemundu,[23] a king otherwise known only from the Pre-Sargonic section of the *Sumerian King List,* opens by commemorating his victory over a grand coalition of enemy forces, but most of the text is concerned with his erection of the Enamzu in Adab, and his provisions for that establishment.[24] The understanding of a difficult line in the *Curse of Agade* was made possible by a gloss to a similar line in that inscription:

mar-ḫa-ši^{ke} le-um-ma gur-ru-dè
That Marḫaši would be reentered on the (tribute) rolls (20)
. . .$^{ki?}$ le-um-ma gur$^{?}$-gur-ru-dam
gloss: *ana le'im utēr*
By reentering . . . on the rolls (gloss: I reentered . . .) (Lugalannemundu 5)

One additional parallel with that inscription involves a topos known from royal inscriptions beginning with Lugalzagesi:[25]

kur-kur ú-sal-la i-im-nú
All foreign lands rested contentedly (38)
un-e kur-kur-ra ú-sal-la mi-ni-in-nú (-a)
The people in all foreign lands rested contentedly (Lugalannemundu 7)

Excursus A: The Divine Alienation of Political Power

The alternation of good times with bad that characterizes, realistically, the ancient Mesopotamians' view of their past, as articulated in Güterbock's classic study,[26] must, as Green demonstrates in her study of the city-laments, be understood as the enactment of divine will.[27] But what motivated that will? When a city or dynasty loses sovereignty or is destroyed, when Sumer is overrun, is there any reason for this display of divine displeasure? In some texts there is, and in some there is not. Royal inscriptions and hymns, from earliest times on, equate a ruler's piety with the power and prosperity that the gods have bestowed or will bestow upon him, and the impiety or dishonor of an enemy was or will be the cause of the enemy's defeat and destruction. But the literary-historical texts do not all make the causal link between royal behavior and the alienation of political power. The *Sumerian King List,* in fact, never even mentions a single deity in its long litany of dynastic change, but simply recounts the transfer of sovereignty from city to city, as a result of military defeat or just "alienation" (kúr).[28] This absence of theological speculation may be attributed to an effort to make the tendentious king list, composed to promote the concept of a single legitimate sovereign at any one time, resemble the true year lists and king lists that were maintained for administrative and legal purposes.

The city-laments, as has been shown above, place the responsibility for the loss of power and destruction of Sumerian cities squarely on the shoulders of the great gods and the divine assembly. Curiously, the city-laments never attribute these divine decisions to any impiety of the sovereign or his people. It was just time:

> urí^{ki}-ma nam-lugal ḫa-ba-sum bala da-rí la-ba-an-sum
> u_4 ul kalam ki-gar-ra-ta zag un lu-a-šè
> bala nam-lugal-la sag-bi-šè è a-ba-a igi
> im-mi-in-du$_8$-a
> True, Ur was given sovereignty, but it was not given an eternal reign,
> From the ancient day that the land was established, among all the numerous
> people (who have lived since)
> Has anyone ever seen a royal dynasty that remained (forever) paramount?[29]
> (LSU 368-70)

A similarly arbitrary view of divine will acting in history can be found in the Ur III Royal Correspondence:

> u_4-da ^{d}en-líl-le gá-e-ra ḫul ba-an-gig
> dumu-ni ^{d}sin-na-ra ḫul ba-an-gig
> urí^{ki} lú kúr-ra bí-in-sum-mu
> At the moment, Enlil hates me, and
> He hates his son Sin;
> He is giving Ur to a foreigner.
> (Letter 20: 5-7)[30]

Thus Ibbisin explains his setbacks, and in Letter 21, his rival, Išbierra, explains how Enlil has granted *him* sovereignty, again, entirely without motive.

In the *Curse of Agade,* it is Naramsin's outrageous attack on the temple of Enlil that causes the Gutian invasion, and leads to the divine execration against Agade. But earlier in the composition, in lines 55ff., Inanna abandons Agade, seemingly at Enlil's behest. No explicit reason for this sudden alienation of divine affection is expressed in the text, but several scholars understand it to be motivated by the flow to Agade of offerings which should be going to Nippur. However, given the absence of any rationale for divine abandonment in other Sumerian historical-literary compositions, the initial displeasure of Inanna and Enlil in the *Curse of Agade* might also have been arbitrary.[31]

Divine whim continues to play a role in literature known from first-millennium sources. Although the *Erra Epic* attributes Erra's decision to destroy Babylonia to the preference of the Babylonians for Marduk rather than for him (I 120ff.), Marduk admits to having unintentionally caused cosmic disruptions when he last left his sanctuary to get his cultic self refurbished, and is tricked into creating chaos again in the same unthinking way (III 44ff.). So, too, in the *Marduk Prophecy,*[32] he absents himself from Babylonia not because he is unhappy with the Babylonians, but for business or touristic reasons.[33] Other prophecy texts[34] parade a succession of good and bad rulers, but the succession itself has no apparent motivation.[35]

But these are exceptions in the first millennium, where one frequently encounters long and elaborate portraits of good and bad rulers, and the rewards and punishments they received from on high.[36] It is this tradition, already present in the Pre-Sargonic royal inscriptions,[37] that we find in the *Curse of Agade,* where Enlil's wrath is very reasonably kindled when his temple is destroyed by the frustrated Naramsin. The notion that the rise and fall of great empires depended on the impious behavior of one or another ruler was developed, by the first millennium, into a pattern that could be superimposed on all of Babylonian history, so that the fortunes of rulers from earliest times to the present could be attributed to their conduct toward the cult of Marduk at Babylon,[38] or Anu at Uruk.[39]

Excursus B: The Subhuman Barbarian

Mesopotamian sources of all periods are surprisingly free of racist ideology. That is to say, different ethno-linguistic groups are rarely characterized as inherently inferior, subhuman, or deserving extermination or servitude, and this is true of groups within Mesopotamia proper[40] as well as groups from neighboring lands.[41] Enemies, to be sure, are reviled in the strongest terms, both as groups and as individuals, but the ruler of a neighboring Babylonian city can be showered with as much (or more) abuse as the ruler of a distant land. In Sumerian literary tradition, there *was* a feeling that sovereignty over Babylonia should rest in native hands,[42] but the only expression of ethno-linguistic superiority in Sumerian literature is placed in the mouth of the ruler of Aratta, who is not a Sumerian.[43]

There are two important exceptions to this absence of ethnic stereotypes: the Gutians and the Amorites, who represent the nomadic and seminomadic hordes of the mountains to the north and east, and the desert to the north and west, respectively.[44] Both are described as subhuman, but in somewhat different terms. The Gutians are characterized as savage, beastlike imbeciles, whereas the Amorites are usually curious primitives, less horrible, if every bit as threatening militarily, than the Guti. In the *Curse of Agade,* the Guti are introduced as follows (154-57):

un-gá nu-sì-ga kalam-ma nu-šid-da
gu-ti-um^{ki} un kéš-da nu-zu

dím-ma lú-ulu$_3^{lu}$ galga ur-ra SIG$_7$.ALAN ^{ugu}ugu$_4$-bi
^{d}en-líl-le kur-ta nam-ta-an-è
Not classed among people, not reckoned as part of the land,
Gutium, people who know no inhibitions,
With human instinct but canine intelligence and monkeys' features—
Enlil brought them out of the mountains.[45]

The first two lines express a total otherness, an inhuman quality that characterizes their behavior. The third line maligns their intelligence and appearance.[46]

The apelike appearance of the Guti figures once again in a fictional letter of Ibbi-Sin, who says, referring back to the period of Gutian domination of Mesopotamia, that when Enlil hated Sumer,

^{ugú}ugu$_4$-bi kur-bi-ta è-dè
nam-sipa kalam-ma-šè mu-un-íl
He raised to the shepherdship of the land
Monkeys who came down from their mountains.[47]

Other sources picture the Guti as "serpents of the mountains"[48] or "dogs."[49] Their lack of intelligence recurs as a stereotype in the inscription of the Kassite king Agumkakrime (mid-second millennium), who calls the Guti *nīšē saklāti* "stupid people."[50] The inhuman quality of the Guti, both physically and behaviorally, persists in the Akkadian literary-historical tradition. The *Cuthean Legend*[51] describes the Ummanmanda who overwhelm Naramsin as "people with sheldrake bodies, men with raven faces," suckled by the monster Ti'amat.[52] They do turn out to be sorts of human beings after all, because they bleed when pricked.[53] A pseudepigraphic Naramsin inscription preserves a similar tradition when it speaks of a Gutian king as "not of flesh and blood."[54] The *Weidner Chronicle* writes of

Qutû ša tazzimte ila palāha la kullumi
parṣī uṣṣurāti šūtešura la idû
Oppressive Guti, who were never shown how to worship god,
Who did not know how to properly perform the rites and observances[55]

These Guti, in their ignorance, take away the fish offering presented to Marduk and thereby lose their sovereignty. The attribution of the loss of sovereignty to ignorance, rather than neglect or hostility, is unique to the Guti in this text.

The *ša tazzimte* "oppressive" of the last citation is a direct translation of lú i-^{d}utu found as an epithet of the Guti in a Shulgi hymn.[56] The expression is used imaginatively in an Urnammu hymn, where it is claimed that the king "loosed the bitter hold of Gutium . . .," and i-^{d}utu ka-ba um-mi-gi$_4$ "put the cry of the oppressed into *their* mouths."[57]

The Amorites' "otherness" is described in more specific terms than that of the Guti.[58] They are ignorant of the fundamental institutions of civilization: fixed shelter and settlements, agriculture, cuisine, and proper burial practices.[59] This ignorance is found in the *Curse of Agade* 46 mar-tu kur-ra lú še nu-zu "the highland Amorites, people ignorant of agriculture," and similarly in the *Lugalbanda Epic*[60] and a Shusin inscription.[61] An Ibbisin year name refers to them as "tempestuous forces who have never known cities (ul-ta uru^{ki} nu-zu)."[62] Their ignorance is described more fully in the *Marriage of Martu*:

lú uzu-diri kur-da mu-un-ba-al-la du_{10} gúr nu-zu-am
uzu nu-$šeg_6$-ga al-kú-e
u_4 ti-la-na é nu-tuk-a
u_4 ba-ug_6-ga-na ki nu-túm-mu-dam
A person who digs for truffles in the highlands, who knows not how to pay homage,
He eats uncooked meat,
Who, as long as he lives, has no house, and
When he dies, receives no burial.[63]

Similarly, in *Enki and the World Order*:

uru nu-tuk é nu-tuk-ra
^{d}en-ki-ke_4 mar-tu máš-anše sag-e-eš mu-ni-rig_7
To the Amorite, who has neither city nor house,
Enki presented livestock.[64]

But the topos of the uncivilized nomad (Amorite) merges with the topos of the animal-like brute from the mountains (Guti)[65] in two other descriptions of the Amorites, one from an Išmedagan hymn, and another from a Shusin inscription:

mar-tu é nu-zu uru^{ki} nu-zu
lú líl-lá hur-sag-gá tuš-a
The Amorite who knows neither house nor city,
The fool[66] who lives in the mountains[67]

u_4-bi-ta / mar-tu lú ḫa-lam-ma
dím-ma ur-ra-gim / ur-bar-ra-gim[68]
From that time, the Amorites, destructive people,
With instincts like dogs or like wolves

And both the Amorite's ignorance of civilization and his lack of intelligence are alluded to in what might be the earliest recorded ethnic joke:

gig-gú-nida(-a) làl-gim íb-ak
mar-tu ì-kú-e níg-šà-bi nu-un-zu
Pease flour is made up like a confection,
The Amorite eats it, but doesn't recognize its ingredients![69]

These ethnic slurs on Amorites and Guti are almost unique.[70] The Elamites, a traditional enemy from time immemorial, are once called ur idim "wild dogs,"[71] and they occur at the head of a passage in a plea from an Old Babylonian letter-prayer of Siniddinam, king of Larsa, in which the kind of imagery usually reserved for the Amorites and Gutians is applied to the Elamites, Subarians, and Su-people:[72]

kur $elam^{ki}$-ma $[buru]_5$ ^{mušen}-gim maḫ-bi lú til-a nu-gál-la
$su\text{-}bir_4^{ki}$ $muru_2$ dugud-da dingir-re-e-ne ní-te-gá nu-zu-a
ma-da-bi nu-ub-ta-ba ud-bi nu-gál-la
lú su(-e) dingir-ra-ni nu-gig lukur íl-la nu-mu-un-zu-a
(var. ki dingir-re-e-ne-ke_4 nu-gig lukur nu-mu-da-íl-e)
$eren_2$-a-ni ú-gim lu-lu-a/àm numun-a-ni/bi dagal-la
za-lam-gar ti-la ki-dingir-re-e-ne-ke_4 nu(-mu-un)-zu-a

ú-ma-am-gin$_7$-nam u$_5$(-a) zìz(-eše) siskur$_2$ (íl-la) nu-mu-un-zu-a
nam-tar ḫul-gál á-sàg níg-gig-ga nu-mu-(un-)na-te
lú mu dingir sal-la-bi níg-gig-ga ì-kú-e
The (inhabitants of the) mountainous land of Elam, overwhelming as lo[cust swarms], who are not among the living,
Subir, the thick fog that knows not how to revere the gods,
Whose land is not . . . and whose storm (to destroy it) is nonexistent,
The Su, whose god knows no consecrated *nugig* or *lukur* priestess,
(var.: who consecrates no *n.* or *l.* priestess in the places of the gods)
Whose population is numerous as grass, whose seed is wide-spread,
Who lives in a tent, and knows not the places of the gods,
Who mates just like an animal, and knows not how to make offerings of (*eše*)-flour,
The evil *namtar*-demon and the dangerous *asag*-demon do not approach him.
Someone who, profaning the name of god, violates taboos . . .

In the well-known letter of Ibbisin to Puzurnumusda, Išbierra is characterized as

lú im-sa$_{10}$-sa$_{10}$ nu-luḫ-ḫa^{sar}
A man who peddles asafetida
numun ke-en-gi-ra nu-me-a
Not of Sumerian stock
lú ma-rí^{ki}-ke$_4$ galga ur-ra
A man from Mari, with a dog's intelligence[73]

Although we have seen (n. 46) that the slur in the last line can be used as a general insult, it and similar expressions occur mainly in descriptions of the Guti and Amorites, and the image in the first line calls to mind the Amorite grubbing for truffles in the *Marriage of Martu* passage quoted earlier. Perhaps the currently accepted opinion that Išbierra did not have an Amorite background[74] needs revision. Certainly his Akkadian name alone does not conclusively prove that he was not an Amorite.[75]

Notes

1. Green Eridu Chap. 9; Krecher, RLA s.v. Klagelied. Cf. Vanstiphout, RAI 26 83f.
2. M. Cohen, SANE 1/2; Krecher, op. cit. Just such a lament is performed by the survivors of the Gutian incursions in *Curse of Agade* 196ff.
3. See Chap. I.
4. LSU 35. Note also the mention of Išmedagan at the end of the Uruk and Nippur laments, in connection with those cities' restoration (Green Eridu 306).
5. See Green Eridu Chap. 9, for an outline of the city-laments and a catalogue of themes and topics.
6. An's frown is followed in LSU 23 by ^{d}en-líl-le igi-ni ki kúr-ra ba-an-gar-ra-a-ba "When Enlil set his eye on a foreign place," i.e., in search of a destructive agent to visit upon Sumer. Cf. *Curse of Agade* 152 (^{d}en-líl-le . . .) kur gú-bí-na-šè igi na-an-íl "Enlil looked toward the Gubin mountains" (whence he brings down the Guti).
7. See Chap. IV.

8. Green Eridu 304ff. The notion that the gods abandon their cities to destruction voluntarily persists into the first millennium in, e.g., the *Marduk Prophecy*, the *Erra Epic*, and Neo-Assyrian and Neo-Babylonian royal inscriptions. Divine abandonment is the mythological expression of the looting of an enemy's sacred images, frequently described in historical inscriptions (See Roberts and Miller, *Hand of the Lord*, 10ff.), and is implied in the descriptions of the looting of sanctuaries in the city-laments (Green Eridu 289f.) as well as in the *Curse of Agade*. The topos can be traced back as far as the *Lagash Lament* of Uru'inimgina (see n. 37), immediately preceding the Sargonic period.

9. At the point when it was decided that Sin must leave his city, but before he did so.

10. Following a suggestion of T. Jacobsen.

11. Green Eridu 300.

12. Ibid. 301. Cf. Vanstiphout, RAI 26 85f.

13. For the description of the Guti, see Excursus B, below.

14. Cf. Green Eridu 295ff. The theme continues, of course, in Akkadian literary and historical texts; cf. the Sargon (of Assyria) and Esarhaddon passages cited by F. Malbran, JA 268 25f., for striking parallels to certain passages in the *Curse of Agade*.

15. Green Eridu 322.

16. The so-called *Königsepen*.

17. ZA 42 37f.

18. JAOS 103.

19. Note that there is no dialogue in the *Curse of Agade*, and the only direct speech in the composition is the long divine curse.

20. Contrast TRS 73 r. 5 šà-ga-né nu-un-zu ugu kin-gi$_4$-a nu-mu-un-du$_{11}$ "He (Lugalzagesi) did not know it deep in his heart, and would not speak to the messenger." Lugalzagesi does not yet understand that his number is up.

21. UET 8 32f., ed. Green Eridu 58 ff., and cf. Michalowski, Essays Finkelstein 155ff., and Hruška, Ar Or 47 8ff.

22. Assuming a sequence UET 8 32r. followed by 33. Note Naramsin's seven-year wait *before* performing extispicy in *Curse of Agade* 92f.

23. See Chap. II n. 32.

24. To be compared, perhaps, with the *Cruciform Monument of Maništusu* (Sollberger, JEOL 20 52ff.).

25. Sjöberg, ZA 54 67.

26. ZA 42 13ff.

27. Green Eridu 325.

28. Jacobsen, AS 11 29ff.; Grayson ABC 197. The same godless change occurs in the related *Dynastic Chronicle* (Grayson ABC No. 18).

29. Compare the similar response given to Gilgamesh in order to explain not the end of his reign, but the end of his own life: ^{d}bìl-ga-mèš nam-zu nam-lugal-šè mu-túm ti da-re-éš nu-mu-un-túm "Gilgamesh, your destiny is supposed to be for kingship; it is not supposed to be for eternal life" (Kramer, BASOR 94 7).

30. Cf. Enmerkar's accusation of arbitrariness to Inanna in Wilcke Lugalbanda lines 311ff. = 377ff. (already Wilcke ad loc.).

31. For the difficulties involved in these lines and their various interpretations, see Chap. I, this chapter, and the Commentary to lines 55f. and 57.

32. Borger, Bi Or 28 3ff.

33. Compare this with the explanation (Marduk's anger) in the text last edited by Lambert, RAI 19 434ff.; and with Nabonidus's attribution of Sennacherib's destruction of Babylon to Marduk's anger at that city (VAB 4 p. 270). Esarhaddon gives a more elaborate, but essentially similar description of the same events (Borger Asarhaddon pp. 12ff.). On the texts dealing with Marduk's absences from Babylon and his anger or indifference toward it, see Roberts and Miller, *Hand of the Lord*, 11ff.; Roberts, Essays Finkelstein 183ff.

34. Grayson and Lambert, JCS 18 7ff. Text A; Hunger and Kaufman, JAOS 95 371 ff. = Hunger Uruk 3 = Hunger UVB 26/27 87 and pl. 25; Grayson BHLT 24 ff. (*Dynastic Prophecy*).

35. Grayson and Lambert, JCS 18 7ff. Text B//Biggs, Iraq 29 117ff., gives astrological justification for the succession.

36. This tradition culminates in the inscriptions of Nabonidus, and in the inscriptions and propaganda of his vanquisher, Cyrus, but it had already flowered in the late second millennium, in compositions like those taking Tukulti-Ninurta I or Nebuchadnezzar I as their subjects.

37. See also, and especially, the so-called *Lagash Lament* (Sollberger Corpus Ukg. 16), where the question of responsibility and punishment is very explicit (cf. Sjöberg Or Su 21 91; Kienast, Or 42 493).

38. The *Weidner Chronicle*, and the *Chronicle of Early Kings* (Grayson ABC Nos. 19 and 20).

39. The *Shulgi Chronicle* (Hunger Uruk 2).

40. Cf., e.g., Or 42 239 ff.

41. Cf. Limet, RAI 18 123 ff.

42. Note Ibbisin's objection to Išbi'erra on the grounds that he was from Mari, of non-Sumerian stock (Royal Letter 22 quoted below), and Utuhegal's account of how the Guti "carried away Sumer's sovereignty to the mountains" (RA 9 113 ff. i 4ff.), and then Enlil commissioned him "to return the sovereignty of Sumer" (ibid. 29f.), which he successfully accomplishes (ibid. edge). Similar feelings are found in the Assyrian description of Shamshi-Adad as *la šīr Aššur* (JCS 8 32). The *Sumerian King List*, however, makes no distinction at all between foreign and Babylonian dynasties.

43. Cohen Enmerkar 566f. lú-bé-ne lú lú-ta dar-a/lú ^{d}dumu-zi-dè lú-ta è-a-me-eš "Its (Aratta's) people are separate from other people, a people that Dumuzi has made superior to other people."

44. For the same phenomenon in Assyrian inscriptions, see Malbran, JA 267 11ff.

45. For this last line in LSU, see above.

46. The insult za-e dím-ma-zu dím-ma ^{ugu}ugu$_4$-bi galga-zu galga ur-gi$_7$-ra-ka "You! Your instinct is a monkey's and your intelligence a dog's!" (Civil, JCS 21 37) demonstrates that such epithets could also be applied to individuals. A similar insult in another texts, ^{ugu2}ugu$_4$-bi (var. $^{a.ugu}$ugu$_4$-bi) kur(-bi) umuš nu-ša$_6$ galga-bi sùh-a "a monkey of? the mountains whose sense is not good and whose intelligence is confused" (Sjöberg JCS 24 107), may be a play on our *Curse of Agade* passage that subsequently became corrupted.

47. Michalowski Royal Correspondence Letter 22:16f. Note also the monkey from the mountains (= Elamites?) in the name of Ibbisin's 23rd year (cf. Klein, JCS 31 153 n. 23)

48. RA 9 113 ff. i 1 and iv 30 (Utuḫegal) muš-gír ḫur-sag-gá (cf. Sjöberg TCS 3 118); LSU 148 muš kur-ra.

49. LW 4:11 gu-ti-um ur-re; Ibid. 20 gu-ti-um^{ki} ur-ra.

50. 5R 33 i 38f.

51. See Chap. II.

52. An St. 5 98 and 100:31ff.; KBo 19 98b 5′ is a Bogh. Akk. parallel.

53. An St 5 100 and 102:64ff.; Hittite version ZA 44 52 ff.

54. RA 70 117 L ii 14′ff.; see Chap. II.

55. Grayson ABC 149f., 56f.; see Chap. II.

56. Castellino Shulgi B 267.

57. ZA 53 120 iv 90f.

58. Buccellati Amorites 89ff. and 330ff.; Alster Studies 124.

59. Limet, RAI 129f., connects this with the anonymous enemies called lú kù nu-zu-ù-ne . . . lú za nu-zu-ù-ne "people who knew neither precious metals nor precious stones" (LU 280f.), and lú ì nu-zu-ne . . . lú ga nu-zu-ne "people who know neither oil nor milk" (LSU 336f.). See also the unique passage in Alster Studies 137:271f.:

dingir kur-ra lú kú-kú-ù-[me]-eš
é lú-gim nu-dù uru lú-gim nu-dù
The gods of the mountains/foreign lands eat men,

They do not build houses like men, they do not build cities like men.

A reflex of the topos of culinary ignorance can be found in broken context at the end of the first millennium Akkadian geographical treatise on the empire of Sargon of Agade (AfO 25 60:59).

60. Wilcke Lugalbanda 304 = 370.

61. JCS 21 31:29.

62. RLA 5 6.

63. SEM 58 iv 26-29.

64. EWO 248f. (~ 131f.).

65. Cf. Malbran, JA 267 28f.

66. Lieberman, JCS 22 58, rejects "fool" for lú-líl-lá, but see now MSL 12 201:14; CAD s.v. *lillu*. "Phantom" seems unlikely here, but "man who lives in the open" is possible. In any case, the lexical evidence suggests contamination between lú-líl-lá and lil by OB. Cf. Yiddish *luftmensh*, which means someone with no visible means of support (lives off the air), but can also suggest a lack of intelligence.

67. Römer Königshymnen 53:271f.

68. JCS 21 31:24-27.

69. Alster, RA 72 104 and 111 (Proverb Collections 3 and 7).

70. The notion that Sum. ḫur-ru(-um) = Akk. *aḫurru* has anything to do with the Hurrians is no longer tenable (see RLA 4 509). But cf. AHW *nullâtu*, which Soden derives from the eastern barbarians, the Lullu(bi).

71. OECT 5 28f. l. 11.

72. OECT 5 25:35ff. / / TRS 56:1ff.; cf. Kramer, OECT 5 p. 5. P. Michalowski has kindly put his unpublished edition at my disposal.

73. Michalowski Royal Correspondence, Letter 22:18, 19, 34.

74. RLA 5 174.

75. For Amorites with Akkadian names in the Ur III period, see Buccellati Amorites 100, and Wilcke, WO 5 24.

CHAPTER IV

POETIC AND NARRATIVE STRUCTURE

The poetry of the *Curse of Agade* is characterized by the same devices common to all Sumerian poetic texts:[1] the artful combination of two and three-line units, which are themselves formed through repetition, parallelism or enjambment; long litanylike sections in which every line repeats the same verb or nominal phrase; and sequences of repeated passages, expressing, in this case, a curse and its fulfillment (264-71 ~ 273-80). Typically Sumerian, too, is the concise obscurity of the lines most crucial to understanding the composition, 55-59 and 98f., those lines which explain Inanna's rejection of Agade, and Naramsin's motives for attacking Ekur. The tone of the composition moves between narrative passages reminiscent of the epic texts and certain literary-historical compositions, and long descriptive passages of the type that characterize the city-laments.[2]

There are five narrative episodes in the composition:

- I. The Rise of Agade (1-54)
    - a. Enlil alienates sovereignty from Kish and Uruk and gives it to Sargon. Inanna establishes her cult in Agade. (1-9)
    - b. Inanna works for Agade's prosperity. (10-24)
    - c. Agade prospers. (25-54)
- II. Withdrawal of Divine Favor (55-93)
    - a. Inanna is displeased and abandons Agade. (55-65)
    - b. Ninurta withdraws emblems of royalty, and other gods withdraw powers. (66-76)
    - c. Agade's reaction. (77-82)
    - d. Naramsin's foreboding dream and depression. (83-93)
- III. Naramsin Destroys Ekur (94-148)
    - a. Unsuccessful extispicy provokes Naramsin's hostility. (94-101)
    - b. Narmsin desecrates, destroys, and plunders Ekur. (102-45)
    - c. Agade becomes irrational. (146-48)
- IV. Enlil and the Guti (149-209)
    - a. In revenge, Enlil unleashes the barbarian Guti. (149-57)
    - b. The Guti devastate Babylonia. (158-92)
    - c. Enlil consolidates his shrines. (193-95)

d. The survivors lament. (196-208)
e. Enlil in retreat. (209)

V. The Gods Curse Agade (210-81)
a. The gods worship Enlil, and offer to curse Agade in revenge. (210-13)
b. The gods curse Agade. (214-21)
c. The gods decide to curse Agade again. (222-26)
d. The second curse and its fulfillment. (227-80)
e. Doxology. (281)

The introductory episode (I), dwelling on Agade's prosperity, stands in opposition to the final episode (V), in which Agade is cursed. Episode III, describing Naramsin's destruction of Ekur, is complemented by episode IV, detailing the depredations of the Guti in Babylonia. There is no apparent patterning of episodes with respect to length,[3] but the first three episodes (1-148), in which all action is done for or by Agade, take up a bit more than half the total number of lines, and the last two episodes (148-281), in which all action is taken against Agade, comprise somewhat less than half. Even so, a difference of nearly 20 lines in the lengths of the two halves precludes any planned division into two equal parts.

More interesting than counting lines or playing with the subdivision of the composition, is observing the manner in which portions of the text refer to one another in both contrasting and complementary ways, not only in the gross, thematic sense mentioned in the preceding paragraph, but on a more detailed level of specific phrases and topoi.[4] Contrast occurs between the images of prosperity in the first episode and the negative images in the four subsequent episodes. Complementary references occur in the description of the destruction of Ekur on the one hand, and the depredations of the Guti and divine curses of Agade on the other. To begin with contrast, the sovereignty (nam-en) and kingship (nam-lugal-la) which Enlil gives to Naramsin in l. 6, are found again in 67ff., where Ninurta withdraws the sovereign symbol (sa nam-en-na) and royal crown (aga nam-lugal-la) into his temple. In lines 7ff., Inanna establishes her cult in Agade, and in 58ff., she removes it in very similar terms:

7. u$_4$-ba èš a-ga-dè^{ki} kù ^{d}inanna-ke$_4$
8. ama$_5$ maḫ-a-ni-šè im-ma-an-dù-dù
9. ul-maš^{ki}-a ^{giš}gu-za ba-ni-in-gub
10. lú-tur gibil-bi é dù-ù-gim
11. dumu-bàn-da ama$_5$ gá-gá-gim
At that time, holy Inanna built
The sanctuary Agade as her grand woman's domain,
Set up her throne in Ulmaš
Like a youngster building a house for the first time,
Like a girl establishing a woman's domain . . .
58. a-ga-dè^{ki} tuk$_4$-e mu-un-na-lá-lá
59. ul-maš^{ki}-a ní im-ma-ni-in-te
60. uru^{ki}-ta dúr-ra-ni ba-ra-gub
61. ki-sikil ama$_5$-na šub-bu-gim
62. kù ^{d}inanna-ke$_4$ èš a-ga-dè^{ki} mu-un-šub
Agade was reduced to trembling before her, and
She grew anxious in Ulmaš.
She withdrew her dwelling from the city,

Like a young woman abandoning her woman's domain,
Holy Inanna abandoned the sanctuary Agade.

Lines 61f. here exactly negate 7f., both containing the names of the goddess and Agade, and the woman's domain, substituting the verb *abandon* for the earlier *build.*

The people of Agade who eat "splendid food" in 15 reappear in 249 as "aristocrats" used to eating "fine food", who will now have to eat grass. The acquaintances eating together in 18, become people eaten together in 186f. (Note also the acquaintances who no longer find one another in 215.) The exotic monkeys on the crowded boulevards of Agade in 21, symbols of cosmopolitanism, return in the guise of the monkey-faced barbarians in 156. The same precious metals that fill Agade's storehouses in 25ff., are grossly devalued in 242ff.

In lines 29ff., a well-endowed populace uses musical instruments to express pleasure; in 196ff., these same population groups (um-ma 29, 196, 202; ab-ba 30, 197, 203; ki-sikil 31, 205; guruš 32, 206) use musical instruments to accompany a lament for their destroyed city. The foreign lands resting contentedly in 38, lose their well-being in 126 and are crying bitterly in 169; in 46ff., foreigners come to Agade bringing exotic tribute on open trade routes, but in 151ff., the marauding barbarian Guti invade Babylonia and disrupt the arteries of communication. The cities of Sumer towed cargo to Agade in 45, but the towpaths are clogged with "long grass" from disuse in 264. The walls of Agade are high as mountains in 42, and from the very heights of these walls laments resound in 227. The wide-open gates of 43f. become the nesting places of the "bird of depression" (258f.).

The complementarity between the destructive deeds of Naramsin at the Ekur and the Gutian depredations or divine curses is less extensive, but nevertheless noteworthy. The desecration of the Giguna̋ (105, 135) is repaid in 228, and the "*laḫama*-figures standing in the (great) gateway" are brought low in 131f. and 229f. The foreign lands are disturbed in 126 and 169, and built-up areas treated like agricultural plots in 127f. and 170. The looting of Ekur's precious woods and metals in 134ff. is balanced by the debasement of Agade's timber and precious metals in 235f. and 242ff.

It is of course true that prosperity and destruction are opposite sides of the same coin, that descriptions of one are bound to have elements found in descriptions of the other, and that the destruction of Ekur by Naramsin could not but contain some of the same topoi used to describe the Gutian depredations. But the similarities are too numerous to be written off as mere lexical exigencies. The resonance of Agade's prosperity throughout its curse, the curse of the same structures in Agade (gi-gun_4-na, dub-lá) that Naramsin destroyed in Nippur, Inanna's departure from Agade as she arrived—all of these correspondences serve to emphasize the main underlying notions of history found in the literary-historical tradition. The first, enunciated by Güterbock in 1934,[5] is the inevitable alternation of good and bad times, which is implicit in the contrast of Agade's prosperity with its downfall, and the second, stressed by Green,[6] is the enactment of divine will expressed by that alternation. Here divine will is the execution of divine justice, visiting upon Naramsin what he visited upon Ekur. This justice, not always an expressed motive for political intervention by the gods in the literary-historical texts,[7] especially those in Sumerian, is made explicit at two points in the composition:

151. Enlil—because his beloved Ekur was destroyed,
what should be destroyed for it?
(Enlil then unleashes the Guti)

212. Enlil, may the city that destroyed your
city be done to as your city,
That defiled your *giguna,* be done to as Nippur!
(The gods then curse Agade)

The unusually explicit account of the reasons for a dynasty's collapse presented by the *Curse of Agade* finds a fitting climax in its terrible and unique doxology: "Agade is destroyed—hail Inanna!"[8]

Notes

1. The question of Sumerian poetics has been broached in many text editions and studies; see, e.g., An Or 52 14ff. At the present stage of Sumerological studies, the poetic analysis of an individual text is no longer a rewarding enterprise in the absence of a broadly based statement of poetic principles which could serve as a theoretical framework for such analysis.

2. See Chap. III.

3. Whereas the regularity of stanzas in Sumerian poetry claimed by Sauren is exaggerated (cf. An Or 52 14 n.2), many Sumerian compositions do have groups of stanzas that are nearly regular in length (e.g., *Angimdima* Sections 1f., 3-5, 6f., and 13f. [See An Or 52 25ff.]).

4. Cf. Edzard's characterization of the composition in *Kindlers Literaturlexikon* 2121f.: "Die vier Teile: Segenszeit, Peripetie, Angriff auf Nippur, Rache und Verfluchung sind auf gekonnte Weise ineinander verarbeitet."

5. ZA 42 13ff.

6. Green Eridu 323.

7. See Chap. III, Excursus A.

8. The parallel with the doxology of *Inanna and Ebiḫ* (see the comm.) does not detract from this uniqueness. Agade was a Babylonian city, whereas Ebiḫ was an enemy land.

CHAPTER V

MANUSCRIPTS AND TEXT

Ur III Manuscripts and Text

The Ur III manuscripts of the *Curse of Agade* (R_3, S_3, K_4), all from Nippur, are fragments of one- and two- column excerpt tablets of ca. 30-50 lines each. With these, compare the Ur III manuscript of the *Sumerian Temple Hymns,* a two-column tablet preserving the first 37 lines of that composition,[1] and the two-column tablet containing part of an Ur III version of *Lugalbanda.*[2] Our fragments preserve only 35 lines or partial lines of text, but this is enough to indicate that we are dealing with a text very close to that of the OB mss., like the *Temple Hymns,* and not with a radically different version, like *Lugalbanda.*

R_3 contains a "colophon": dub-sag is written at the end of the rev., after a large blank space following the last line of text. The same "colophon" occurs at the end of 6NT 638, the Ur III ms. of *Lugalbanda.* Since the term occurs on the rev. of each tablet, and neither R_3 nor 6NT 638 contain the beginnings of their respective compositions, the equations (from Antagal) with Akk. *muttu* and *qudmu* "front" are useless for interpreting dub-sag in this context.[3]

Most of the differences between the Ur III and OB manuscripts of the *Curse of Agade* are orthographic. Phonetic spellings occur in the following instances:

85 S_3 sàg-di for ság-di (but note R_3 *ság*—du_{11} in 100)
101 R_3 zi-KA—gar for zi gú— or zi-ga—gar[4] (but R_3 writes *gú*—gar in 100, where Y_2 has KA—gar)
114 S_3 ù-*sa-ar* for ù/u_4-*sar.*
127 R_3 S_3 $ugur_2$ for a-gàr[5]
188 K_4 TU.TU for KU.KU (also Y_2; the OB KU.KU must be interpreted as dab_5-dab_5, but K_4 and Y_2 read, or were read, /ku-ku/ and interpreted ku_4-ku_4 [TU.TU])[6]

Compare in the *Temple Hymns* Ur III rig_7-ga for OB ri-da (4), mus̆ for mùs̆ (13), pa_5-ar for bar and ùn for un (30); and Sauren's remarks on the orthography of Ur III legal and administrative documents from Nippur in ZA 59 14ff. In three instances, there are what might be called period orthographies, spellings that were orthographically standard in Ur III, but were modified in the Old Babylonian academies:

74 tár-GAG for OB targul (also H_3)
104 $lirum_3$ (KIB) for lirum (ŠU.KAL)
114 *ù*-sa-ar for *u_4*-sar (also O_1)

The only other occurrences of tár-GAG are in Ur III PNN; $lirum_3$ occurs in literary context in a Shulgi hymn; and ù- can become u_4- in OB because of the homonymy of ù-sar "sharpen" and u_4-SAR "crescent."[7]

The writing of determinatives in the Ur III mss. is less consistent than in the OB mss.:

giš—112 R_3 omits before eren; 125 S_3 omits before al
urudu[8]—113 R_3 ḫa-zi-in^{urudu}, R_3 omits with gí-dim; 128 S_3 eren[*sic!*]^{urudu}, R_3 omits
ki—106 R_3 uru as one-half the OB mss. (others uru^{ki})[9]
ku_6—127 R_3 eštub, S_3 eštub^{ku_6}
^{d}—86 S_3 omits before RN (as one-half OB mss.), but inserts before DN; 193 K_4 ^{d}DN

No similar inconsistency is observable in the Ur III *Temple Hymns* and *Lugalbanda* mss.

The Ur III mss. are often marked by the *absence* of nominal and nominalizing suffixes found in the OB text, or by the use of suffixes different from those in the OB text, but without any noticeably consistent pattern. The absence of -a(-) is found in lines:

72 S_3 im-ús-bi for OB im-ús-sa(-a)-bi, but cf. S_3 im-da-dù-a-bi (74) and R_3 ì-sì-ga-na (98) and gú-gar-ra-na (99)
105 R_3 gi-gun_4-šè for OB gi-gun_4-na-aš/bi/Ø
127 S_3 dagal-gim for OB dagal-la-gim, but cf. R_3 dugud-a-gim here.

Not apparent in the Ur III *Temple Hymns* or *Lugalbanda* mss., it occurs in the Salabikh *Instructions of Shuruppak* and *Kesh Hymn*[10] (E.g., *Shuruppak* OB 44 zuḫ-a, Sal. zuḫ; OB 47 ù-nu-gar-ra, Sal. ù-nu-gar; OB 52 ḫul-a, Sal. ḫul; OB *Kesh* 22f. dù-a, Sal. dù). The suffix -e is absent in S_3 125 al for OB ^{giš}al-e, but it is utilized by S_3 in 73 (an-né) and R_3 in 117 (é-e). In 114, S_3 (with one OB ms.) has mìn-na-bi for OB min-na-bi-da/ta.

In l. 86, the Ur III ms. S_3 is marked by the *presence* of an ergative -e, seemingly justified, that is absent in all OB mss. In 128, S_3 has a plene writing é-kur-ra-a, where the OB mss. have é-kur-ra/re/e/.[11]

Differences in suffixes between Ur III and OB mss. occur in the following instances:

-e < -a
101 R_3 eren-na-na for OB eren-na-né (but both R_3 and OB gú-gar-ra-né in 100)
191 K_4 mèš-a for OB mèš-e

-e < -ra
192 K_4 lú zi-ra for OB lú zi-da-ke_4[12]

-šè < -a
102 R_3 kisal-mah-a for OB kisal-mah-šè (but R_3 and OB both é-kur-šè in 103)

-bi < -šè
84 S_3 egir-šè for OB egir-bi

The most marked and consistent orthographic difference between the Ur III and OB mss. is the absence in the former of preradical -n- in verbal prefix chains (all beginning ba-). This absence is found in lines 71, 73,[13] 101, 103, 105, 107, 114, 124, 125, and 128. The absence of the -n- is also found in the Ur III *Temple Hymns* ms. to lines 13 and 37 of that composition. The verb forms in question are all active, and the absence of -n- in the Ur III mss. reflects the use of ba-an-√ in that period for passive forms.[14] Thus, the Ur III ms. K_4 has ba-an-√ for OB ba-√ in 188 (2×) and 189, in contexts where the verb form is most easily interpreted as a passive.

Completely different prefix chains are found in only four instances:

101 R_3 ság mu-na-ab-du$_{11}$ for OB ság ba-an-da-ab-du$_{11}$
113 R_3 ì-ma-ta-dé for OB ba-ši-in-dé-dé
191 K_4 ba-[ ] for OB i-im-nú
192 K_4 [ ]-ma-[ ] for OB nu-mu-un-gub

Lines 101 and 113 occur within a long series of lines whose verbs begin with the prefix ba-. One might imagine either that the OB text changed the original prefixes of these two lines to conform to the others, or that the breaking of the series in the Ur III ms. is aberrant. In 191, the verbs of the preceding six lines all have the prefix ba-, and again, one can imagine either that ba- in 191 is original and constituted a seventh line of the series, or that the Ur III ms. replaced the original prefix with ba- under the influence of the preceding series.

Finally, there remains to be mentioned S_3 im-da-dù-a-bi in 74 for OB im-dù-dù-bi, which can be explained as an auditory error in either direction; and R_3 šu-bal-e-gim in 98 for OB šu-a bal-e-dè.

Word absences vis-à-vis the OB text are few: R_3 eren-na for OB ^{giš}eren kù, perhaps due to a resemblance between NA and KUG; in 128, R_3 omits é-kur-ra, which *is* present in S_3, and neither ms. reduplicates kùš; K_4 has no u$_4$-ba at the beginning of 193. All could occur in contemporary mss. of the same composition, as could the omission or absence of three lines: 99 is absent in R_3; R_3, but not S_3, omits 114, because both 113 and 114 begin with a copper implement; K_4 does not have 190, probably because of the similarity between the KA beginning 189 and the SAG of 190.

In eight instances there are actual *lexical differences* between the Ur III and OB mss.:

1) 106 R_3 lú KÍD for OB lú la-ga
2) 125 S_3 ru for OB ra
3) 126 S_3 gul for OB kúr
4) 127 R_3 dugud for OB dagal (S_3 with OB)
5) 128 S_3 eden for OB gí-dim (R_3 with OB)
6) 192 K_4 ù-ri-in for OB úš (or read OB uri$_4$)[15]
7) 193 K_4 é for èš[16]
8) 195 K_4 [sig]-ta igi-nim$^{!}$-šè for utu è-ta utu šú-uš

Nos. 2)-5) can be explained as auditory errors, and the cases of 4) and 5), in which one and then another Ur III ms. agrees with the OB text, suggest that it is the Ur III mss. that are erring in all of these cases, and not the hypothetical collateral ancestor (see below) of the OB mss. In 3) and 4), the auditory error is contextually determined, the original word being replaced by a partial synonym.[17] In Nos. 6)-8), the partial synonym replacements may or may not represent a text closer to the hypothetical original than is the OB text. Compare from the Ur III *Temple Hymns* ms., en for OB kin (10), sá nu-èš for sá nu-sá (11), and ki ninda for gir$_4$ ninda (17).

Division into lines is different from the OB text twice in ms. R_3: 98 and 100 are written in one case (99 is absent), as are 106f. In the latter instance, this has led to the erroneous exchange of verbs between the two lines. Both R_3 and S_3 put OB 127f. before 115, probably because of the attraction between gí-dim in 115 and 128. Since it is easier to explain an original line order represented by the OB texts being changed because of this attraction, rather than two originally adjacent gí-dim's being separated by twelve lines for no apparent reason, the Ur III mss. are probably aberrant here.

Evaluating the Ur III mss. is difficult. On the one hand, they represent a witness to the text several hundred years earlier than the OB witnesses, and are perhaps chronologically not very distant from the time of composition. On the other, they contain enough demonstrably erroneous readings to seriously mitigate their value in reconstructing an original text. In two cases in lines 72f., however, an Ur III reading, found also in a minority of OB mss., has been followed because it yields better sense—in 73, Y_2 ba-e-e_{11} is followed with S_3 ba-e_{11} against è and túm in other OB mss (BCU_2)—or because the OB majority is clearly corrupt—in 72, S_3 [me]-lam an-né (also H; B -na) has been misconstrued in $EU_2V_2Y_2$ as /melam-ani/. In these same two lines, another problem becomes obvious: despite the occasional agreement of one or another OB ms. with an Ur III ms. against other OB mss., we cannot demonstrate a direct relationship between the Ur III mss. and any particular OB ms. In l. 72, it is H and B that with S_3 preserve the best reading against $EU_2V_2Y_2$, but in 73, it is Y_2 that preserves the best reading with S_3 against BCU_2V_2. Similarly, in 114 O_1 preserves the older (and more correct) orthography *ù*-(sar) with S_3, but in 74 it is H_3 that with S_3 writes tár-GAG for the targul of O_1 and other OB mss. The writing TU.TU for KU.KU in both K_4 and Y_2 in l. 188 is best explained by the propensity of both Y_2 and the Ur III mss. for phonetic orthographies and auditory errors, and not by a more profound relationship between the two mss.

We have, then, fragments of an older recension of the *Curse of Agade,* which sometimes offer a text inferior to that of more recent manuscripts, perhaps because of the particular scribe(s) or school responsible for these Ur III mss. It is clear that this particular Ur III tradition at Nippur cannot have been the sole direct ancestor of the Nippur tradition of the OB mss., nor can random agreement between certain OB mss. and an Ur III ms. be used to accord a position of privilege to particular OB mss. The situation is, in fact, very similar to the relationship of the Middle Assyrian and Neo-Assyrian mss. of *Angim* discussed in An Or 52 51f.

Old Babylonian Manuscripts and Text

Provenience

There are 96 separate OB manuscript witnesses to the *Curse of Agade* listed at the beginning of Chapter VII, a number which uncertain or unnoticed indirect joins and long-distance joins might reduce by about 10. Only 12 of these mss. were not excavated at Nippur: A and B are from Kish, M_2 and D_4 from Ur, B_4 from Susa, C_4 from Isin, and the provenience of $CWU_2V_2T_3$ and U_3 is unknown. Similarities between A and U_3 suggest that the latter might also be from Kish.

Manuscript Typology

Curse of Agade mss. are of five types: originally complete editions on a six-sided prism and three- and two-column tablets (i.e., columns per side), and excerpts of varying lengths on one- and two-column tablets.[18] The prism, with ca. 45-50 lines per side, has been reconstructed from pieces in Philadelphia, Jena, and Istanbul. Although indirect long-distance joins are risky propositions even with photos, these are fairly certain, since none of the prism fragments overlap, and the first lines of the Jena fragment's (R) cols. ii and iii are consecutive with the last lines of the Philadelphia fragment's (G) i and ii. The reconstruction is as follows: i = G (31-45); ii = R (46-57) (+) G (77-92); iii = R (93-104) (+) G (CBS 7858; 99-101); iv = G (CBS 7858; 148-52) (+) Z_1 (171-93); v = Z_1 (224-35); vi = G (275-81). Another prism is represented by the fragment C_4, from Isin.

The three-column tablet fragments are C, O, Q, G_1, X_1, W_1, U_1 +, I_2[19], Y_2+, X_2, and L_4. They had between 41 and 50 lines per column. Y_2, a nearly complete three-column tablet,[20] underestimated the space necessary to complete the composition and was forced to write the final four lines on the left edge.

Mss. D and S_1+ are two-column tablets that originally contained complete editions of the composition. The columns on the obverse of S_1 contained 61 and 65 lines each, and those on the reverse 75 and 80 lines. Similar crowding of the reverse due to underestimation of space needed when writing the obverse can be demonstrated for D.

All but one of the two-column excerpts seem to be parts of two-tablet editions of the composition, although there is no sequence of two tablets which can be shown to be part of the same edition (i.e., tablet I ending at line x, and II beginning at x + 1). Each column contained from 30 to 39 lines. Tablet I is represented by I+, O_1, T_2, W_2, and O_3; tablet II by S and J_1. V_3 seems to have been a two-column exerpt that contained the first ca. 200 lines of the composition in columns of ca. 50 lines each.

Fragments of multi-column tablets which may be parts of two- *or* three-column tablets are Y, H_1, H_2[21], L_2[21] W_3, Y_3, and H_4. Fragments which may be of either single or multi-columned tablets are Z(+), D_1, A_4, E_4, and F_4.

Single-column tablets preserve excerpts ranging in length from 21 lines (N_1, E_3) to 72 (B) and possibly 80 (U_2) or even perhaps 90 (N_3) lines. Despite 25 first and 25 last lines preserved on the 65 single-column tablets and fragments, only two pairs of sequential tablets occur:

Q_2 (167-201) and K (202-42)
C_3 (151-83) and G_3 + (184-216)

If, however, Heimpel is correct and a scribe began a single tablet of a multi-tablet edition of a composition with the *same* line that ended the previous tablet (not with the following line)[22] then the following might represent four tablets of a five-tablet edition:

M_1 [ ]-112
T 112-171
P_1 171-223
I_1 223-[281]

Two excerpt tablets are labeled the work of one *Qurdi-ištar.*[23] The first, P, covers 81-145, over sixty lines, and the second, A_2, ends at 281 (with blank space after that line), and could not have begun before 230. If the tablets were part of a series, there would have had to be either two tablets of ca. 40 lines each, or one of over 80 lines to cover 146-229, that is, tablets of a very different size than the 60-line tablets represented by P and A_2. The enigmatic 8 written between the date and the scribe's name on A_2 cannot be the number of the tablet in a series completing the composition, since an eight-tablet edition implies much smaller excerpts of only 35 lines each. Thus the question remains whether these single-column excerpt tablets of this and other Old Babylonian Sumerian literary compositions were parts of series of tablets written by individual scribes or students containing the entire text, or whether they were just random excerpts done as exercises. There is no skewing of the excerpt tablets toward the beginning of the composition, but rather a relatively even distribution over the entire 281 lines.

Manuscript quality at Nippur cannot be correlated with format. The worst manuscript in terms of omissions and errors is unquestionably Y_2, a complete six-column edition, and the likewise complete G (prism) and S_1 are not especially impressive. In fact, the necessity of crowding and anxiety about whether there would be enough room to complete a line or the composition may have had a deleterious effect on the texts of Y_2 and S_1.[24] Thus, it would be incorrect to characterize any of the complete editions as master exemplars as opposed to school exercises represented by the excerpt tablets.[25]

Colophons

There are colophons or other notations on thirteen Mss., all excerpt tablets except for the prism G:

G end: [ ] x x
[ ] LÚ BI/GA MIN
P left edge: u$_4$ 25-a-kam im-gíd-da *qù-ur-di-ištar$_2$*
V rev., after double ruling: ŠEŠ x x [ ] (= PN?)
X left edge: [ ]x ÍB x x (=PN?)
[u$_4$]-⌈x⌉-a-[kam]
P_1 lower edge: ur$_5$-ra (6 × 3600) + (4 × 600) + (2 × 60) + [x]
Y_1 left edge: [mu-šid-bi (-im) 60 +] 12 u$_4$ 25$^?$-a-k[am]
A_2 left edge: [u$_4$-x-a-ka]m 8 im-gíd-da *qù-ur-di-ištar$_2$*
E_2 end: 46 (after line 46)
M_2 lower edge: 60 (number of lines actually on tablet)
U_2 left edge: mu-šid-bi 81
G_3 lower edge: u$_4$-kúr-šè (= [to continue] on another day?)
B_4 left edge: 71 mu-bi-im
I_4 end: [ ] LÚ (= PN?)

Where intelligible, the colophons seem restricted to, at most, number of lines, day of the month, and the name of the scribe. G_3 perhaps, has another sort of notation; P_1 is a mystery. The incipit of the composition is never mentioned.

Textual Variants

The frustrations of working with textual variants among Old Babylonian Sumerian literary mss. are well known.[26] The main problems are deciding whether a particular type of variant is idiosyncratic or recensional, and finding mss. that overlap sufficiently to provide a significant number of correlations in variants. What an exhaustive tabulation of variants for this composition generally shows, is that every time an apparent grouping of mss. arises, the members of the group diverge a few lines later. With the aid of a computer, it would be possible to assign mss. coefficients of relative distance from one another, but would such results be sufficiently useful to justify the effort? As an example of the difficulties involved, here are the significant variants in lines 89-91:[27]

89	^{gi}kid-má	$C_1N_1T_2J_3$	vs. ^{gi}má	$PR_1S_1L_2$
	šú-a	C_1T_2	vs. šà-ga	$PN_1R_1S_1L_2J_3$
90	si ^{giš}má-gur$_8$	S_1B_4	vs. ^{giš}má-gur$_8$	$GPC_1H_1N_1R_1L_2T_2J_3E_4$
91	á-šita$_4$-a	$YC_1N_1R_1S_1L_2B_4$	vs. á-šu-du$_7$-a	GPT_2J_3

Looking at the mss. preserved in all four instances (8 out of 13), the number of times one ms. agrees with another can be charted as follows:

	P	C_1	N_1	R_1	S_1	L_2	T_2	J_3
P	*	1	2	3	2	3	2	3
C_1	1	*	3	2	1	2	3	2
N_1	2	3	*	3	2	3	2	3
R_1	3	2	3	*	3	3	1	2
S_1	2	1	2	3	*	3	0	1
L_2	3	2	3	3	3	*	1	2
T_2	2	3	2	1	0	1	*	3
J_3	3	2	3	2	1	2	3	*

In no instance is there unanimous agreement, and in only one case is there no agreement.

In the preceding example, the addition of si in line 90 is found in S_1, a Nippur ms., and B_4, from Susa, which illustrates the fact that in general, there is no tendency for non-Nippur mss. to group together against Nippur mss. It happens sometimes, but just as often there are Nippur mss. with the same variant as the non-Nippur mss., or the non-Nippur mss. for a line will oppose each other, with Nippur mss. also witnessing one or both of the opposing variants found in the non-Nippur mss. The single exception is the pair of manuscripts A and U_3, which agree 14 times against all the preserved Nippur mss., and disagree with one another only twice. No other two mss., including those from Nippur, can be shown to be so close, and this strongly implies that U_3, like A, must come from Kish. A notion of the problem of trying to establish Nippur and non-Nippur recensions can be seen from the variants to the fifth sign in l. 23 (non-Nippur mss. marked *):

dara$_3$	H S_1 U_2*
kušu	A* O_1 W_1 Y_2
anše	Y_1 U_3*

Compare these with the distribution of variants for the verb in̆ 27, and for the fifth sign of 28:

27. du$_{11}$-du$_{11}$	A* H_1 O_1 S_1 Y_1 U_2*
dù-dù	B* Y_2 U_3*
28. im	H_1 O_1 S_1 U_2* Y_2 H_4
um	A* X_1 U_3*

Again, a computer would be a useful sorting and correlating tool, if one thinks the results would justify the effort.

In choosing readings, I have tried to follow what seem to be the best Nippur alternatives in every instance, but in the few cases where the Nippur mss. are poorly preserved or yield no sense, I have not hesitated to prefer a ms. from elsewhere. Among the Nippur variants, the choice is frequently easy, because the "incorrect" variants can be explained by text-critical principles. When there seems to be no criterion for choosing, I have followed the majority of witnesses. Certain choices have been made arbitrarily for technical reasons: the mss. are nearly evenly divided between those that write uru and those that write uru^{ki} (with a few writing either, inconsistently), and I have always written uru^{ki} in my composite text. Likewise, I have followed full writings, such as mu-un-na-, over writings such as mu-na-, because it is easier to show the absence of signs in the apparatus than to add them.

It has been stated above that there is no correlation between ms. format and quality. In fact, it is usually difficult to make qualitative distinctions between mss. (again, the computer . . .). One glaring exception is Y_2, whose auditory errors, phonetic writings, omissions and other obviously erroneous deviations from the text can only be described as outrageous.

Lineation

The only variants in line order are V_2's insertion of 76 between 71 and 72, and the exchange of 255 and 263 (both lines contain the phrase eden ki si-ga) by L_1 and W_1.[28] There is disagreement about writing lines 5f., 36, 72f., 115f., 151, 222, and 281 as two lines or one, but except for 5f., where the mss. are nearly evenly divided, there are usually one or sometimes two mss. opposing all others in each instance. One, or, rarely, two mss. omit the following lines, always due to errors that are obvious: 54f., 96f., 112-18, 119, 141, 221, 233f., 244, and 248. Half the preserved mss. include 93a, a repetition of 87 due to the similar endings of 86 and 93. B_4 then added a line-pair equivalent to 94f. after 87 to create the symmetry of 87-87a-87b = 93a-94-95. Finally, D_4, from Ur, is an excerpt that gives four pairs of lines: 126f., 173f., 200f., and 213f. The jump from 127 to 173 can be explained because both begin a-gàr, but the other jumps seem arbitrary.

Notes

1. TCS 3 mss. A_1 + A_2.
2. S. Cohen, *Enmerkar and the Lord of Aratta* 10ff., n. 22.
3. Note that dub-sag does seem to mean "(tablet) beginning" on the OB Lipitishtar prism AO 8863 (TRS 87; cf. Vanstiphout, JCS 30 34), where it precedes the first line.
4. See the comm.
5. Or auditory error?
6. Cf., e.g., Y_2 in 104, where it read/heard lirum as ŠU.KAL and wrote lú kal.
7. See the comm. to the lines in question, and Klein, JCS 31 151 n. 10.
8. According to Limet Métal 191, ^{urudu} always precedes copper objects in Ur III (as it does in later periods). Its postposition here may reflect Pre-Sargonic scribal practices. Cf. Bauer Wirtschaftsurkunden Glossar s.v. alal^{urudu}, A.EN-da^{urudu}; Deimel SF 20 (Limet Métal p. 254) with ^{urudu} following nouns; Pettinato, OLA 5 204 i 2 gu-kak-šub-gíd^{urudu}; Edzard Rechtsurkunden Nos. 65f. and Glossar s.v. ḫa-zi^{urudu} and ḫa-zi-sipar^{urudu}. For the Sargonic period, cf. MAD 4 No. 134 ^{urudu}šum, and MAD 3 s.v. *ḫassinnum*, where ^{urudu} precedes the noun in every case but one.
9. See the discussion of the OB mss.
10. Alster, *The Instructions of Šuruppak*. and Biggs., ZA 61 193ff.
11. See Sauren, ZA 59 50 for plene writings in legal and administrative documents from Ur III Nipp
12. See n. 15.
13. Here the three preserved OB mss. from Nippur have -e-, and only the non-Nippur mss. have -n-.
14. See Krecher, ZA 69 1-3 (suggestion of C. Wilcke).

15. Note that the Ur III var. here is closer to other OB parallels cited in the comm., just as, in the same line, Ur III lú zi-ra is closer to the parallels than is OB lú zi-da-ke$_4$.

16. Cf. An Or 52, p. 40 No. 18.

17. Cf. An Or 52 44.

18. Note that all non-Nippur mss. except C and C$_4$ are single column.

19. Probably the same tablet as fragments H$_2$ and L$_2$.

20. The physical joining was realized through the generosity of the Oriental Institute, which entrusted its fragments to the University Museum for that purpose.

21. Probably part of I$_2$.

22. In his introduction to the Nanshe Hymn, JCS (forthcoming).

23. See below for the colophons.

24. See Civil, RA 60 13f. for crowding leading to incomplete writings.

25. Cf. Hallo, YNER 3 38f., and Civil's remarks on Proto-Ea mss. from Nippur in MSL 14 7f.

26. See, e.g., An Or 52 39; Römer, AOAT 209/1 8ff.; Civil MSL 14 15f.

27. Omitting Y$_2$, which is very aberrant and idiosyncratic.

28. These two mss. do not otherwise show a special affinity for one another.

CHAPTER VI

COMPOSITE TEXT AND TRANSLATION

Composite Text[1]

1. sag-ki gíd-da ^{d}en-líl-lá-ke$_4$
2. kiš^{ki} gu$_4$ an-na-gim im-ug$_5$-ga-ta
3. é ki unu^{ki}-ga gu$_4$-maḫ-gim saḫar-ra mi-ni-ib-gaz-a-ta
4. KI.UD-ba šar-ru-GI lugal a-ga-dè^{ki}-ra
5. sig-ta igi-nim-šè ^{d}en-líl-le
6. nam-en nam-lugal-la mu-un-na-an-sum-ma-ta
7. u$_4$-ba èš a-ga-dè^{ki} kù ^{d}inanna-ke$_4$
8. ama$_5$ maḫ-a-ni-šè im-ma-an-dù-dù
9. ul-maš^{ki}-a ^{giš}gu-za ba-ni-in-gub
10. lú-tur gibil-bi é dù-ù-gim
11. dumu-bàn-da ama$_5$ gá-gá-gim
12. é níg-ga-ra níg sá-di-dè
13. uru^{ki}-bé dúr ki-gar sum-mu-dè
14. un-bé ú nir-gál kú-ù-dè
15. un-bé a nir-gál nag-nag-dè
16. sag a-tu$_5$-a kisal ḫúl-le-dè
17. ki ezem-ma un sig$_7$-ge-dè
18. lu zu-ù-ne téš-bi kú-ù-dè
19. lú bar-ra mušen nu-zu-gim an-na nigin-dè
20. mar-ḫa-ši^{ki} le-um-ma gur-ru-dè
21. ^{ugu}ugu$_4$-bi am-si maḫ áb-za-za ú-ma-am ki bad-rá
22. šà sila-dagal-la-ke$_4$ téš-bi tag-tag-ge-dè
23. ur-gi$_7$ ur-nim dara$_3$[2] kur-ra udu-a-lum SÍG.BU-si
24. kù ^{d}inanna-ke$_4$ ù nu-um-ši-ku-ku
25. u$_4$-ba a-ga-dè^{ki} é-ÁŠ-a-ba kù-GI mi-ni-in-si
26. é-ÁŠ babbar-ra-ba kù-babbar mi-ni-in-si
27. araḫ$_4$ še-ba urudu an-na na$_4$-lagab za-gìn-na sá im-mi-in-du$_{11}$-du$_{11}$[3]
28. gur$_7$-bi bar-ta im[4] ba-an-ùr

Translation[5]

I. The Rise of Agade

After Enlil's frown
Had slain Kish like the Bull of Heaven,
Had slaughtered the house of the land of Uruk in the dust like a mighty bull,
And then, to Sargon, king of Agade,
Enlil, from south to north,
Had given sovereignty and kingship—
At that time, holy Inanna built
The sanctuary Agade as her grand woman's domain,
Set up her throne in Ulmaš.
Like a youngster building a house for the first time,
Like a girl establishing a woman's domain,
So that the warehouses would be provisioned,
That dwellings would be founded in that city,
That its people would eat splendid food,
That its people would drink splendid beverages,
That those bathed (for holidays) would rejoice in the courtyards,
That the people would throng the places of celebration,
That acquaintances would dine together,
That foreigners would cruise about like unusual birds in the sky,
That (even) Marḫaši would be reentered on the (tribute) rolls,
That monkeys, mighty elephants, *water buffalo,* exotic animals,
Would jostle each other in the public squares—
Thoroughbred dogs, lions, mountain ibexes,[6] *alu*-sheep with long wool—
(So that all this might happen), Holy Inanna did not sleep.
At that time, she filled Agade's . . . with gold,
She filled its shining . . . with silver,
Delivered copper, tin, and blocks of lapis to its granaries,
Sealed them away in its silos.

29. um-ma-bé ad-gi$_4$-gi$_4$ ba-an-sum
30. ab-ba-bé inim-inim-ma ba-an-sum
31. ki-sikil-bé ki-e-ne-di ba-an-sum
32. guruš-bé á ^{giš}tukul-la ba-an-sum
33. di$_4$-di$_4$-lá-bé šà-ḫúl-la ba-an-sum
34. emeda[7]-ga-lá[8] šu-gíd[9] dumu šagina[10]-ke$_4$-ne
35. ^{giš}al-gar-sur$_9$-da e-ne im-di-ne
36. uru^{ki} šà-bé tigi-a bar-bi-ta gi-gíd za-am-za-am-ma
37. kar ^{giš}má ús-bé mud$_5$ me-gar-ra
38. kur-kur ú-sal-la i-im-nú
39. un-bé ki ša$_6$-ga[11] igi bí-ib-du$_8$
40. lugal-bi sipa ^{d}na-ra-am-^{d}sin-e
41. bara$_2$ kù a-ga-dè^{ki}-šè u$_4$-dè-éš im-è
42. bàd-bi ḫur-sag-gim[12] an-né im-ús
43. abul-a-ba ^{id}idigna a-ab-ba-šè du[13]-ù-gim
44. kù ^{d}inanna-ke$_4$ ka-bé gál bí-in-tag$_4$
45. ki-en-gi-ra níg-ga ní-ba-ke$_4$ ^{giš}má im-da-gíd-dè
46. mar-tu kur-ra lú se nu-zu
47. gu$_4$ du$_7$ máš du$_7$-da mu-un-na-da-an-ku$_4$-ku$_4$
48. me-luḫ-ḫa^{ki} lú kur gi$_6$-ga-ke$_4$
49. níg-šu kúr-kúr[14]-ra mu-un-na-ra-ab-e$_{11}$-dè
50. elam^{ki} su-bir$_4$^{ki} anše bara$_2$ lá-gim níg mu-na-ab-lá-lá
51. ensi$_2$-ensi$_2$ sanga[15]-e-ne
52. sa$_{12}$-du$_5$ gú-eden-na-ke$_4$-ne
53. nidba itu-da zag-mu-bi si àm-sá-e-ne

54. abul a-ga-dè^{ki}-ka a-gim x[16] mi-ni-ib-gál[17]
55. nidba-bé kù ^{d}inanna-ke$_4$ šu-te-gá nu-zu
56. dumu-gi$_7$-gim é ki-gar di-da[18] la-la[19]-bi nu-um-gi$_4$
57. inim é-kur-ra me-gim ba-an-gar
58. a-ga-dè^{ki} tuk$_4$-e mu-un-na-lá-lá
59. ul-maš^{ki}-a ní im-ma-ni-in-te

60. uru^{ki}-ta dúr-ra-ni ba-ra-gub[20]
61. ki-sikil ama$_5$-na šub-bu-gim
62. kù ^{d}inanna-ke$_4$ èš a-ga-dè^{ki} mu-un-šub
63. ur-sag ^{giš}tukul-a sag-gá-gá-gim
64. uru^{ki}-ta[21] mè šen-šen im-ma-ra-è[22]
65. lú kúr-ra-ra gaba ba-ni-in-ri
66. u$_4$ nu-iá-àm u$_4$ nu-u-àm
67. sa nam-en-na aga nam-lugal-la
68. ma-an-si-um ^{giš}gu-za nam-lugal-la sum-ma
69. ^{d}ninurta-ke$_4$ é-šu-me-ša$_4$-na ba-ni-in-ku$_4$
70. uru^{ki} inim-inim-ma-bi ^{d}utu ba-an-túm
71. geštu$_2$-bi ^{d}en-ki-ke$_4$ ba-an-túm[23]
72. me-lám an-né[24] im-ús-sa-a-bi

She endowed its old women with advice,
She endowed its old men with counsel,
She endowed its young women with dances,
She endowed its young men with martial might,
She endowed its little ones with joy.
The *viceroy's* children, (still) cradled[25] by nursemaids.
Played *algarsur*-instruments,
Inside the city was the *tigi*-drum, outside it, the flute and *zamzam.*
Its harbor, where ships docked, was full of excitement,
All foreign lands rested contentedly,
Their people experienced happiness.[26]
Its (Agade's) king, the shepherd Naramsin,
Rose like the sun on the holy throne of Agade.
Its city-wall touched heaven, like a mountain,[27]
Holy Inanna opened wide
The portals of its city-gates, as if for the Tigris, going to[28] the sea,
Ships brought the goods of Sumer itself upstream (to Agade),
The highland Amorites, people ignorant of agriculture,
Came before her (Inanna) there with spirited bulls and spirited bucks,
Meluḫḫans, people of the black mountains,
Brought exotic wares[29] down to her,
Elam and Subir carried goods to her like packasses,
All the governors, temple administrators,[30] and land registrars of the Gu'edena,
Regularly supplied monthly and New Year offerings there.
How/thus in Agade's city-gate . . . !

II. The Withdrawal of Divine Favor

Holy Inanna knew not how to accept those offerings there;
Like an aristocrat, talking about founding a house,[31] she could not get enough of those luxuries,
But the word from Ekur was as silence.
Agade was reduced to trembling before her, and
She grew anxious in Ulmaš.
She withdrew her dwelling from the city,
Like a young woman abandoning her woman's domain,
Holy Inanna abandoned the sanctuary Agade.
Like a warrior advancing to arms,
She removed[32] battle and combat from[33] the city, (and)
Confronted the enemy.
It was not five days, it was not ten days, when
Ninurta brought (back) into his (temple) Ešumeša
The sovereign insignia, the royal crown,
The . . . and the royal throne which had been bestowed (on Agade).
Utu took away the city's counsel,
Enki took away[34] its wisdom,
Its (Agade's) radiant aura, that reached heaven,

73. an-né an šà-ga ba-e-e$_{11}$[35]
74. ^{giš}targul[36] kù im-dù-dù-a-bi
75. ^{d}en-ki-ke$_4$ abzu-a mi-ni-in-bu
76. ^{giš}tukul-bi ^{d}inanna-ke$_4$ ba-an-túm
77. èš a-ga-dè^{ki} zi-bi suḫur^{ku_6} tur-ra-gim engur-ra ba-an-til

78. uru^{ki} téš-bi igi-bi àm-da-gál
79. am-si maḫ-gim gú ki-šè mi-ni-ib-gar
80. gu$_4$ maḫ-gim si àm-da-íl-íl
81. ušumgal idim-a-gim sag àm-ma-zé-re
82. mè-gim nam-dugud-ba àm-da-ab-laḫ$_4$-laḫ$_4$-e
83. nam-lugal a-ga-dè^{ki} ki-tuš gi-na du$_{10}$ nu-tuš-ù-dè
84. egir-bi níg-na-me nu-ša$_6$-ge-dè
85. é tuk$_4$-e erim$_3$ ság di-dè[37]
86. ^{d}na-ra-am-^{d}sin máš-gi$_6$-ka igi ba-ni-in-du$_8$-a
87. šà-ga-ni-šè mu-un-zu eme[38]-na nu-um-gá-gá lú-da nu-mu-un-da-ab-bé[39]
88. nam-é-kur-ra-šè ^{túg}mu-sír-ra ba-an-mu$_4$
89. ^{giš}gigir-ra-né ^{gi}kid-má šà-ga[40] ba-an-šú[41]
90. ^{giš}má[42]-gur$_8$-ra-né MUNSUB ba-ra-an-si-ig
91. á-ŠITA$_4$[43]-a nam-lugal-la-ka-ni im-ma-ra-an-ba-ba
92. ^{d}na-ra-am-^{d}sin mu imin-àm mu-un-ge-en
93. lugal mu imin-àm šu sag-gá du$_{11}$-ga a-ba igi im-mi-in-du$_8$-a
93a.[44] šà-ga-ni-šè mu-un-zu eme-na[45] nu-gá-gá lú-da nu-mu-un-da-[ab-bé]

94. é-šè máš-àm šu[46]-gíd-dè
95. é dù-a máš-a nu-mu-un-dè-gál
96. mìn-kam-ma-šè é-šè máš-àm šu[47]-gíd-dè
97. é dù-a máš-a nu-mu-un-dè-gál
98. ì-sì-ga-na šu-a bal-e-dè
99. ^{d}en-líl níg-du$_{11}$-ga-ni ba-en-dè-kúr
100. gú-gar-ra-né ság ba-an-da-ab-du$_{11}$
101. erén-na-né zi-ga[48] ba-ni-in-gar
102. á tuk kisal-maḫ-šè ku$_4$-ku$_4$-gim
103. é-kur-šè šu-kéš ba-ši-in-ak
104. du$_{10}$ tuk lirum-šè gam-e-gim
105. gi-gun$_4$-na-aš eše gín ba-ši-in-ak
106. nita lú-la-ga uru^{ki} laḫ$_5$-gim
107. é-šè ^{giš}kun$_5$ gal-gal ba-ši-in-ri-ri
108. é-kur ^{giš}má maḫ-gim gul-gul-lu-dè
109. kur kù ba-al-gim saḫar du$_8$[49]-ù-dè
110. ḫur-sag ^{na_4}za-gìn-na-gim ku$_5$-re-dè
111. uru^{ki} ^{d}iškur-re ba-an-dé[50]-a-gim gú ki-šè gá-gá-dè[51]
112. é-e kur ^{giš}eren ku$_5$ nu-me-a
113. ^{urudu}ḫa-zi-in gal-gal ba-ši-in-dé-dé[52]
114. ^{urudu}aga-silig-ga á min-na-bi-da u$_4$-sar ba-an-ak
115. úr-bi-a ^{urudu}gí-dim ba-an-gar

An took up[53] into heaven's midst,
Its well-anchored holy mooring pole,
Enki tore down into the Abzu,
Inanna took away its weapons.
Sanctuary Agade's life, as if it were a tiny carp, was brought to an end in the deep waters.
The city held up its face in unison,
As a mighty elephant, it bent its neck to the ground,
As a mighty bull, it raised its horns,
As a raging dragon, it slithered its head along,
As in a battle, it *plundered its own riches.*
That the kingdom of Agade would no longer occupy a good, lasting residence,
That its future was altogether unfavorable,
That its temples would be shaken and their stores scattered[54]—
This is what Naramsin saw in a dream!
He understood it, but would not articulate it, nor would he talk with anyone about it.[55]
Because of Ekur he donned mourning garb,
Covered his chariot with reed mats,[56]
Tore the *reed canopy* off[57] his processional ship, and
Gave away his royal paraphernalia.
Naramsin was immobile for seven years!
Who has ever seen a king act so anomalously for seven years?[58]

III. Naramsin Destroys Ekur

Performing extispicy with regard to the temple,
The (omen for) building the temple was not present in the extispicy,
Performing extispicy for a second time with regard to the temple,
The (omen for) building the temple was not present in the extispicy.
In order to effect a change *in his situation,*
He tried to alter Enlil's pronouncement,
He scattered what he had gathered together,
And mustered his troops.
Like an athlete coming into the great courtyard,
He *clasped his hands in triumph* over Ekur,
Like a runner bent to start a race,
He treated the *giguna* as (if it were worth only) thirty shekels,
Like a robber plundering the city,
He set tall ladders against the temple.
To demolish Ekur as if it were a huge ship,
To break up[59] its soil, like mountains where precious metals are mined,
To splinter it, like the lapis lazuli mountain,
To prostrate it, like a city inundated by Iškur—
For the temple—though it was not the mountains where cedars are felled—
He had large axes cast,[60]
He had double-edged *agasilig*-axes sharpened.
He set spades against its roots, and

116. suḫuš kalam-ma-ka ki ba-e-lá
117. pa-bi-a ^{urudu}ḫa-zi-in ba-an-gar
118. é-e guruš ug$_5$-ga-gim gú ki-šè ba-an-da-ab-lá[61]
119. gú kur-kur-ra ki-šè ba-an-da-ab-lá
120. ^{giš}alal-bi im-ma-ra-an-zil-zil
121. im šèg-šèg an-na ba-e-e$_{11}$
122. giš-ká-na-bi ba-ra-an-si-ig téš kalam-ma ba-kúr
123. ká še nu-ku$_5$-da še i-ni-in-ku$_5$
124. šu[63] kalam-ma-ta še ba-da-an-ku$_5$
125. ká silim-ma-bé ^{giš}al-e bí-in-ra
126. kur-kur-re silim-silim-bi ba-kúr
127. a-gàr[63] maḫ a-eštub^{ku6} dagal-la-gim
128. é-kur-ra ^{urudu}gí-dim[64] gal-gal-bi kùš-kùš-a bí-in-sì-sì[65]
129. itima é u$_4$ nu-zu-ba un-e igi i-ni-in-bar
130. ^{urudu}šen kù dingir-re-e-ne-ke$_4$ uri^{ki} igi i-ni-in-bar
131. la-ḫa-ma dub-lá gal é-e su$_8$-ga-bi
132. lú an-zil kú-a nu-me-eš-a
133. ^{d}na-ra-am-^{d}sin šà izi-ka ba-an-sìg
134. ^{giš}eren ^{giš}šu-úr-mìn ^{giš}za-ba-lum ^{giš}taskarin
135. giš gi-gun$_4$-na-bé-eš GUM ba-an-sur-sur
136. kù-GI-bi mi-si-IŠ-ra bí-in-ak
137. kù-babbar-bi KUŠ.LU.ÚB / KUŠ.LU.ÚB-šir-ra bí-in-ak
138. urudu-bi še maḫ DU-a-gim kar-ra bí-in-si-si
139. kù-bi kù-dím-e im-dím-e
140. za-bi za-dím-e im-dím-e
141. urudu-bi simug im-tu$_{11}$-bé
142. níg-ga uru^{ki} ḫul-a nu-me-a
143. é-e ^{giš}má gal-gal kar-ra ba-an-ús
144. é ^{d}en-lil-lá-šè ^{giš}má gal-gal kar-ra ba-an-ús
145. níg-ga uru^{ki}-ta ba-ra-è
146. níg-ga uru^{ki}-ta è-da-ni
147. a-ga-dè^{ki} dím-ma-bi ba-ra-è
148. ^{giš}má-e kar íb-tuk$_4$[66]-e umuš a-ga-dè^{ki} ba-kúr[67]

149. ud te-eš du$_{11}$-ga kalam téš-a gar-ra
150. a-ma-ru zi-ga gaba-šu-gar nu-tuk
151. ^{d}en-líl-le nam-é-kur ki-ág-gá-ni ba-ḫul-a-šè a-na-àm im-gu-lu-a-ba

152. kur gú-bí-na-šè igi na-an-íl
153. ḫur-sag dagal téš-bi nam-ta-an-si-ig
154. un-gá nu-sì-ga kalam-ma nu-šid-da
155. gu-ti-um^{ki} un kéš-da nu-zu
156. dím-ma lú-ulu$_3^{lu}$ galga[68] ur-ra SIG$_7$.ALAN ^{ugu}ugu$_4$-bi
157. ^{d}en-líl-le kur-ta nam-ta-an-è

It sunk low as the foundation of the land,
He set axes against its branches, and
The temple, like a dead soldier, fell prostrate—
All the foreign lands fell prostrate—
He ripped out its drain pipes, and
The heavens' rains came down into it,
He removed its door frames, and the land's vigor was subverted.
At its "Gate from Which Grain Is Never Diverted," he diverted grain(-offerings), and
Grain was thereby diverted from the "hand"[69] of the (home)land,
At its "Gate of Well-Being," the pickax struck, and
Well-being was subverted in all the foreign lands,
As if for[70] great tracts of land with wide-spreading carp ponds,
He cast large spades[71] *in moulds* for the Ekur.
The people saw the bedchamber, its room which knows no daylight,
Akkad saw the holy vessels of the gods,
Naramsin cast down into the fire
Its *laḫama*-figures, standing in the great gateway at the temple,
Though they had committed no sacrilege.
The cedar, cypress, juniper, and boxwood,
Wood for its *giguna*, he . . . ,
He put its gold in containers,

He put its silver in leather bags,

He filled the docks with its copper, as if he were delivering huge ears of grain.
Metalsmiths were to work its precious metals,
Lapidaries were to work its precious stones,
Smiths were to beat its copper.
Though they were not the goods of a plundered city,
Large ships were docked at the temple,
Large ships were docked at Enlil's temple, and
The goods were removed from the city.
As the goods were removed from the city,
So was the good sense of Agade removed,
The ships jarred[72] the docks, and Agade's intelligence was displaced.[73]

IV. Enlil and Gutium

The roaring storm that subjugates the entire land,
The rising deluge that cannot be confronted,
Enlil, because his beloved Ekur was destroyed, what should he destroy (in revenge) for it?
He looked toward the Gubin mountains;
He *scoured* all of the broad mountain ranges—
Not classed among people, not reckoned as part of the land,
Gutium, a people who know no inhibitions,
With human instincts, but canine intelligence,[74] and monkeys' features—
Enlil brought them out of the mountains.

158. ŠID.ŠID buru$_5$ ^{mušen}[75]-gim ki àm-ú-ús
159. á-bi gu[76] máš-anše-gim eden-na mu-un-na-an-lá
160. níg-na-me á-bi la-ba-ra-è
161. lú-na-me á-bi la-ba-an-tag$_4$-tag$_4$
162. lú-kin-gi$_4$-a ḫar-ra-an-na nu-mu-un-gin
163. ^{giš}má ra-gaba íd-da nu-mu-un-dab$_5$-bé[77]
164. ùz gi ^{d}en-líl-lá amaš-ta ba-ra-ra-aš na-gada[78]-bi bí-in-ús-ú-ús

165. šilam[79] tùr-bi-ta ba-ra-ra-aš unu$_3$[80]-bi bí-in-ús-ú-ús
166. giš-gú-ka en-nu-un ba-e-dù
167. ḫar-ra-an-na lú-sa-gaz ba-e-tuš
168. abul kalam-ma-ka ^{giš}ig im-ma ba-e-gub[81]
169. kur-kur-ra bàd uru^{ki}-ne-ne-ka gù gig mi-ni-ib-bé-ne
170. uru^{ki} šà eden bar dagal nu-me-a mú-sar mu-un-dè-gál[82]
171. u$_4$ uru^{ki} ba-dím-dím-ma-ba ba-sì-sì-ga-ba
172. a-gàr[83] gal-gal-e še nu-um-túm
173. a-gàr[84] sù-sù-ge ku$_6$ nu-um-túm
174. pú-^{giš}kiri$_6$ làl geštin nu-um-túm
175. IM.UD sír-da la-ba-šèg ^{giš}maš-gurum la-ba-mú
176. u$_4$-ba ì diš gín-e ba$_7$ sila$_3$-àm
177. še diš gín-e ba$_7$ sila$_3$-àm
178. síg diš gín-e ba$_7$ ma-na-àm
179. ku$_6$ diš gín-e ^{giš}ba-an-e íb-si
180. ganba uru^{ki}-ba-ka ur$_5$-gim íb-sa$_{10}$-sa$_{10}$
181. ùr-ra nú-a ùr-ra ba-ug$_7$
182. é-a nú-a ki nu-um-túm
183. un šà-gar-bi-ta ní-bi-a šu im-dúb-dúb-ne
184. ki-ùr ki gal ^{d}en-lil-lá-ke$_4$
185. ur sila si-ga KA ba-ni-ib-kéš
186. šà-ba lú min DU téš-e ba-ni-ib-kú
187. lú eš$_5$ DU téš-e ba-ni-ib-kú
188. KA ba-dub-dub sag ba-dab$_5$-dab$_5$[85]
189. KA ba-dub sag numun-e-eš ba-ab-gar
190. sag zi sag lul-la šu-bal ba-ni-ib-ak
191. mèš mèš-e an-ta i-im-nú
192. úš lú lul-e úš lú zi-da-ke$_4$ an-ta na-mu-un-DU
193. u$_4$-ba ^{d}en-líl-le èš gal-gal-la-ni-ta
194. èš gi TUR.TUR im-ma-ra-an-dù[86]
195. utu è-ta utu šú-uš erim$_3$-bi ba-tur
196. um-ma u$_4$-ta ba-ra-ab-tag$_4$-a
197. ab-ba u$_4$-ta ba-ra-ab-tag$_4$-a
198. gala-maḫ mu-ta ba-ra-ab-tag$_4$-a
199. u$_4$ imin gi$_6$ imin-šè
200. balag imin-e an-úr gub-ba-gim ki mu-un-ši-ib-ús
201. ùb me-zé li-li-ìs[87] ^{d}iškur-gim šà-ba mu-na-an-tuk
202. um-ma a uru$_2$-mu nu-gá-gá

Like hordes of locusts[88] they lie over the land,
Their arms are stretched over the plain for him (Enlil) like a snare for animals,[89]
Nothing leaves their arms,
No one escapes their arms.
Messengers no longer travel the highways,
The courier's boat no longer takes to[90] the rivers.
They (the Guti) drive the trusty goats of Enlil from the fold, and make their herdsmen[91] follow,
They drive the cows from the pens, and make their cowherds[92] follow.
The *criminal* manned the watch,
The brigand occupied the highways,
The doors of all the city-gates of the land lay dislodged in[93] the dirt, and
All the foreign lands uttered bitter cries from the walls of their cities.
In the cities' midst, though not the widespread exterior plains, they planted gardens,
(For the first time) since cities were built and founded,
The great[94] agricultural tracts produced no grain,
The[95] inundated[96] tracts produced no fish,
The irrigated orchards produced neither syrup nor wine,
The gathered clouds did not rain, the *mašgurum* did not grow.
At that time, one shekel's worth of oil was only one-half quart,
One shekel's worth of grain was only one-half quart,
One shekel's worth of wool was only one-half mina,
One shekel's worth of fish filled only one *ban*-measure—
These sold at such (prices) in the markets of all the cities!
He who slept on the roof, died on the roof,
He who slept in the house, had no burial,
People were flailing at themselves from hunger.
In the *ki'ur,* Enlil's great place,
Dogs were gathered together in the silent streets,
Two men would come therein, and be eaten together,
Three men would come, and be eaten together,
Mouths were crushed, heads were crashed,
Mouths were crushed, heads sown like seeds,
Honest people were confounded with liars,
Young men lay upon young men,
The blood of liars ran upon the blood of honest men.
At that time, Enlil remodeled
His great sanctuaries into tiny reed sanctuaries, and
From east to west he reduced their stores.
The old women who survived those days,
The old men who survived those days,
The chief lamentation singer who survived those years,
For seven days and seven nights,
Put in place seven *balag*-drums, as if they stood at heaven's base, and
Played *ub, meze,* and *lilis*-drums[97] for him (Enlil) among them (the *balags*).
The old women did not restrain (the cry) "Alas my city!"

203. ab-ba a lú-bi nu-gá-gá
204. gala-e a é-kur nu-gá-gá
205. ki-sikil-bé SÍG.ŠAB-bi nu-gá-gá
206. guruš-bé gír-kin nu-gá-gá
207. ír-bi ír ama a-a ^{d}en-líl-lá-ke$_4$
208. du$_6$-kù su-zi gùr-ru du$_{10}$ kù ^{d}en-líl-lá-ke$_4$ i-im-gá-gá-ne
209. nam-bé-éš ^{d}en-líl itima kù ba-an-ku$_4$ šà ka-tab-ba ba-an-nú

210. u$_4$-ba ^{d}sin ^{d}en-ki ^{d}inanna ^{d}ninurta ^{d}iškur ^{d}utu ^{d}nusku ^{d}nisaba dingir gal-gal-e-ne[98]

211. šà ^{d}en-líl-lá-ke$_4$ a šed$_{10}$ im-šed$_{10}$[99] -e-ne a-ra-zu-ta ba-ab-bé-ne
212. ^{d}en-líl uru uru-zu im-ḫul-a uru-zu-gim ḫé-dù
213. gi-gun$_4$-na-zu šu bi-in-lá-lá[100] nibru^{ki}-gim ḫé-dù
214. uru-zu sag PU-ba ḫé-ni-ib-si-si
215. lú lú ù-zu-dè na-an-ni-in-pà-dè
216. šeš-e šeš-a-né giskim na-an-ni-in-è
217. ki-sikil-bé ama$_5$-na giš ḫul hé-en-da-ab-ra
218. ad-da-bé é dam ug$_7$-a-na gù gig-bi ḫé-em-me
219. tu^{mušen}-bé ab-làl-ba še ḫé-ni-in-ša$_4$
220. buru$_5$^{mušen}-bé á-búr-ba níg ḫe-ni-ib-ra
221. tu^{mušen} ní-te-a-gim ur$_5$-da ḫé-ak-e
222. mìn-kam-ma-šè ^{d}sin ^{d}en-ki ^{d}inanna ^{d}ninurta ^{d}iškur ^{d}utu ^{d}nusku ^{d}nisaba dingir ḫé-em-me-eš
223. uru^{ki}-šè igi-ne-ne i-im-gá-gá-ne
224. a-ga-dè^{ki} áš ḫul-a im-ma-ab-bal-e-ne
225. uru^{ki} é-kur-šè ba-e-a-ul$_4$-en ^{d}en-líl ḫé-àm[101]
226. a-ga-dè^{ki} é-kur-šè ba-e-a-ul$_4$-en ^{d}en-líl ḫé-àm[102]
227. bàd kù-zu en-na sukud-rá-bi a-nir ḫé-em-da-sá
228. gi-gun$_4$-na-zu saḫar-gim ḫé-dub
229. dub-lá la-ḫa-ma su$_8$-su$_8$-ga-bi
230. guruš maḫ geštin nag-a-gim ki-šè ḫé-em-ta-gá-gá
231. im-zu abzu-ba ḫé-eb-gi$_4$
232. im ^{d}en-ki-ke$_4$ nam-kud-rá ḫé-a
233. še-zu ab-sín-ba ḫé-eb-gi$_4$
234. še ^{d}ezinu$_2$-e nam-kud-rá ḫé-a
235. giš-zu tir-bi-a ḫé-eb-gi$_4$
236. giš ^{d}nin-ildu$_2$-ma-ke$_4$ nam-kud-rá ḫé-a
237. gu$_4$ gaz-gaz-e[103] dam[104] ḫé-en-gaz-e
238. udu šum-šum-zu[105] dumu[106] ḫé-en-šum-e
239. ukú-zu dumu kù-ge-eš pà-da-na a ḫé-em-ta-ab-ra-ra
240. kar-kid-zu ká éš-dam-ma-na-ka ní ḫa-ba-ni-ib-lá-e
241. ama nu-gig-zu ama nu-bar-zu dumu[107] ḫé-en-gi$_4$-gi$_4$
242. kù-GI-zu kù-šè ḫé-sa$_{10}$-sa$_{10}$.
243. kù-babbar-zu níg za-ḫa-am-šè[108] ḫé-sa$_{10}$-sa$_{10}$
244. urudu-zu a-gar$_5$-šè ḫé-sa$_{10}$-sa$_{10}$

The old men did not restrain (the cry) "Alas its people!"
The lamentation singer did not restrain (the cry) "Alas the Ekur!"
Its young women did not restrain from tearing their hair,
Its young men did not restrain their sharp knives.
Their laments were (like) laments which Enlil's ancestors
Perform in the awe-inspiring *duku,* the holy lap of Enlil.
Because of this, Enlil entered his holy bedchamber, and lay down fasting.

V. The Gods Curse Agade

At that time, Sin, Enki, Inanna, Ninurta, Iškur, Utu, Nusku, and Nisaba, the great gods,[109]
Cooled[110] Enlil's (angry) heart with cool water, and prayed to him:
"Enlil, may the city that destroyed your city, be done to as your city,
"That defiled[111] your *giguna,* be done to as Nippur!
"(Because of) your city, may heads fill its wells!
"May no one find his acquaintance there,
"May brother not recognize brother!
"May its young woman be cruelly killed in her woman's domain,
"May its old man cry bitterly for his slain wife!
"May its pigeons moan in their holes,
"May its birds be smitten in their nooks,
"May they, like frightened pigeons, become immobilized!"
Once again, Sin, Enki, Inanna, Ninurta, Iškur, Utu, Nusku, and Nisaba—all the gods whosoever—
Turned their attention to the city, and
Cursed Agade severely:
"City that attacked Ekur—it was Enlil![112]
"Agade that attacked Ekur—it was Enlil![113]
"May your holy walls, to their highest point, resound with mourning!
"May your *giguna* be piled up like dirt!
"May your *laḫama*-figures that stand in the gateway,
"Lie on the ground, like giants drunk on wine!
"May your clay be returned to its Abzu,
"May it be clay cursed by Enki!
"May your grain be returned to its furrow,
"May it be grain cursed by Ezinu!
"May your timber be returned to its forest,
"May it be timber cursed by Ninildum!
"May the[114] cattle slaughterer slaughter his wife,
"May your[115] sheep butcher butcher his child,
"May your pauper drown the child who seeks money for him!
"May your prostitute hang herself at the entrance to her brothel,
"May your cult prostitutes and hierodules, who are mothers, kill their children!
"May your gold be bought for the price of silver,
"May your silver be bought for the price of *pyrite,*[116]
"May your copper be bought for the price of lead!

245. a-ga-dè^{ki} á-tuk-zu á-ni ḫé-eb-ta-ku$_5$
246. ^{kuš}lu-úb dag-si-né na-an-íl-íl-e
247. anše ni-is-kum-zu á-ni na-an-ḫúl-e u$_4$ šúš-a ḫé-nú
248. uru^{ki}-bi šà-gar-ra ḫé-ni-ib-ug$_7$-e
249. dumu-gi$_7$ ninda ša$_6$-ga kú-kú-zu ú-šim-e ḫa-ba-nú
250. lú sag$_5$-e ba-zi-ga-zu
251. tag-tag ^{giš}ùr-ra-na ḫé-kú-e
252. ^{giš}ig gal ^{kuš}gur$_{21}$ é ad-da-na-ka
253. ^{kuš}gur$_{21}$-bi KA-ni-ta ḫé-ḪAR-re
254. é-gal šà ḫúl-la dù[117]-a-za šà-sìg ḫé-en-šub
255. lú-ḫul[118] eden ki-si[119]-ga-ke$_4$ gù ḫu-mu-ra-ra-ra
256. ki-us-ga šu-luḫ-ḫa gar-ra-zu
257. ka$_5$ du$_6$ gul-gul-la-ke$_4$[120] kun ḫé-ni-ib-ùr-ùr-re
258. abul kalam-ma gar-ra-zu
259. ù-ku-ku^{mušen} mušen šà-sìg-ga-ke$_4$ gùd ḫé-em-ma-an-ús
260. uru^{ki} tigi-da ù nu-ku-ku-za
261. šà ḫúl-la-da nu-nú-za
262. tùr-e si gu$_4$ ^{d}nanna-ke$_4$
263. eden ki-si[121]-ga-ke$_4$ nigin-na-gim[122] še$_{26}$[123] ḫu-mu-un-gi$_4$-gi$_4$-gi$_4$
264. gú ^{giš}má gíd-da íd-da-zu ú gíd-da ḫé-em-mú
265. ḫar-ra-an ^{giš}gigir-ra ba-gar-ra-zu ú a-nir ḫé-em-mú
266. mìn-kam-ma-šè gú má gíd-da ki a-lá íd-da-zu
267. šeg$_9$-bar mul muš-ul$_4$ kur-ra-ke$_4$[124] lú na-an-ni-ib-dib-bé
268. eden šà ú ša$_6$-ga mú-a-zu[125] gi ír-ra ḫé-em-mú
269. a-ga-dè^{ki}[126] a du$_{10}$-ga dé[127]-a-zu[128] a mun-na ḫé-em-dé[129]
270. uru^{ki}-bi-a ga-tuš bí-in-du$_{11}$-ga ki-tuš na-an-ni-du$_{10}$-ge

271. a-ga-dè^{ki}-a ga-nú bí-in-du$_{11}$-ga ki-nú na-an-ni-du$_{10}$-ge

272. i-ne-éš ^{d}utu u$_4$-dè-e-a ur$_5$ ḫé-en-na-nam-ma-àm
273. gú ^{giš}má gíd-da[130] íd-da-ba[131] ú gíd-da ba-an-mú
274. ḫar-ra-an ^{giš}gigir-ra ba-gar-ra-ba[132] ú a-nir ba-an-mú
275. mìn-kam-ma-šè gú ^{giš}má gíd-da ki a-lá íd-da-ba[133]
276. šeg$_9$-bar mul muš-ul$_4$ kur-ra-ke$_4$ lú nu-mu-ni-in-dib-bé
277. eden šà ú ša$_6$-ga mú-a-bé gi ír-ra ba-an-mú
278. a-ga-dè^{ki} a du$_{10}$-ga dé[134]-a-bi a mun-na ba-an-dé[135]
279. uru^{ki}-bi-a ga-tuš bí-in-du$_{11}$-ga ki-tuš nu-um-ma-an-da-du$_{10}$

280. a-ga-dè^{ki}-a ga-nú bi-in-du$_{11}$-ga ki-nú nu-um-ma-an-na-du$_{10}$

281. a-ga-dè^{ki} ḫul-a ^{d}inanna zà-mí

"Agade, may your athlete be deprived of his strength,
"May he be unable to lift his gear bag *onto its stand*!
"May your *niskum*-ass not enjoy its strength, but lie about all day,
"May that city thereby die of hunger!
"May your aristocrats, who eat fine food, lie (hungry) in the grass,
"May your upstanding nobleman
"Eat the *thatching* on his roof,
"The leather hinges on the main door of his father's house—
"May he *gnaw* at those hinges!
"May depression descend upon your palace, constructed[136] in joy!
"May the 'evil one' of the silent plains scream out!
"In your fattening pens, established for purification ceremonies,
"May[137] foxes that frequent ruined[138] mounds sweep with their tails!
"In your city-gate, established for the land,
"May the 'sleep bird,' the bird of depression, establish its nest!
"In your city that couldn't sleep because of the *tigi*-drum music,
"That couldn't rest because of its rejoicing,
"The cattle of Nanna, that fill the pens—
"May they shriek like the 'wandering one' of the silent plains!
"May long grass grow on your canal bank tow-paths,
"May 'mourning grass' grow on your highways laid for coaches!
"Moreover, on your tow-paths, places (built up) with canal sediment,
"May *recurved* mountain sheep and mountain *ul*-snakes[139] allow no one to pass!
"On your[140] plains, where fine grass grows, may 'lamentation reeds' grow!
"Agade,[141] may your[142] flowing sweet water flow as brackish water!
"Whoever says, 'I would dwell in this city!'—may no dwelling place be acceptable to him there!
"Whoever says, 'I would rest in Agade!'—may no resting place be attractive to him there!"
And with the *rising* of the sun, so it was!
On its[143] canal bank tow-paths,[144] long grass grew,
On its[145] highways laid for coaches, "mourning grass" grew.
Moreover, on its[146] tow paths, places (built up) with canal sediment,
Recurved mountain sheep and mountain *ul*-snakes allowed no one to pass,
On its plains, where fine grass grew, "lamentation reeds" now grew,
Agade's flowing sweet water flowed as brackish water.
Whoever said, "I would dwell in that city!"—there was no acceptable dwelling place for him there,
Whoever said, "I would rest in Agade!"—there was no attractive resting place for him there!
Agade is destroyed—hail Inanna!

Notes

1. This eclectic transliteration, with significant variants noted, is for the convenience of the reader, who should, however, refer to the critical text and apparatus for scholarly purposes.

2. Vars. kušu and anše.
3. Vars. -dù-dù.
4. Vars. um.
5. The translation is meant to be literal, without being excessively awkward. For further interpretation, see the commentary. Variants in the Sumerian text that can be meaningfully translated, are noted.
6. Vars. "mountain *beasts*" and "horses."
7. See comm.
8. Vars. la and Ø.
9. Vars. omit.
10. Vars. add -ma-.
11. Vars. ki-sì-ga and níg ša$_6$-ga for ki ša$_6$-ga.
12. Var. gal for -gim.
13. Vars. dé for du.
14. Vars. kur-kur-.
15. Var. GÌR.NITA$_2$.
16. X = DÙL, ki-šè, sag.
17. Vars. gar.
18. Vars. dù-ù-dè for di-da(m).
19. Vars. a-la.
20. Var. è.
21. Var. -šè.
22. Vars. -an-ri.
23. Var. dé.
24. Vars. me-lám-(m)a-ni for me-lám an-né.
25. Vars. omit.
26. Vars. "funeral observances" for "happiness."
27. Var. "a great mountain" for "like a mountain."
28. Var. "flowing into."
29. Var. "wares of foreign lands" for "exotic wares."
30. Var. "generals" for "temple administrators."
31. Vars. "building a well-founded house."
32. Vars. "carried forth."
33. Var. "against."
34. Var. "spilled out."
35. Vars. ba-an-è and ba-an-túm.
36. Vars. [giš]tár-GAG.
37. Var. sì-sì-ge for ság di-dè.
38. Var. inim.
39. B_4 adds the equivalent of 93f. here.
40. Vars. [gi]kid-má-šú-a and [gi]gag-bar-ra for [gi]kid-má šà-ga.
41. Var. -si.
42. Vars. si [giš]má- etc.
43. Vars. šu-du$_7$.
44. Line in ½ the mss. only.
45. Var. inim-ma.
46. Var. ši-.
47. Var. ši-.
48. Var. gú.
49. Vars. dù.

50. Vars. DU.
51. Vars. ba-an-da-ab-lá for gá-gá-dè.
52. Var DU.DU.
53. Vars. "out" and "away."
54. Var. "thrown about."
55. B_4 adds the equivalent of 94f. here.
56. Var. "Pulled out the outside pin on his chariot."
57. Vars. add "the prow of."
58. Half the mss. add 93a = 87.
59. Vars. "work."
60. Var. "brought."
61. Vars. gá-gá-dè for ba-an-da-ab-lá.
62. Var. suḫuš.
63. Vars. a-šà a-gàr.
64. Var. ḫa-zi-in.
65. Var. dé-dé.
66. Vars. kúr.
67. Var. gul.
68. Vars. arḫuš.
69. Var. "foundation."
70. Vars. add "fields."
71. Var. "axes."
72. Vars. "displaced."
73. Var. "destroyed."
74. Vars. "wombs."
75. Var. $u_5^{mušen}$.
76. Var. gu_4.
77. Vars. -dib-bé and -tag_4-tag_4.
78. Var. unu_3.
79. Var. áb-šilam.
80. Vars. na-gada.
81. Var. dul.
82. Var. bí-in-mú.
83. Vars. a-šà a-gàr.
84. Vars. a-šà a-gàr (gal).
85. Vars. TU.TU.
86. Var. du_8.
87. Vars. šèm li-li-ìs and $šèm^{zabar}$, for me-zé li-li-ìs.
88. Var. "*u*-birds."
89. Vars. "like cattle and animals."
90. Vars. "passes along" and "leaves on."
91. Var. "cowherds."
92. Vars. "herdsmen."
93. Var. "were covered with."
94. Vars. add "fields and."
95. Var. adds "great."
96. Vars. add "fields and."
97. Vars. "*šem* and *lilis*-drums" and "bronze *šem*-drums" for "*meze* and *lilis*-drums."
98. Var. ḫé-em-me-eš for gal-gal-e-ne.
99. Vars. su_{13} and su.

100. Var(s). bí-in-dù-a for šu bí-in-lá-lá.
101. Vars. ul_4.
102. Vars. ul_4.
103. Vars. -zu.
104. Var. adds -ni.
105. Vars. -e.
106. Var. adds -ni.
107. Var. adds -ni.
108. Var. NÍG za$\breve{h}$an$_2$-šè and NÍG za-$\breve{h}$a-an-šè.
109. Var. "all the gods whosoever."
110. Var. "sprinkled."
111. Var. "built."
112. Vars. "it attacked Enlil!"
113. Vars. "it attacked Enlil!"
114. Var. "your."
115. Vars. "the."
116. Var. "za$\breve{h}$an" (a foodstuff).
117. Var. gál.
118. Var. adds gál.
119. Var. si-si- for ki-si-.
120. Var. ka$_5$-zu ki du$_6$-ul-du$_6$-ul-la-ke$_4$.
121. Var. si-si for ki-si-.
122. Var. omits nigin-na-gim.
123. Vars. še$_{25}$.
124. Var. anše-kur-ra-ka for muš-ul$_4$ kur-ra-ke$_4$.
125. Var. -bi.
126. Var. íd-da for a-ga-dè[ki].
127. Vars. túm.
128. Vars. -bi.
129. Vars. túm.
130. Var. omits gíd-da.
131. Var. -zu.
132. Var. -zu.
133. Vars. -zu.
134. Var. túm.
135. Var. túm.
136. Var. "which existed."
137. Var. adds "your."
138. Var. omits.
139. Var. "horses" for "mountain *ul*-snakes."
140. Vars. "its."
141. Var. "In the canal."
142. Vars. "its."
143. Var. "your."
144. Var. omits.
145. Var. "your."
146. Vars. "your."

CHAPTER VII

CRITICAL TEXT AND APPARATUS

List of Manuscripts

Work on this edition began with the list of tablets in the preliminary version of M. Civil's catalogue of Sumerian literary texts, supplemented by certain texts given in Wilcke Kollationen, and a British Museum tablet (C) identified by Kramer in 1973. Following Civil, the list was ordered by museum or excavation number, and because the number of available manuscripts had quadrupled since the publication of Falkenstein's edition, it was decided, perhaps unwisely, to abandon his sigla entirely and assign new ones according to the order of Civil's supplemented list of tablet numbers. New texts discovered since 1975 by the editor and others (from T_3 on) were added at the end in the order of their discovery. When all collations had been completed (mid-1977), the existence of numerous new joins and manuscripts suggested that a revision of sigla might be in order, but because the sigla themselves are essentially arbitrary, it was decided that the danger of error caused by such a revision would be greater than any possible esthetic benefits, and the sigla have remained as assigned in early 1976.

Joined manuscripts are subsumed under the lowest number, except that those joined after summer, 1977, are sometimes subsumed under higher numbers, because work on the final edition of the critical text had by then made certain changes of sigla impractical. Only definite indirect joins and long-distance joins are listed as such. Other probable and possible joins are indicated in the notes.

When giving the lines of text covered by a manuscript, commas are used to separate text portions on the same side of a tablet; semicolons are used to separate obverse from reverse (or the sides of a prism from one another). The relationship between the line numbers of this edition and those of Falkenstein's edition is given in the chart immediately following the list of manuscripts.

Every tablet has been collated by the editor (for tablets in Baghdad, casts were used), with the exception of those in Jena, for which I have relied on Wilcke Kollationen, written communication from J. Oelsner, and photos supplies by S. N. Kramer; and Mss., W, C_4, D_4, and K_4, which have been collated by generous colleagues.

All manuscripts are Old Babylonian except R_3, S_3, and K_4, and from Nippur, with the following exceptions:

A Kish
B Kish
C unknown
W unknown
M Ur
U_2 unknown
V_2 unknown
T_3 unknown
U_3 unknown
B_4 Susa
C_4 Isin
D_4 Ur

Siglum	Museum and/or Excavation No.	Publication	Lines of Text	Falkenstein Siglum
A	AO 6890	TRS 64	1-29; 30-60	A
B	AO 6892	TRS 66	1-8, 27; 35-72	B
C	BM 54696	pl. I	67-88, 120-40	
D	CBS 2213	pl. II	108-24; 195-206	
E	CBS 6813	STVC 101	64-74	R
F	CBS 7805	(see S_1)		
G (+)	CBS 7820 + 7830 (+) 7858 (+)	PBS 13 47; and pl. II (7858)	31-45; 45-57, 77-92; 93-104; 148-52, 171-93; 224-35; 275-81	E
R (+)	HS 1489 (+)	TuM NF 3 29		V
Z_1	Ni 4248	SLTN 104		I
H	CBS 8137	STVC 111	16-24	P
I +	CBS 8408 +	STVC 100	1-8, 34-39, 43f.?; 77-79,	Q
C_2 (+)	Ni 4416 (+)	ISET 1 154	110-18, 138-44	
M	CBS 14227	PBS 13 15		C
J	CBS 9233	PBS 13 43	123-46; 147-68	D
K	CBS 13110	STVC 135	202-20; 228-42	AA
L	CBS 13946	STVC 94	155-66; 167-76	G
M	CBS 14227	(see I)		
N	CBS 15076	pl. II	149-58; 159-70	
O	CBS 15127	pl. III	194-207, 246-53	
P	HS 1446	TuM NF 3 27	81-108; 116-45	T
Q	HS 1465	TuM NF 3 28[1]	3-17, 47-59; 220-33, 266-81	U
R	HS 1489	(see G)		
S	HS 1514	TuM NF 3 30[2]	151-80, 181-213; 214-51, 252-281	W
T	HS 1521	TuM NF 3 31	112-39; 140-71	X
U	HS 1541	TuM NF 3 33	154-75; 180-202	Z
V +	HS 1584 +	TuM NF 3 32	104-29; 130-45, 149-51	Y
K_1	N 4201	pl. III		
W	IM 12183a	TIM 9 4	152-63; 191-202	AB
X	N 1066	pl. III	246?-55; 256-63	
Y	N 1344	pl. IV	42-47, 91-97	
Z (+)	N 1346 + 1596 (+)	pl. IV	171-78, 182-91; 192-98,	
B_1	N 1546		204-12	
A_1	N 1444	pl. IV	257-63; 267-69	

Siglum	Museum and/or Excavation No.	Publication	Lines of Text	Falkenstein Siglum
B_1	N 1546	(see Z)		
C_1 +	N 1765 +	pl. IV	38-47, 86-94; 192-201,	
U_1	Ni 4057	TAD 8/2 pl. 8	244-50	
D_1	N 2655	pl. V	93a-100	
E_1[3]	N 2707	pl. V	180?-98; 199-214?	
F_1	N 3561	pl. V	211-21; 235-44	
G_1	N 3618	pl. V	?, 126-33; 134-42, 185f.	
H_1	N 3633 + 1390	pl. VI	27-45, 79-91	
I_1	N 3743	pl. VI	223-32	
J_1	N 4161	pl. VI	145-51	
K_1	N 4201	(see V)		
L_1 +	N 4288	pl. VI	246-64; 265-81	
S_2	UM 29-16-87			
M_1	N 6274 + 7328	pl. VI	97-112	
N_1	Ni 2373	BE 31 1	88-98; 99-108	H
O_1	Ni 2398	SLTN 106	20-31, 53-64; 72-85, 106-21	L
P_1[4]	Ni 2497	SRT 2	171-79; 216-23	F
Q_1[5]	Ni 2727	SLTN 105	1-11; 46-51	K
R_1	Ni 2728	SLTN 108	85-94; 103-115	N
S_1 +	Ni 4008 +	SLTN 107	3-61, 83-124; 127-71, 200-272	M
N_2 +	UM 29-13-92 +	pl. VIIf.		
F	CBS 7805			
T_1	Ni 4032	SLTN 109	100-111, 119-22;[6] 137-47	O
U_1	Ni 4057	(see C_1)		
V_1	Ni 4109	ISET 1 130	216-23[7]	
W_1	Ni 4155	TAD 8/2 pl. 2 and 10	2-25, 45-56; 207-16, 247-74	S
X_1[8]	Ni 4192	pl. IX	12-29; 227-31, 267-81	
Y_1	Ni 4242	ISET 1 142	17-32; 42-58	
Z_1	Ni 4248	(see G)		
A_2	Ni 4350	ISET 1 146	237-48; 281	
B_2[9]	Ni 4411	ISET 1 151	38-45	
C_2	Ni 4416	(see I)		
D_2	Ni 4453	ISET 1 120	229-49; 250-62	
E_2 +	Ni 4542 +	ISET 1 157	29-46	
R_2	Um 29-15-639	pl. X		
F_2	Ni 4559	ISET 1 148	198-210	
G_2	Ni 9532	ISET 1 171	5-14, ?	
H_2[10]	Ni 9583	ISET 1 205	100-110	
I_2[11]	Ni 9757	ISET 2 113	216-225, 264-71	
J_2	Ni 9842	ISET 1 199	54-63	
K_2	Ni 9883	ISET 1 193	101-3; 105-10	
L_2[12]	Ni 9912	ISET 1 195	87-93	
M_2	U 16846	UET 6/2 145	110-39; 140-69	
N_2	UM 29-13-92	(see (S_1)		
O_2	UM 29-13-575	pl. X	250-56; 281?	
P_2	UM 29-13-576 + N 1830	pl. X	255-62; 263-71	
Q_2	UM 29-13-744	pl. XI	167-82; 191-201	
R_2	UM 29-15-639	(see E_2)		
S_2	UM 29-16-87	(see L_1)		
T_2	UM 29:16-420	pl. XI	28f.?, 56-65; 87-91, 124-27	
U_2	YBC 4611	pl. XIIf.	3-38; 41-77	

Siglum	Museum and/or Excavation No.	Publication	Lines of Text	Falkenstein Siglum
V_2	YBC 7171	pl. XI	57-74, 76[13]	
W_2	2N T84 = IM 58944	pl. XII	1-14, 42-56; 92-95, 126-39	
X_2	3N T125 = IM 58344	pl. XIII	49-54, 94-105; 189-98	
Y_2 +	3N T298 = UM 55-21-301 +	pl. XIVf.	2-41, 42-81, 82-125; 126-69, 170-216, 217-65, 278-81[14]	
Z_2 +	3N T303 = A 30204 +			
A_3 +	3N T405 = A 30235 +			
B_3 +	3N T424 = UM 55-21-324 +			
K_3	3N T900, 26 +	OPBF 4 11		
M_3 +	3N T901, 53	OPBF 4 11		
Z_2	3N T303 = A 30204	(see Y_2)		
A_3	3N T 405 = A 30235	(see Y_2)		
B_3	3N T424 = UM 55-21-324	(see Y_2)		
C_3	3N T433 = IM 58480	pl. XV	151-57; 179-83	
D_3	3N T509 = A 30255	pl. XIV	214-28; 236-50	
E_3	3N T510 = IM 58529	pl. XVI	238-47; 248-58	
F_3[15]	3N T544 = IM 58543	pl. XVII	225-30; 231-38	
G_3 +	3N T550 = IM 58547 +	pl. XVII	184-201; 202-16	
I_3	3N T780 = A 30296			
H_3	3N T670 = IM 58606	pl. XVIII	72-81; 92-97	
I_3	3N T780 = A 30296	(see G_3)		
J_3	3N T825 = UM 55-21-380	pl. XVIII	82-94; 119-23	
K_3	3N T900, 26	(see Y_2)		
L_3	3N T901, 36	OPBF 4 10	211-17; 234-39	
M_3	3N T901, 53	(see Y_2)		
N_3	3N T903, 62	OPBF 4 11	36-43; 47-56	
O_3	3N T906, 244	OPBF 4 10	55-61; 62-68	
P_3[16]	3N T917, 370	OPBF 4 10	241-50	
Q_3	3N T923, 501	OPBF 4 10	2-11	
R_3	6N T76 = IM 70097	pl. XIX	98, 100-107; 112f., 115, 127f.	
S_3	6N T935 = IM 70122	pl. XIX	71-75, 84-86; 114, 124-28	
T_3	AUM 73.3175	pl. XX	215-25; 226-39	
U_3	YBC 13249	pl. XXI	2-30; 32-59	
V_3	Ni 1071	pl. XX	32-47; 177-98	
W_3	Ni 4285	pl. XXI	232-39	
X_3	3N T918, 405	OPBF 4 9	258-69; 272-81	
Y_3	N 2574	pl. XX	152-57	
Z_3	3N T901, 44	OPBF 4 10	33-37	
A_4	N 6273	pl. XXI	270-79	
B_4	Sb 12364 + 14154	pl. XXIIf.	74-94; 110-36	
C_4	IB 815		186-210; 237-77	
D_4	U (unnumbered)	UET 6/3 176*	126f.?, 173f., 200f., 213f.	
E_4	N 7289	pl. XXIV	85-91	
F_4	CBS 3957	pl. XXIV	92-94	
G_4	UM 29-13-551	pl. XXIV	237-45; 266-70	
H_4	3N T903, 111	OPBF 4 9	27-32	
I_4	N 3473	pl. XXIV	225-43; 280-81[17]	
J_4	N 7199	pl. XXIV	184-91; 193-98	
K_4	6N T988 = IM 70124	pl. XIX	?, 188-95	
L_4	N 7253	pl. XXIV	209f., 256f.[18]	

Line Numbering

Falkenstein	This Edition
1-30	same
31-34	32-35
35f.	36
37-71	same
72	72f.
73-77	74f.
78-212	subtract 2
213f.	211
215-52	subtract 3
253	250f.
254-83	subtract 2

Notes

1. Obverse according to new copy in Wilcke Kollationen 31.
2. Plus small unnumbered fragment given in Wilcke Kollationen 32.
3. Probable indirect join with P_1.
4. Probable indirect join with E_1.
5. Possible indirect join with B_2.
6. Skips 112-18, but has end of either 115 or 117 on edge.
7. There is a trace of an earlier line (ca. 213).
8. Possible indirect join with H_2, I_2, and L_2.
9. Possible indirect join with Q_1.
10. Probable indirect join with I_2 and L_2; possible indirect join with X_1.
11. Probable indirect join with H_2 and L_2; possible indirect join with X_1.
12. Probable indirect join with H_2 and I_2; possible indirect join with X_1.
13. Between lines 71 and 72.
14. 278-81 are on the edge.
15. Possible indirect join with P_3.
16. Possible indirect join with F_3.
17. Traces of several lines preceding 280.
18. Rev. only; obv. has trace of one sign.

Note to the Critical Text and Apparatus

The composite text presented for each line is eclectic, based on what appear to be the best readings of all manuscripts. Although methodologically unfashionable, this is unavoidable, because the most extensive manuscripts, such as Y_2, are often the most erroneous, and those best preserved, such as the Yale and Louvre tablets for the first sixty lines, often represent recensions at variance with the great majority of other manuscripts. When recensional differences occur, the Nippur tradition is followed, unless it is clearly the worse reading for the line in question. When the reason for choosing one reading over another is not obvious from the context, justification is provided in the commentary. Sign index numbers conform to Ellermeier, *Sumerisches Glossar.*

To facilitate the presentation of the apparatus, full writings and determinatives have been favored in the eclectic text (e.g., mu-un-na- over mu-na-, uru^{ki} over uru). A dash (-) in the apparatus always indicates the presence of the same sign given above it in the eclectic text. Partially preserved signs preceding and following breaks are indicated by ⊦ and ⊣ respectively. Other symbols used are:

- / indented line
- // new line
- . . . traces
- > one line with the following
- < one line with the preceding
- * refers to marginal note

Manuscripts are presented in the order of their sigla, with the exception of the Ur III mss. (R_3 S_3 K_4), which, where preserved, are set off after the Old Babylonian texts.

1.	sag-	ki	gíd-	da	^{d}	en-	líl-	lâ-	ke$_4$
A	[ ]	⸢-	-⸣	-	-	-	-	-	-
B	[					-]	⸢-⸣	-	-
I	-	-	-	-	-	-	-	-	-
Q$_1$	-	-	⸢-	-	-	-	-	-	-⸣
W$_2$	-	-	-	-	-	-	[		]

2.	kiš	^{ki}	gu$_4$	an-	na-	gim	im-	ug$_5$-	ga-	ta
A	-	-	-	-	-	gí	-	-	-	a -
B	[						-]⸢	-	-⸣	a -
I	-	-	-	-	-	- i	-	-	-	-
Q$_1$	-	-	-	-⸢	-	-	-	-	-	- a$^{?}$⸣
W$_1$	. . .									
W$_2$	-	-	-	-	-	-	-	-	⸢-⸣[	]
Q$_3$	⸢-	-⸣	-]	⸢-⸣	-	[				]
U$_3$	. . .									

3. é ki unu^{ki}-ga gu$_4$-mah-gim sahar-ra mi-ni-ib-gaz-a-ta

A - - - - ∅ - - - - - - - - - - -[ ]

B [ ] - -[ ] ⸢ - re ∅ ∅ ∅ -$^?$⸣- -

I - - - - ∅ - - - / - - - - íb - ∅ -

Q ⸢-⸣ . . .

Q_1 - - - - - -⸢ - - - - - -⸣ - - - -

S_1 [ ]⸢- -⸣ -[ ]

W_1 [ɫ - ƚ / ɫ - - - za ƚ]

U_2 [ɫ ƚ]

W_2 - - - - ∅ - - - - ƚ/]- - - - za ƚ]

Y_2 ⸢- - - -! ∅⸣ ƚ]

Q_3 - ⸢- -⸣ƚ /] - - - - - [ ]

U_3 - - ƚ

4. KI.UD-ba šar-ru- GI lugal a-ga-dè^{ki}-ra

A - - - ^{d}- - - - - - - ƚ]

B [ɫ⸢-⸣ -

I [ɫ$^?$bi - - - - - - - - -

Q [ ] - - - - - ƚ]

Q_1 - - - - - um ki in ⸢- - - - -⸣ -

S_1 [ ] - - - ƚ]

W_1 [ɫ - - - - - - - ƚ]

U_2 [ɫ ⸢-⸣ ƚ]

W_2 - - - ⸢- -⸣ - - - - - - - ƚ]

Y_2 ⸢- -⸣ - - ƚ ɫ - - - ƚ]

Q_3 - - - - - - - [ ]

U_3 - - - ^{d}⸢- -⸣ ƚ ɫ

5. sig-ta igi-nim -šè̌ ^{d}en-líl-le

	sig	ta	igi	nim	-šè	^{d}	en	líl	le	
A	-	-	-	- ^{ki}	-	-	-	-	-	
B	[							]	-	
I	[	ǂ	-	-	-	-	-	-	-	
Q	-	-	-	-	-	-	-[	-	-]	>
Q_1	-	-	-	-	-	-	-	-	Ø	>
S_1	[	]	-	-	-	-	-	-	lá	>
W_1	[			ǂ	-	-	-	-	-	
G_2	[	]	-	ƚ					]	
U_2	[		]	ƚ?					]	
W_2	ƚ	ǂ	-	-	-	-	-	-	Ø	>
Y_2	ƚ]	-	-	-	-	-	-	-	Ø	>
Q_3	-	-	-	-	-	-	-	-	-*	>
U_3	-	-	-	- ^{ki}	-	-	-	-	-	

*gloss above and right?

6. nam-en nam-lugal mu-un-na-an-sum-ma- ta

	nam	en	nam	lugal		mu	un	na	an	sum	ma		ta
A	-	-	-	-	la	-	-	-	-	-	-		-
B	[					ǂ⸢-		-	-	-	-⸣	a	-
I	[	]	-	-		-	∅	-	-	-	-		-
Q	< -	-	-	-		-	∅	-	-	[ǂ	a		-
Q_1	< -	-	-	-		-	∅	-	x	-	-		-
S_1	< ƚ				] /	-	-	-	-	-	-	[	]
W_1	⸢-⸣	-	-	-		-	∅	-	-	-	-		-
G_2	[	ǂ	-	-	x̶*								]
U_2	. . .												
W_2	< -	-	-	-	l[a]/	-	∅	-	-	-	-	[	]
Y_2	< -	-	∅	-		-[							]
Q_3	< ƚ				]/	-	∅	-	-	ƚ			]
U_3	[ǂ	-	-	-	la	-	-	-	-	-	-		-

* x = l[a] or m[u]

7. u_4-ba èš a-ga-dè[ki] kù [d]inanna-ke_4

	u_4	ba	èš	a	ga	dè	ki	kù	d	inanna	ke_4
A	-	-	ƚ]	-	-	-	-	-	-	-	-
B	[										]-
I	[				ǂ	-	-	-	-	-	ƚ]
Q	-	-	-	-	-	-	-	-	-	-	-
Q_1	[	ǂ⸢-⸣		-	-	-	-	-	-	-	-
S_1	[	]-		-	-	-	-	-	-	-	[ ]
W_1	[	ǂ -		-	-	-	-	-	-	-	-
G_2	[	ǂ		-	-	-⸢-⸣[					]
U_2	[	]⸢-⸣		-	ƚ						]
W_2	ƚ	ǂ -		-	-	-	-	-	-	-	-
Y_2	[ǂ	-	-	-	-	-	-	-	-	-	ƚ]
Q_3	-	-	-	-	-	-	-	ƚ			]
U_3	[ ]	-	-	-	-	-	-	-	-	-	-

```
8.    ama5 mah-a-ni-šè im-ma-  an-dù-dù

A      -    -  -  -  -  -  -    -  - ⌈-⌉

B     [                            ]⌈-⌉

I     [                  ]⌈-  -    -  -⌉[ ]

Q      -    -  ∅  -  -  - m[i] in  -  -

Q1    [           ɬ  -  -  -    -  -  -

S1    [     ɬ  -  -  -  -  -    -  ɫ   ]

W1    [ ]   -  -  -  -  -  -    -  -  -

G2    [     ɬ  ∅  - ⌈-⌉ -  ɫ           ]

U2    [ ]   -  -  - [                  ]

W2     ɫ    ɬ  -  -  -  -  - da -  -   ∅

Y2    [ ]   -  -  -  -  -  -    -  ɫ   ]

Q3     -    -  -  -  -  - [            ]

U3     -    -  -  -  -  -  -    -  -  -



9.    ul-maš^ki-a ^giš gu-za ba-ni-in-gub

A      -  -  -  -  -  -  -  -  ɫ      ]

Q      -  -  ∅  -  -  -  - [   ]⌈-⌉ -

Q1    [              ɬ ⌈-⌉ -  -  -  -

S1    [        ɬ  -  -  -  -  -  - [ ]

W1    [   ɬ!   -  -  -  -  -  -  -  -

G2    [      ɬ  -  -  - ⌈-⌉[          ]

U2    [ ] - ⌈- -  -⌉[                 ]

W2     ɫ  ɬ  - -  -  -  -  -  -  -  -

Y2    [ ] -  ∅ e  -  - [ ] -  -  - [ ]

Q3     -  -  - -  -  -  -  ɫ          ]

U3     -  -  - -  -  -  -  -  -  -  -
```

10. lú-tur gibil -bi é dù-ù-gim

A - - gibil$_4$ - ⸢-⸣ - [-]

Q - - - - [- -] -

Q_1 [ ]- dè

S_1 [ ] - - - - - [ ]

W_1 [-] - - - - - - -

G_2 [-] - - [-]

U_2 [ ]⸢-⸣[ ]

W_2 [-] - - - - - -

Y_2 [ ] - gibil$_4$ - - ⸢- - x⸣* *x = gim or dè

Q_3 ⸢-] - ⸢-⸣ - [ ]

U_3 - [-] - - - - -

11. dumu-bàn-da ama$_5$ gá-gá-gim

A - - - - - - ⸢x⸣* *x more like gim than dè

Q ⸢ -] - - - [- -] -

Q_1 . . .

S_1 [-] - - - [ ]

W_1 [-] - - - - - -

G_2 [-] ⸢-⸣ - [-]

U_2 [ ] - [ ]

W_2 [ ] - - - - - -

Y_2 [-] - - - dè

Q_3 - [-] - [ ]

U_3 [ ] - - - -

12. é níg-ga-ra níg sá-di-dè

A	- - - - - - - da[m]
Q	⌈-⌉ - - ⌈-⌉ - si x -
S_1	[ ] - - - - [ ]
W_1	⌈-⌉ - - - - - - -
X_1	[ ] - - - [ ]
G_2	[ ] - - - [ ]
U_2	[ ] - - . . .
W_2	[ ] - - - - - - -
Y_2	[ ]⌈-⌉ - - - ⌈-⌉ - -
U_3	[ ] - - - dam

13. uru^{ki}-bé dúr ki-gar sum-mu-dè

A	- - - - - - - - -
Q	⌈- -⌉ - - - - - - -
S_1	[ ] - - - - - [ ]
W_1	[ǂ Ø - - - - - - -
X_1	[ǂ Ø - - - [ ]
G_2	[ǂ - [ ]
U_2	[ǂ* Ø - - - ⌈-⌉ ŧ ǂ
W_2	[ǂ ⌈- -⌉ - - - -
Y_2	[ǂ - - ⌈-⌉ - - - -
U_3	[ ] - - -

*x is either [ur]u or [k]i. The sign seems to be the second rather than the first on the line, suggesting ki, but U_2 consistently writes uru without the determinative (lines 60, 64, 70)

14. un-bé ú nir-gál kú-ù-dè

```
A      -  - -  -   -   - -! -
Q      -  - -  -   -   - -  -
S1    [       ] -  ⌈-   -⌉-[ ]
W1    []̶  - -  -   -   - -  -
X1    []̶  - -  [̶              ]
G2    [                []̶⌈-⌉[]
U2    [ ] - -  -   -  []⌈-?-?⌉
W2    . . .
Y2    [ ] - -  -   -   - -  -
U3    [              ] - -  -
```

15. un-bé a nir-gál nag-nag-dè

```
A      -  - -  -   -   -   -  -
Q     []̶  - -  -   -   -   -  -
S1    [       ] -  [             ]
W1    []̶  - -  -!  -   -   -  -
X1    []̶  - - [                  ]
U2    [ ] - -  -   -  ⌈-⌉  - ⌈-⌉
Y2    [ ] - -  -   -   -   -  -
U3    [              ] -   -  -
```

16. sag a-tu$_5$-a kisal húl-le-dè

A - - - - - - - -

H [ǂ ŧ]

Q [ǂ ⌈- -⌉ ∅ - - ⌈- -⌉

S_1 . . .

W_1 [ǂ - - - - - - ⌈-⌉

X_1 [ ]⌈- -⌉[ ]

U_2 [ ] - - - - - - [ǂ

Y_2 [ǂ - ∅ - ŧ]⌈-⌉

U_3 [ ] ⌈-⌉ - - -

17. ki ezem-ma un sig$_7$-ge-dè

A - - - - - - -

H [ ] - sì [ ]

Q . . .

S_1 [s]ì ŧ]

W_1 [ǂ - - - - -

X_1 [ ]

Y_1 - - [ ]

U_2 [ǂ - - ⌈-⌉ - [ǂ

Y_2 [ ] ⌈-⌉ -

U_3 [ ] - - - -

```
18.  lú zu-ù-ne téš-bi kú-ù-dè

A      -  - ∅ ke4 -  -  -  -  -

H     [            ⊣  -  ⊢     ]

S1    [              ⊣  - [   ]

W1    [            ⊣  ba -  ∅  -

X1    [          ]⌈-⌉ -  - ⌈- -⌉

Y1     -  - - ⌈-⌉ ⊢            ]

U2    [ ] - ∅ ke4 - ⌈-  -  - -⌉

Y2    [              ] -  ∅  -

U3    [            ⊣  -  -  - -
```

```
19.  lú bar-ra mušen nu-zu-gim an-na nigin-dè

A      -  -  -   -   -  -  -  -  -  -  -

H     [                 ⊣  -   -  - [      ]

S1    [                         ⊣  -   ⊢   ]

W1    [    ]⌈-   -   -  -  -⌉ -  -  -   -

X1    [    ] -  ⌈-   -  -  -  -⌉ -  -   -

Y1     -  -  -   -   -  - [                ]

U2    [ ] -  -   -   - ⌈-⌉ -  - [ ]  ⊢   ⊣

Y2    [                          ]  -   -

U3    [          ⊣   ⊢       ] -  -  -   -
```

```
20.    mar-ha-šiki    le-um-    ma gur-ru-dè

A        - - - -      - -      - - - -
H      [              ǂ -      - ǂ     ]
O1     [                           ǂ -
S1     [          ] ⸢- -⸣    ∅   - - [ ]
W1     [   ǂ - -    GUD.AN.NA-   - - ǂ]
X1     [               ]⸢-     -⸣ - - ⸢-⸣
Y1       - - -⸢-⸣* - - [               ]     *or giš
U2     [ ] - - - šè⸢-⸣ -    ǂ         ǂ
Y2     [                        ] - ⸢-⸣
U3     [          ] - -      - - - -
```

```
21.  uguugu4-bi am-si mah áb-za-za ú-ma-am ki bad-rá

A    a-ga_ - - - - - -! - - u4 - - -   - -
H    [                ǂ -! - - [               ]
O1   [                        ]-! - - -   - -
S1   [            ǂ - - - - - - - - - [     ]
W1   [                        ]- - - - [     ]
X1   [                  ]⸢- - -⸣ - - - ⸢-  -⸣[ ]
Y1      - - - - - -[                          ]
U2   [ ǂ - - - ǂ ǂ - - - [     ǂ - - -
Y2   [ ] - - ⸢-⸣[     ]⸢- -/ -⸣ - ∅ -  - dè
U3   [               ] - - - - - - - - - -
```

22. šà sila-dagal-la-ke$_4$ téš-bi tag-tag-ge-dè

A	- - - - - - - - - - -
H	[ǂ - - [ ]
O_1	[ ] - - - - -! -
S_1	[ǂ - - - - - - -
W_1	[ǂ - ka - ba ŧ]
X_1	[ǂ ⌈- - -⌉[ ]
Y_1	- - ⌈-⌉ - - ŧ]
U_2	[ ] - - - - ⌈- -⌉ - ⌈-⌉[ǂ
Y_2	[ ] - - - - - - - ∅
U_3	[ǂ - - - - - -

23. ur-gi$_7$ ur-nim dara$_3$ kur-ra udu-a-lum SÍG-BU si

A	- - - - kušu - - - - - - - -	
H	[ǂ - - [ ]	
O_1	[ ]-ki⌈kušu⌉ - - - - - - - -? e	
S_1	[ ]- - - - - - - - ⌈x(x)⌉* a	*x(x)≠BU si
W_1	[ǂ kušu - ŧ]	
X_1	[ ]( )*⌈- x (x)⌉	*a?]-lum-udu
Y_1	- - - - an⌈še -⌉ ŧ	
U_2	[ǂ - - - - - - ⌈-⌉ - - [ ]x*	*x could=si, but is not like si in 25f.
Y_2	[ǂ - - kušu - - - - - - - ∅ ∅	
U_3	[ǂ anše - - - -[ǂ - -	

24. kù ^{d}inanna-ke$_4$ ù nu-um-ši-ku-ku

A - - - - - - - - - -

H [ ]-[ ]

O_1 [ǂ - - - - - - - -

S_1 [ǂ - - - - - ⌈-⌉-

W_1 [ǂ - [ ]

X_1 [ ]- - ǂ]

Y_1 - - - - ⌈-⌉ -[ ]

U_2 [ǂ - - - - - - ⌈- -⌉-

Y_2 [ǂ - - - mu un - - -

U_3 [ǂ - - - - - - - -

25. u$_4$-ba a-ga-dè^{ki} é-ÁŠ-a-ba kù-GI mi-ni-in-si

A - - - - - - - - - - - - - - - -

O_1 [ ]- - - - - - - - - - - - - -

S_1 [ǂ - - - - - - - - ⌈- - - -⌉

W_1 [ǂ ǂ]

X_1 [ ]⌈-⌉ - - - ǂ]

Y_1 - - - - - - [ ]

U_2 - - - - - - - - - - ⌈-⌉ - ⌈- -⌉ - -

Y_2 [ ]- - - - - - - - - - - -/ ø -

U_3 [ ]⌈- -⌉ - - - - - - - - ǂ]

26.	é-	ÁŠ	babbar-	ra-	ba	kù-	babbar	mi-	ni-	in-	si
A	-	-	babbar$_2$	-	∅	-	-	-	-	-	-
O_1	[		ǂ	-	-	-	-	-	-	-	-
S_1	[	ǂ	-	-	-	-	-	-	⌈-	-	-⌉
X_1	[							ǂ	-	-	[ ]
Y_1	[		ǂ	-	-	-	[				]
U_2	-	-	-	-	-	-	-	-	⌈-	-⌉	-
Y_2	[	]	-	-	-	-	-	-	-	∅	-
U_3	[		b]abbar$_2$	⌈-⌉	∅	-	-	-	-	-	⌈-⌉

27.	arah$_4$	še-	ba	urudu	an-	na	na$_4$-	lagab	za-	gìn-	na	sá	im-	mi-	in-	du$_{11}$-	du$_{11}$
A	-	-	-	-	-	-	-	-	-	-	-	-	-	-	- /	-	-
B	[											]	mi	ni	-	dù	dù
H_1	[											]	⌈-?⌉	[	/	]-	-
O_1	[ǂ	-	bi	-	-	- /	-	∅	-	-	-	-	-	-	-	-	-
S_1	-	ŧ	ǂ	⌈-⌉	-	- /	-	-	⌈-⌉	-	-	⌈-	x	x⌉[		]⌈x	-⌉
X_1	[					]	-	-	-	ŧ							]
Y_1	[ǂ	-	-	ŧ							/			]	-!	-	ŧ]
U_2	-	⌈-	-⌉	-	-	-	ŧ	ǂ	-	-	-/	-	⌈-	-⌉	-	[ ]	-
Y_2	[ǂ	-	-	-	-	-	∅	-	-	-	∅/	∅	-	∅	∅	dù	dù
U_3	[ǂ	-	-	-	-	-	-	-	-	-	-	-	-	-	∅	dù	⌈dù⌉
H_4	[								ǂ	-	-	⌈-⌉	ŧ				]

28. gur$_7$-bi bar-ta im ba-an-ùr

	gur$_7$-bi bar-ta		im ba-an-ùr	
A	⌈-⌉ - - -		um - - -	
H_1	[		ǂ[!] - ∅ -	
O_1	[ǂ - - -		- - ∅ -	
S_1	- - - ⌈-		-⌉ - ⌈- -⌉	
X_1	[ ]	DI*	um ma[ ]	*or KI
Y_1	[ ] - - ŧ		]	
T_2?	[		ǂ?	
U_2	- - ⌈-⌉[		] - - [?] -	
Y_2	[ǂ - - -		- ta - -	
U_3	[ǂ ⌈-⌉ - -		um - - -	
H_4	[ǂ		- - ⌈-⌉[ ]	

29. um-ma-bé ad-gi$_4$-gi$_4$ ba-an-sum

	um-ma-bé ad-gi$_4$-gi$_4$ ba-an-sum
A	⌈-⌉ - - - - - - - -
H_1	[ ] - - - - -
O_1	[ ] - - - - - ∅ -
S_1	- - - ⌈- - - - -⌉ -
X_1	[ ] - ŧ]
Y_1	[ǂ - - ŧ]
E_2	[ǂ - ŧ]
T_2?	[ǂ
U_2	- - ⌈-⌉[ ] - - [ ] -
Y_2	[ǂ - - - - - - -
U_3	[ ]⌈- - - -⌉ - - -
H_4	[ǂ - - - - [ ]

30. ab-ba-bé inim-inim-ma ba-an-sum

A	- - - - - - - - -
I	⌈-⌉ [̶]
H_1	[ ] ⌈-⌉ - - - -
O_1	[ ] ⌈- -⌉ - - Ø -
S_1	- - - ⌈- - ⌉[ ] ⌈-⌉
Y_1	[ ] - - [̶]
R_2	[ ] - - -
U_2	- - ⌈-⌉ [ ]̶ - ⌈-⌉[ ] -
Y_2	[ ] - - - - - - - -
U_3	[ ] ⌈- -⌉ - - - -
H_4	[ ]̶ - - - - [ ]

31. ki-sikil-bé ki-e-ne-di ba-an-sum

A	omits
G	⌈- - - -⌉ - [̶]̶
I	- ⌈-⌉[ ]
H_1	[ ]̶ - - - -
O_1	[ ]⌈-⌉
S_1	- - - - ⌈- - - - -⌉ -
Y_1	[ ]̶ - - [̶]
E_2	[ ]̶ - - -
U_2	- - [ ]̶ a - ⌈- - -⌉ -
Y_2	[ ]̶ - ⌈- - -⌉ - - - -
U_3	omits
H_4	[ ]̶ - -* - - [ ] *adds -dè

32. guruš-bé á ^{giš}tukul-la ba-an-sum

A ⌈-⌉ - - - - - - - -

G - - - - - lá [ǂ -

I ŧ]

H_1 [ǂ - - - - - -

S_1 - - a ⌈- - - - - -⌉

Y_1 [ ]⌈- -⌉[ ]

E_2 [ ] e - - -

U_2 - ø ⌈- - -⌉ a [ǂ - -

Y_2 [ǂ - - - ø - - -

U_3 ⌈- - -⌉ - - ŧ]- - ⌈-⌉

V_3 [ ]⌈- - - - -⌉ - [ ]

H_4 [ ]⌈- -⌉ [ ]

33. di_4-di_4-lá-bé šà húl-la ba-an-sum

A - - - - - - - - - - -

G - - - - - ⌈-⌉ - ⌈- -⌉ -

I ŧ]

H_1 [ ] - - - - - - -

S_1 - - - - ⌈- -⌉ - - - [-]

E_2 [ ] - - - -

U_2 ⌈- -⌉[ ] - ⌈-⌉ - - - -

Y_2 [ǂ - - - ⌈-⌉ ø - - -

U_3 ⌈- -⌉ - - - - - - - - -

V_3 - ⌈- -⌉ - - - - - - - [ ]

Z_3 [ ] - - ŧ]

```
34.   emeda-ga-lá šu-gíd dumu šagina-   ke4-  ne

A       x*  -  ∅  -   -   -   kiš^ki      -    -       *see comm.

G       ƚ?] -  -  ∅   ∅   ⌈-     -⌉       -    -

I       ƚ?] -  ∅  ∅   -   ƚ                    ]

H1    [                  ]  -      ma  -    -

S1      ƚ ] -  -  ∅   ∅   -      -        -   ƚ]

E2    [                      ɟ            -    -

U2    [               ]⌈-⌉   -      ma  -    -

Y2      ƚ?] -  la bi  ∅   -   ⌈alim?⌉ ma  -    -

U3      x*  -  ∅ ⌈-⌉  -   -      -        -    -       *see comm.

V3     ⌈-⌉ ƚ]  ∅  ∅   ∅   -      -        - e [ ]

Z3    [         ] -   -   -      ƚ             ]
```

```
35.   gišal-gar-sur9-da e-ne im-di-  ne

A      -  -  -   -   -  -  -  -    -

B     [                        ]-   ƚ ]

G      - ⌈-  -   -⌉  -  -  -  ƚ        ]

I      -  -  -   ƚ         ] ƚ        ]

H1    [           ] -  -  -  -  -  e -

S1     - ⌈-  -   -   -  -⌉-  -  - ƚ*(x)]       *x looks most like
                                                N[I]

E2    [           ɟ  -  -  -  -     -

U2    [           ɟ  -  - ⌈-⌉ ƚ     ɟ

Y2     -  -  ∅   -   - ⌈-⌉- ∅  -     -

U3     -  ƚ  ɟ   -   - ⌈-⌉- -  -     -

V3    ⌈-  - -⌉   -   - ∅ i  -  - e [ ]

Z3    [  ɟ  -   -   - ƚ              ]
```

36. uru[ki] šà-bi tigi-a bar-bi-ta gi-gíd za-am-za-am-ma

A	- - - - - - // - - - - - - - - - - e
B	[ɟ ŧ ɟ - - - - - - ŧ]
G	- - - - ŧ]⸢-⸣ ŧ]/ - - - ŧ ɟ [ ]
I	- ∅ - - ŧ]/ - - - ŧ]
H_1	[ɟ - ⸢-⸣ - - - - - - - - -
S_1	- - - - ⸢-⸣ - - - [ɟ / - - - - ⸢- - -⸣
E_2	[ɟ àm - - - - - - - - ŧ (?)]*
U_2	[ɟ àm - - - ŧ]
Y_2	- - - - - - - ∅ - - - - - - ∅ ∅ ∅
N_3	-⸢- - - -⸣[ ]/⸢- - - - -⸣[ ]
U_3	[ɟ - - // [ɟ - - - ⸢- -⸣
V_3	⸢-⸣∅ - - ⸢- - -⸣ - - - ŧ/]⸢-⸣[ ]⸢-⸣ - ŧ]**
Z_3	[ ] - - - -[/ ɟ ⸢-⸣ - - - [ ]

*a[m] probably final sign

**x could be ma or e

37. kar ^{giš}má ús-bi mud$_5$-me-gar-ra

	kar	^{giš}	má	ús	bi	mud$_5$	me	gar	ra	
A	-	-	-	-	-	-	-	-	-	
B	[	ǂ	-	⌈-	-⌉	-	-	-	-	
G	-	-	-	-	-	ǂ			]	
I	-	∅	-	-	-	ǂ			]	
H_1	[		ǂ	-	-	-	-	-	-	
S_1	[ǂ*	-	-	⌈-	-	-⌉	-	-	⌈-⌉	*beginning possibly [kar-r]a
E_2	[				]	-	-	-	-	
U_2	[				]	-	-	ǂ	]	
Y_2	-	∅	-	-	∅	GIŠ.Ú	-	-	-	
N_3	ǂ	ǂ	⌈-	-	-⌉	ǂ			]	
U_3	[				ǂ	-	-	-	-	
V_3	-	∅	⌈-	-	-	-⌉	-	⌈-⌉[	]	
Z_3	[					ǂ[			]	

38. kur-kur ú-sal-la i-im-nú

	kur	kur	ú	sal	la	i	im	nú
A	-	-	-	-	-	-	-	-
B	[ ]	-	-	-	-	-	-	-
G	-	- re	-	-	-	ɫ		]
I	-	-	-	-	-	-	ɫ	]
C_1	[				]	⌈-	-	-⌉
H_1	[	]	-	-	-	-	-	⌈-⌉
S_1	[ǂ	[ ]	⌈-	-	-⌉	-	-	-
B_2	⌈-	- re	-⌉[					]
E_2	[				ǂ	-	-	-
U_2	[				ǂ	ì[		]
Y_2	[ǂ	-	-	-	-	ì	∅	-
N_3	-	-	-	-	-	-	-	ɫ]
U_3	[				]	-	-	-
V_3	⌈-	- re	-⌉	-	-	-	⌈-⌉	ɫ]

```
39.   un-bé ki  šà6-ga igi bí-ib-du8
A       - - níg - -   - - -   -
B       - - - sì  -   - - -  ŧ]
G       - ⌈-⌉ -  - -  ŧ       ǂ
I       - - -  - -  - ŧ       ]
C1    [               ǂ - -   -
H1    [           ǂ  -  - - ⌈in⌉ -
S1    [ ] - - sì ⌈-⌉  - - -   -
B2      - - - ŧ               ]
E2    [            ] ⌈-⌉ - in -
Y2    [     ǂ sì  -   - bi - ⌈x⌉
N3      - - -  - -  - - -    ŧ]
U3    [            ] - - -    -
V3    [- - -  - -] - ⌈-⌉ -    -


40.   lugal-bi sipa dna-ra-am-dsin-e
A        -   -   -   - - - -  - - -  -
B        -   -   -   - - - -  - -[   ]
G        -   -   -   Ø⌈- -⌉ - ⌈- -⌉  -
C1    [                       ] - -  Ø
H1    [                 ǂ -  ŧ] - -* Ø        *dEN.(eras.)ZU
S1    [  ]   -   -   -⌈- -⌉ - - -    -
B2       -   -   -   Ø - ŧ           ]
E2    [                       ǂ - -  -
Y2    [     ]    -   Ø - -  - - -    Ø
N3       -   -   -   Ø - -  - - -  ⌈-⌉
U3    [            ] - - - [ǂ - -    -
V3    ⌈. . .                  -⌉- [  ]
```

41. bara$_2$ kù a-ga-dè^{ki}-šè u$_4$-dè-éš im- è

A - - - - - - ka - - eš - mi in -

B - - - - - - ka - - - ∅ -

G - ⸢-⸣ -⸢- -⸣- ⸢-⸣[ ] - - -

C$_1$ [ ] - - -

H$_1$ [ǂ eš*- - *adds MA?

S$_1$ [ǂ - - - - - ⸢- -⸣ - -

B$_2$ LU - - - - - - [ ]

E$_2$ [ǂ - - -

U$_2$ [ ]⸢-⸣[ ]

Y$_2$ [ǂ - ⸢x⸣ eš - me

N$_3$ [ ] ⸢-⸣ - - - - ka - ǂ]

U$_3$ [ ] eš - mi in -

V$_3$ ⸢ . . . -⸣ ke$_4$⸢- - - -⸣[ ]

42.	bàd-	bi	hur-	sag-	gim	an-	né	im-		ús
A	-	-	-	-	-	-	-	-	ú	-
B	-	-	-	-	-	-	-	-	mi	-
G	⸢-⸣	-	⸢-⸣	-	-	ǂ]	-	-		-
Y	[					]	⸢-	-		-⸣
C_1	[						ǂ	-		-
H_1	[			ǂ	gal	-	-	-		-
S_1	[	ǂ	-	-	-	-	e	⸢-		-⸣
Y_1	[		ǂ	-	ǂ					]
B_2	[ǂ	-	-	-	-	ǂ				]
E_2	[						ǂ	-		-
U_2	[	]	-	[						]
W_2	ǂ									]
Y_2	[								]	⸢-⸣
N_3	[ǂ	-	-	-	-	-[				]
U_3	[									]
V_3	⸢-	-	-	-	-	-	-⸣[			]

43.   abul -a-ba ́id idigna a-ab-ba-šè du-ù-gim

A   -   - bi -   -   - - - - dé-a -

B   - ∅ -   -   -   - - - - ⌈dé a⌉ -

G   - -⌈- -⌉ -   - - - - - - - ŧ]

I   ŧ   ]

Y   [   ] - - - - - ∅ -

C_1 [ɟ - - da ∅ -

H_1 [ɟ - - - - -! - - -

S_1 [ ] ∅ -   -   -   - - - - x* ∅ -   *x=du or da

Y_1 ⌈ - ⌉ -⌈-   -   -⌉[   ]

B_2 [ɟ - -   - ŧ   ]

E_2 ⌈. . .- -⌉[ɟ - [   ]

U_2 [   ] - [   ]- - ⌈- -⌉[   ]

W_2 ŧ   ]

Y_2 [   ]⌈-⌉

N_3 [   ]⌈- -   -   -⌉[   ]

U_3 [   ]

V_3 [   ]⌈ -   -   - - - -⌉[   ]

44. kù ^{d}inanna-ke$_4$ ka-bé gál bí-in-tag$_4$

	kù	d	inanna	ke$_4$	ka	bé	gál	bí	in	tag$_4$
A	-	-	-	-	-	-	-	-	-	-
B	-	-	-	[-]	-!	-	[	-]	-	-
G	-	-	-	-	-	-	-	-	-	-
I	[-									]
Y	[				]	-	-	-	-	-
C_1	[						-]	-	-	-
H_1	[			-]	-	-	-	-	-	[-]
S_1	⸢-⸣	-	-	-	-	-	-	⸢-⸣	[ ]	⸢-⸣
Y_1	-	-	-	-	-	[				]
B_2	[		-]	-	-	[-				]
E_2	[	]	-	[-						]
U_2	[-			-]	-	-	-	bi	[-	]
W_2	-	[								]
Y_2	[									]⸢-⸣
U_3	[ ]	⸢-	-	-⸣	[-					]
V_3	⸢-⸣	[		]-	⸢-⸣	-	⸢-	bi⸣	[	]

45.	ki-en-gi-ra níg-ga ní-ba-ke$_4$ ^{giš}má im-da-gíd-dè
A	- - - - - - - - - ta - - hé - - - da
B	[ ] - - re - - - - - ta - ⌈- -⌉ - - -
G	[ǂ - gi$_4$⌈-⌉ - - - bi ta - - ⌈x x⌉*[ ]
Y	[ ] - - - /[ǂ - - -
C_1	[ ] bi ta /[ǂ - -
H_1	. . .
S_1	- - - - - - ⌈- - -⌉ - ⌈- x x⌉ ǂ ǂ
Y_1	- - - - - - [ ]
B_2	[ǂ - ǂ]
E_2	[ǂ - - - ⌈- - - - - . . . /- dè?⌉
U_2	-[ǂ - - - - - - - ∅ - ǂ]
W_2	-[ ]
Y_2	[ǂ ta - ∅
U_3	[ ] - - - - - - - ta - - hé - ǂ]
V_3	[ ]⌈- - . . .⌉ bi ta ǂ /] ⌈- - x (x)⌉

*x x could be hé-im or i-im

46. mar-tu kur-ra lú še nu-zu

	mar	tu	kur	ra	lú	še	nu	zu
A	-	-	-	-	-	-	-	-
B	[ŧ	-	-	-	-	-	⌈-	-⌉
G	[				ŧ	-	-	-
Y	[			]	-	-	-	-
C_1	[				]	-	-	-
Q_1	[	]	⌈-	-	-	-⌉	ŧ	]
S_1	-	-	-	-	-	⌈-	-	-⌉
W_1	ŧ							]
Y_1	-	-	-	-	[			]
E_2	[		ŧ	-	-	-	-	-
U_2	-	ŧ]	-	-	-	-	ŧ	]
W_2	ŧ							]
Y_2	[						ŧ	-
U_3	[ŧ	-	-	-	-	-	-	-
V_3	[		ŧ	-	-	⌈ki$^{?}$-	-⌉[	]

47.	gu_4	du_7	máš	du_7-	da	mu-	un-	na-	da-	an-	ku_4-	ku_4
A	-	-	-	gu_4	du_7	-	-	-	-	-	-	-
B	[ ]	-	-	-	-	-	-	-	-	-	-	-
G	[				]x*	àm	Ø	ma	-	-	-	-
Q	-	-	-	-	-	[						]
Y	[			]x	-	-	-	-	-	-	/[]x	-
C_1	[								]x	-	-	Ø
Q_1	[		]x	-	-	àm	Ø	ma	x[			]
S_1	-	⸢-⸣	-	-	dè	-	-	-	-	⸢-	-	-⸣
W_1	-	[				/]x[?						]
Y_1	-	-	-	-	[							]
U_2	-	-	-	-	-	-!	Ø	-	-	-	x[	]
Y_2	[								]x	Ø	-	-
N_3	. . .											
U_3	[]x	-	-	gu_4	du_7	-	-	-	-	-	-	-
V_3	[				]	⸢-	-	-	-⸣[			]

*x can be [d]a or [d]è

48. me-luh-ha^{ki} lú kur gi$_6$-ga-ke$_4$

A	- - - Ø - - - - kam
B	[ ]⌈-⌉ - Ø - - - - ɫ]
G	[ǂ - - - -
Q	- - - Ø - - ɫ]
Q_1	[ ]⌈-⌉- - - - ɫ]
S_1	[ǂ - Ø - [ǂ - - -
W_1	- - ɫ]
Y_1	- - - - [ ]
U_2	- - - - - - - - - [ ]
Y_2	- ɫ ǂ -
N_3	⌈- -⌉ - Ø [ǂ - - - [ ]
U_3	- - - Ø - - - - kam

49. níg-šu kúr-kúr-ra mu-un-na-ra-ab-e$_{11}$-dè

A	- - - - - - - - - - - - -
B	⌈- -⌉ kur kur - - - - - - - ⌈-⌉[ ]
G	[ ]- Ø - - - - - -
Q	- - kur kur - ⌈- -⌉[ ]
Q_1	[ ]⌈-⌉ - - - - Ø - [ ]
S_1	[ ] - - - - - - - - - -
W_1	- - kur kur - [ ]
Y_1	- - - - - ɫ]
U_2	- - - - ⌈- - Ø -⌉ - - - [ ]
X_2	[ǂ
Y_2	- ɫ ǂ - Ø
N_3	- - - ɫ ǂ Ø ⌈- -⌉ - ɫ]
U_3	- - - - - - - - - - - - -

50. elam^ki su-bir$_4$^ki anše bara$_2$ lá- gim níg mu-na-ab- lá-lá
A - - - búr e^ki - - - - - - š[i i]b - -
B [ǂ - - - ø - - - - - - - - [ ]
G [ ]⌈e -⌉ - - - /[ǂ - - -
Q - - - - - - -!? - [ ]
Q$_1$ - - - - - - - - a - ǂ]
S$_1$ [ ] - a - - - - - - ni i[b?]
W$_1$ - - - - - [ ]
Y$_1$ - - ⌈- - -⌉[ ]
U$_2$ - - - - - a - - - - - [ ]
X$_2$ [ǂ - -
Y$_2$ - - ǂ ǂ - x ø ø ø
N$_3$ - - - [ ]⌈- - -⌉ - ǂ]
U$_3$ - - - búr e^ki - - - - - - ši ib - -

51. ensi$_2$ ensi$_2$ sanga- e-ne
A - - - ø -
B [ǂ GIR.NITA$_2$ǂ]
G [- - - -
Q - ǂ]
Q$_1$ - - - ⌈-⌉ǂ]
S$_1$ [ǂ - - - ǂ]
W$_1$ - ǂ]
Y$_1$ - ǂ]
U$_2$ - - - -⌈-⌉
X$_2$ [ ]-
Y$_2$ - ǂ ǂ -
N$_3$ - ⌈-⌉ - -[ ]
U$_3$ - - - ø -

52.	sa_{12}-	du_5	gú-		eden-	na-	ke_4-	ne
A	-	-	-		-	-	-	-
B	-	-	-		-	-	-	[ ]
G	[		]		-	-	-	-
Q	-	-	-		-	-	[	]
S_1	[	]	-	⌜un⌝	-	-	-	⌜-⌝
W_1	-	-	- [					]
Y_1	-	-	-[					]
U_2	-	-	-		-	-	-	⌜-⌝
X_2	[						]	-
Y_2	-	- [					-]	-
N_3	-	-	⌜-⌝		-	-	-	[ ]
U_3	-	⌜-⌝	-		-	-	-	-

53.	nibda	itu-	da	zag-	mu-	bi		si	àm-		sá-	e-	ne
A	-	-	dè	-	-	-		-	-	ma	-	-	-
B	-	-	-	-	-	-	im	-	-		⌜-	x⌝	[ ]
G	[	]	⌜-⌝	-	⌜-⌝	-		-	-		-	-	-
Q	-	-	- [										]
O_1	[-												]
S_1	[				-]	⌜-		-	x	(x)	-	sá⌝	e
W_1	-	-	- [										]
Y_1	-	-	⌜-⌝[										]
U_2	-	-	-	-	-	-		-	-		-	-	-
X_2	[								x]		-	sá	-
Y_2	[-												-]
N_3	⌜-⌝	[			-]	-		[-					]
U_3	⌜-⌝	[	d]è	⌜-⌝	-	-		-	-	ma	-	-	-

54.	abul a-ga-dè^{ki}-ka a-gim x mi-ni-ib-gál	
A	⌈-⌉ - - - - - - - DÙL - - ŧ]	
B	⌈-⌉ - - - - - - - ki šè* - - - ⌈-⌉	*or šu
G	[ŧ - ke$_4$ - - x* - - in -	*for x, see the comm.
Q	- - - - ŧ]	
O$_1$	- [ ]	
S$_1$	omits	
W$_1$	- - - ŧ]	
Y$_1$	omits	
J$_2$	[ ]⌈- - x . . .⌉[ ]	
U$_2$	- - - - - - - - - sag - - in gar$^{?}$	
X$_2$	[ǂ -	
Y$_2$	- [ŧ	
N$_3$	ŧ ǂ - ŧ]	
U$_3$	[ŧ DÙL - - - gar	

55.	nidba-	bé	kù	^{d}	inanna-	ke$_4$	šu-	te-	gá	nu-	zu
A	-	-	-	-	-	-	-	-	-	-	-
B	-	-	-	-	-	-	-	-	- e	-	[ ]
G	[		ƚ	-	-	-	- nu	-	-	- um	-
Q	-	-	⸢-⸣[								]
O_1	ƚ										]
S_1	omits										
W_1	-	ƚ									]
Y_1	omits										
J_2	[		]	-	-	-	-	-	ƚ		]
U_2	-	-	-	-	-	-	-	-	-	-	-!
Y_2	-	-	-	-	[				]	-	-
N_3	[					ƚ	-	ƚ			]
O_3	[					]⸢-	-	-	-	-⸣	ƚ]
U_3	[						ƚ	-	-	-	-

56. dumu-gi$_7$-gim é ki-gar di- da la-la-bi nu-um-gi$_4$

A	- - - - - - - dam a - - - - gi
B	[ ] - - - - - dù ù dè - - - - un[ ]
G	[ ] - ù⌈-?⌉ a - - [ ]
Q	- - - -[ ]
O_1	- - - [ ]
S_1	[ǂ
W_1	- - ⌈-⌉[ ]
Y_1	[ǂ - -⌈- -⌉[ǂ [ ]
J_2	[ ] - dù ù dè - - [ ]
T_2	[ǂ ǂ /] a ǂ]
U_2	- - - - - - - dam a - - - ∅ -
Y_2	- - - - - ǂ ǂ ∅ - ∅ -
N_3	. . .
O_3	[ǂ - - - - - - - ǂ]
U_3	[ǂ - - gi

57.	inim	é	kur	ra	me	gim	ba	an	gar
A	-	-	-	-	-	-	-	-	-
B	-	-	-	-	-	-	-	-	⌜-⌝
G	. . .								
Q	-	-	-	- [					]
O_1	-	-	- [						
S_1	[					]	⌜-⌝	[ ]	⌜-⌝
Y_1	[ɫ	-	-	-	⌜-	-⌝[			]
J_2	[				ɫ	-	-	- [	]
T_2	[ɫ	-	-	-	- [				]
U_2	-	-	-	-	-	-	-	-	-
V_2	-	-	-	-	-	-	-	-	-
Y_2	-	-	-	-	a [				ɫ
O_3	[			]	-	-	-	-	-
U_3	[								ɫ

58. a-ga-dè^{ki} tuk$_4$-e mu-un-na-lá-lá

```
A      - - - -  -  - - - - - -
B     ⌈-⌉- - -  -  - - - - - -
Q      - - - +                ]
O1     - - +
S1    [                x̶ na ra ⌈x -⌉
Y1    [ ]⌈- - -⌉ x̶            ]
J2    [             ] - - ∅ - - -*
T2     - - - -  -  -[          ]
U2     - - - -  -  - - ∅ - - - e
V2     - - - - ⌈-⌉ - - - - - -
Y2     - - -⌈-⌉[              +
O3    [             ] - - ∅ - - -
U3    [                     ] -
```

*break at end possibly had one more sign

59. ul-maš^{ki}-a ní im-ma-ni-in-te

A - - - - - um - da an⌈-⌉

B - - - e - - - da an -

Q ⌈- -⌉[ ]⌈-⌉[ ]

O_1 - - ǂ]

S_1 [ ] - - - -

J_2 [ ] - - - - ǂ]

T_2 - - - - - - - [ ]

U_2 - - - - - - - - - -

V_2 - - - - - um - da an -

Y_2 ⌈-⌉[ ]

O_3 [ǂ - - - - -

U_3 [a]n -

60. uru^{ki}-ta dúr-ra-ni ba-ra- gub

A [ǂ - - - - - - ⌈x⌉

B ⌈-⌉- - - a - - - è

O_1 - ∅ - [ ]

S_1 [ ] - an -

J_2 [ ] - šè - - [ ]

T_2 - ∅ - - - - - - [ ]

U_2 - ∅ - - - - - - -

V_2 - - - - - - - - -

Y_2 - - ǂ ǂ

O_3 [ ] - šè - - -

61. ki-sikil ama_5-na šub-bu-gim

	ki	sikil	ama_5	na	šub	bu	gim
B	⌈-	-⌉	-	-	-	-	-
O_1	-	- [					]
S_1	[			]	-	-	-
J_2	[			]	-	-	ƚ]
T_2	-	-	-	ni	-	-	ƚ]
U_2	-	-	-	-	-	-	-
V_2	-	-	-	-	-	-	-
Y_2	-	-	-	ƚ			] -
O_3	[		ƚ?	∅?	-	-	-

62. kù ^{d}inanna-ke_4 èš a-ga-dè^{ki} mu-un-šub

	kù	d	inanna	ke_4	èš	a	ga	dè	ki	mu	un	šub
B	⌈-⌉	-	-	-	-	-	-	-	-	-	-	-
O_1	-	-	ƚ									]
J_2	[						ƚ	-	-	ƚ		]
T_2	[ƚ	-	-	∅	-	-	-	-	-	-	ƚ	]
U_2	-	-	-	-	-	-	-	-	-	-	-	-
V_2	-	-	-	-	-	-	-	-	-	-	-	⌈-⌉
Y_2	-	-	-	∅	-	[			ƚ	-	∅	-
O_3	[			x*	-	-	-	-	-	-	-	⌈-⌉

*x can be [inann]a or $[ke]_4$

63. ur-sag ^{giš}tukul-a sag-gá-gá-gim

B [-] - - - e - - - -

O_1 [-]

J_2 [ ]- - [ ]

T_2 [-] - - la - - - -

U_2 - - - - e - - - -

V_2 - - - ⌈-⌉ e ⌈-⌉ - - -

Y_2 - - - - ⌈-⌉[-] -

O_3 [-] - - - - - - -

64. uru^{ki}-ta mè šen-šen im-ma-ra è

B - - šè - - - na - - - an[ ]

E [-] - [-]

O_1 [-]

T_2 [-] - - - - - an ri

U_2 - ∅ - - - - - - da an ri!

V_2 - - - - - - ⌈- -⌉ - ri

Y_2 - - - - - [-] - -

O_3 [ ]⌈-⌉ - - - - -

65. lú kúr-ra-ra gaba ba-ni-in-ri

B ⸢- -⸣ - - - - - - ŧ]

E [ǂ - i [ ]

T_2 [ǂ - ⸢- - -⸣

U_2 - - - - - - - - -

V_2 - - - - - ⸢- - -⸣ -

Y_2 - - - - - - ŧ ǂ

O_3 [ǂ - - ∅ -

66. u_4 nu-iá-àm u_4 nu-u-àm

B ⸢-⸣- - - - - ⸢-⸣ŧ]

E [ǂ - - - []

U_2 - - - - - - - -

V_2 - - - ⸢-⸣[ǂ - -

Y_2 - - - ∅ - - -⸢-⸣

O_3 [ǂ - - ŧ]

67. sa nam-en-na aga nam-lugal-la

B ⸢-⸣ - - - ⸢- - -⸣ -

C [ ] -

E [ǂ - - - [ ]

U_2 - - - - - - - -

V_2 - - [ ] ⸢-⸣ -

Y_2 - - - ∅ - - - ⸢-⸣

O_3 [ǂ - - -

68. ma-an-si-um ^{giš}gu-za nam-lugal-la sum-ma

B - - - - - - - - - - e - -

C [ƚ - -

E [ƚ - - - - ⸢-⸣ ƒ]

U_2 - - - - - - - - - - - - mu

V_2 - - -! - - ƒ ƚ e - mu

Y_2 - - - úm - - - - - ƒ ƚ Ø

O_3 [ ]⸢- - - . . .⸣

69. ^{d}ninurta-ke_4 é-šu-me-$ša_4$-na ba-ni-in-ku_4

B - - - - - - - - - - - - -

C [ƚ - - - Ø - - - -

E [ƚ - ⸢-⸣- - - - [ ]

U_2 - - - - - - - - - - - - -

V_2 - - - ⸢- . . . ⸣

Y_2 - - - - - - - Ø ƒ ƚ

70. uru^{ki} inim-inim-ma-bi ^{d}utu ba-an-túm

B [ƚ - - - - - - - - - - -

C [ ] - - - - - - -

E [ ] - - - - - - ƒ]

U_2 - Ø - - - - - - - - - -

V_2 - - - ƒ]⸢- - - -⸣

Y_2 - - - - - - ⸢- -⸣ - ƒ ƚ

71. ĝeštu$_2$-bi ^{d}en-ki-ke$_4$ ba-an-túm

B	[ǂ - - - - - - - dé
C	[ ] - - - [ǂ - - -
E	[ǂ - - - - - - [ ]
U$_2$	[ǂ - - - - - - - -
V$_2$	- - [ǂ - [ǂ ⌈- - -?⌉*
Y$_2$	- - - - - - - - - ǂ]
S$_3$	[ǂ - Ø ǂ]

*V$_2$ inserts 76 after 71

72. me-lám an-né im-ús-sa-a-bi

B	[ ] - - na - - - - ba/ >
C	[ ] - - - - -
E	[m]a ni - - ǂ]
O$_1$	- ǂ]
U$_2$	[ ] - ma ni - - - Ø -
V$_2$	- - ma ni[ ] - - -⌈ba?⌉
Y$_2$	- - a ni - - - - ba
H$_3$	- [ǂ - - - [ ]
S$_3$	[ ] - ⌈-⌉ -/[ ] - Ø Ø - >

73. an-né an šà-ga ba-e -e_{11}

B < - na - - - - - an è

C [† - - an è

E [† - - - ⌈-⌉[ ]

O_1 - †]

U_2 [† - - - - an túm

V_2 [n]a⌈-⌉ † † ⌈-⌉ è

Y_2 - e - - - - - - -

H_3 - - - - - - - [ ]

S_3 < ⌈- -⌉/[ ] - - - ∅ -

74. ^{giš}targul -kù im-dù-dù-a-bi

C [† - - - - - -

E [† - [ ]

O_1 - †]

U_2 [†* - i - - - - †] *x can be [targ]ul or [tar-]GAG

V_2 [† - - [ ]

Y_2 ∅ ⌈-⌉ ta - - - - ba

H_3 - tár GAG⌈-⌉ - †]

B_4 †]

S_3 [ ]tár GAG⌈-⌉ - /da⌈-⌉ - -

75. ^{d}en-ki-ke$_4$ abzu-a mi-ni-in-bu

C [ɫ - - - - - - -

O_1 ⌈- - - -⌉ [ ]

U_2 [ɫ - - - - - - ⌈]

Y_2 - - -$^{!}$ - - - - - - ɫ]

H_3 - - - - - - - [ ]

B_4 - - - - [ ] ⌈-⌉[ ]

S_3 [ɫ/[ ]

76. ^{giš}tukul-bi ^{d}inanna-ke$_4$ ba-an-túm

C [ɫ - - - - - - -

O_1 ⌈- - - ⌉ ɫ]

Y_2 - - - - ⌈-⌉ - - ɫ]

U_2 [ɫ [ɫ - [ ]

V_2 *- - - [ɫ - - ⌈- -⌉

H_3 - ⌈-⌉ - - - ɫ]

B_4 - - - - - - [ ]

*V_2 inserts this line between 71 and 72

77. èš a-ga-dè^{ki} zi-bi suhur^{ku_6} tur -ra-gim engur-ra ba-an-til

C [ɫ - - - - - - - - - - - / - - - - -

G - - - - - ɫ]

I - ɫ]

O_1 - - - - ɫ]

U_2 . . .

Y_2 ⌈-⌉- - -[ɫ ∅ - ∅ ⌈-⌉ ɫ]

H_3 - -⌈- - -⌉ - [/] - ⌈-⌉ - ⌈-⌉[ ]

B_4 - - - - - - - - ∅ ɫ$^{?}$]

78. uru[ki] téš-bi igi-bi àm-da-gál

C [ǂ - - -* - ⸢-⸣ - - - *gloss; téš-ba

G - - - - ŧ]

I ŧ]

O_1 - ∅ - - ŧ]

Y_2 ŧ ǂ [ ]

H_3 - - - - - - - ⸢- -⸣

B_4 - ∅ - - - ŧ]

79. am-si mah-gim gú ki-šè mi-ni-ib-gar

C - - - - * - -⸢-⸣ - - - - *gloss before gú: ŠU.x

G - - - - [ ]

I ŧ]

H_1 - - [ ]

O_1 -! -! - ŧ]

Y_2 - ⸢-⸣ - ŧ]

H_3 [ǂ ⸢-⸣ - -⸢- - -⸣ - [x]

B_4 - - - - - - - - [ ]

80. gu_4 mah-gim si àm-da-íl-íl

C [ǂ - - ⸢- -⸣ - - -

G - - - - ŧ]

H_1 - - [ ]

O_1 - - - ⸢-⸣[ ]

Y_2 [ǂ - - - ⸢an⸣NI[ ]

H_3 [ ] - ⸢- -⸣[ ]

B_4 - - - - an ŧ]

81.	ušum-gal	idim	-a	-gim	sag	àm	-ma	-zé	-re	
C	-	-	-	-	-	-	-	-	-	
G	-	-	⌜-⌝	-	ƚ				]	
P	ƚ								]	
H_1	-	ƚ							]	
O_1	-	-	-	-	-	b[a[?]			]	
Y_2	[ǂ	x*	∅	-	-	b[a[?]			]	*x≠BAD
H_3	[				]	⌜-⌝				
B_4	-	-	-	-	-	im	[		]	

82.	mè	-gim	nam	-dugud	- ba	àm	-da	-ab	-lah$_5$	-lah$_5$	-e	
C	-!	*-	-	-	bi	-	-	-	-	-	-	*AK
G	⌜-⌝	-	-	-	[						]	
P	-	ƚ									]	
H_1	-	-	ƚ								]	
O_1	-	-	-	-	-	an	ƚ				]	
Y_2	-	-	-	-	-	ƚ*					]	*x=beginning of horizontal
J_3	-	bi	-	-	ƚ					ǂ	-	
B_4	-	ba	-	-	-	im	ƚ				]	

83. nam-lugal a-ga-dè[ki] ki-tuš gi-na du_{10} nu-tuš-ù-dè

C - - - - - - ka - - - - - - - - dam

G [ɨ - - - - -[ ]

P - - - ɨ]

H_1 - ɨ]

O_1 x DU - - - - - - [ ]

S_1 ɨ ɨ[ ]⌈-⌉[ ]

Y_2 - - - - - - - [ ]

J_3 - - - - - - - - [ ] - - -

B_4 - - - - - - ka - - - [ ]

84. egir-bi níg-na-ma nu-$ša_6$-ge-dè

C - - - - - - - - dam

G - - - - [ ]

P - - - ɨ]

H_1 - ɨ]

O_1 - - - - [ ]

S_1 - - - - - [ ]

Y_2 - - - - - - sì [ ]

B_4 - - - - - [ ]

S_3 ⌈- se -⌉ - - /- - ∅ -

85. é tuk$_4$-e erim$_3$ ság di-dè

C - - - ⌈- ⌉ sì sì ge ⌈dam⌉

G - - - - ŧ]

P - - - - ŧ]

H$_1$ - - [ ]

O$_1$ - ŧ]

R$_1$ - - - - - [ ]

S$_1$ - - - - - [ ]

Y$_2$ - - - - maš gi ne⌈dè[?]⌉

J$_3$ - - - - ma -[!]*- [ ] *see the comm.

B$_4$ - - - ŧ]

E$_4$ - ⌈-⌉ [ ]

S$_3$ - ⌈-⌉ - ⌈-⌉ sàg -/ -

86. ^{d}na-ra-am-^{d}sin máš-gi$_6$-ka igi ba-ni-in-du$_8$-a

C	[⸗⸢ - -⸣ - -	-	-	-	-	-	-	⸢-⸣	-
G	∅ - - - - - [								]
P	∅ - - - - -	ƒ							]
C_1	⸢-⸣ƒ]⸢- - - -	-⸣	ƒ						]
H_1	∅⸢-⸣ ƒ								]
R_1	- - - - - -	-	-	-	⸢-	-	-⸣	∅$^?$	[⸗ [ ]
S_1	- - - - - -	-	-	ƒ		⸗	-	∅	- -
Y_2	∅ - - - - -	-	ƒ						]
J_3	- - - - - -	-	- [						]
B_4	∅ - - - - -	-	-	ƒ					]
E_4	- - - - [								]
S_3	∅ - - - - - e/	-	-	-	-	-/[			]

87. šà-ga-ni-šè mu-un-zu eme-na nu-um-gá-gá lú-da nu-mu-un-da-ab-bé

C	[ǂ - - ⌈- -⌉ - - - /[ǂ ǂ]⌈- -⌉
G	- - - - ǂ]
P	- - - - - - - - - ǂ]
C_1	- - - - - - - - inim [/]- - - - ǂ]
H_1	[ ]
R_1	- - - - - - - - - - [ ]/- - - - - - - ⌈-⌉[ ]
S_1	⌈- - -⌉ - - - - - ǂ ǂ - - - - - - - - - - - - -
L_2	. . .
T_2	⌈- - - - - - -⌉- - ∅ - ǂ]/- - - - - - - - -
Y_2	- - - - - - KA⌈-⌉ [ ]
J_3	- - - - - - - - - ǂ]/- - - - ǂ]
B_4	[ǂ - - - - ǂ?]*
E_4	[ǂ - - ǂ]/-[ ]

*B_4 adds:

87a) ⌈é - šè⌉[ ] (=94)

87b) é dù máš[ ] (=95)

88.	nam-é-kur-ra-šè ^{túg}mu-sír-ra ba-an-mu$_4$
C	[ ] ⌈-⌉
P	- - - - - - - - - ŧ]
C_1	- - - - - - - - - ŧ]
H_1	⌈-⌉[ ]
N_1	- - - - - - - - - - - - Ø -
R_1	- - - - - - - - - - - - - [ ]
S_1	⌈- -⌉ - - - - - ŧ] - - -
L_2	⌈-⌉ - - - - - - [ ]
T_2	- - - - Ø - - - - - - - -
Y_2	- - - - - - -⌈-⌉ - - - Ø -
J_3	- - - - Ø - - - ŧ]
B_4	- - - - [ ]
E_4	[ŧ - - - ŧ]

89. ^{giš}gigir-ra-né ^{gi}kid-má-šà-ga ba-an-šú

G	- - - na -[ ]
P	- - - - - ∅ - - - [ ]
C_1	- - - na - - - šú a - [ ]
H_1	- ⸸]
N_1	- - - - - - - - - - - -]
R_1	- - - na - ∅ - - - - - [ ]
S_1	[ ]⌈na⌉- ∅ - - - - - -
L_2	- - - - - ∅ - ⸸]
T_2	- - - na - - - šú a - - -
Y_2	- - - a- - GAG ∅ bar ra ∅ - si
J_3	- - ⌈re⌉∅ - - - ⌈-⌉[ ]
B_4	- - ⌈-⌉ - [ ]
E_4	- - - n[a]

90. ^{giš}má-gur$_8$-ra- né MUNSUB ba-ra-an-si-ig

		giš	má	gur$_8$	ra	né	MUNSUB	ba	ra	an	si	ig
F		[								]-	-	-
G		-	-	⌈-	-	-⌉[						]
P		-	-	-	-	-	-	- [				]
C_1		-	-	-	-	-	-	-	-	- [		]
H_1		-[										]
N_1		-	-	-	-	-	-	-	-	-	-	-
R_1		∅	-	-	-	na	-	-	-	-	ƚ	]
S_1	si	-⌈	-⌉	-	-	na	-	ƚ	]	-	-	-
L_2		[ǂ	-	-	-	-	-	ƚ				]
T_2		∅	-	-	-	na	-	-	-	-	-	-
Y_2		ƚ	ǂ	-	-	a -	-	-	-	-	-	∅
J_3		-	-	-	-	⌈-	-⌉[					]
B_4	si	-	-	ƚ								]
E_4		-	-	-	- [							]

91. á-ŠITA$_4$- a nam-lugal-la-ka-ni im-ma-ra-an-ƀa-ba

G	- šu du$_7$ [ ]
P	- šu du$_7$ - - - - - n[a]
Y	⌈- -⌉[ ]
C_1	- - - - - - - na - ƚ]
H_1	ƚ]
N_1	- - - - - - - - - - - - - ∅
R_1	- - - - - - - na/- - - - - - -
S_1	- - - - ⌈-⌉ - ƚ ƚ - - - - - -
L_2	⌈-⌉ - - - - lá ƚ /]- - - - [ ]
T_2	- šu du$_7$ - - ⌈-⌉ ƚ]
Y_2	[ƚ - - - - - - - - - ni ∅ babbar$_2$
J_3	- šu du$_7$ - - ƚ]
B_4	- - - ƚ]
E_4	. . .

92. ^{d}na-ra-am-^{d}sin mu-imin-àm mu-un-ge-en

G	- - - -[ ]	
P	- - - - - - - - - -[-]	
Y	- - - -[-]	
C_1	- - - - - - - - - - -[-]	
N_1	- - - - - - - - a - - - -	
R_1	- - ⌈- - - -⌉ - - -/ [-] -	
S_1	-⌈-⌉ - - - - - - -[-*]- - -	*or a[ ]
L_2	[-] - - - - -[-]	
W_2	- -[-]	
Y_2	[ ] - - - ø - ø x ø	
H_3	[ ] - - -[-]	
J_3	⌈- -⌉ - - - - -[-]	
B_4	ø - - - - -*[ ]	*adds -⌈e⌉
F_4	[ ]⌈- - - - -⌉[ ]	

93. lugal mu-imin-àm šu sag-gá du_{11}-ga a-ba igi im-mi-in-du_8-a

G	⌈ - -⌉ - - - - [ ]
P	- - - - - - - - ⌈- ⌉ - - ƚ]
Y	- - - ƚ]
C_1	- - - - - - - - - - - ƚ]
N_1	- - - e - - - - -/ - - a - - - - - -
R_1	- [ƚ - -/[à]m
S_1	⌈-⌉ e ∅ - e ⌈- -⌉ - [ ] a - ∅ mu un - -
L_2	[ ]⌈- -⌉ - ƚ]
W_2	- ƚ]
Y_2	[ƚ - - ⌈- ∅ - -⌉ - - ∅ - - - ∅ ∅
H_3	[ ] - - - -*/[ ] ⌈a -⌉ ∅ mu un - àm
J_3	[ ] - - - - - - [ ]
B_4	- - - a ⌈-⌉ - [ ]
F_4	[ ] - - - - - - - - [ ]

*adds ⌈àm⌉

93a. šà-ga-ni-šè mu-un-zu eme-na nu-gá-gá lú-da nu-mu-un-da-[ab-bé]

Y	- - - - - ƚ]
C_1	- - - - - - - inim ma[/] - - - - - - [ ]
D_1	[ ] - ⌈-⌉ ƚ /] - - [ ]
N_1	- - - -⌈- ∅ -? - - -⌉ - - - - ∅ ∅ ∅ ∅ ∅ ∅
W_2	- ƚ]
B_4	- - - ∅⌈- - -⌉[ ]
F_4	[ƚ - -⌈- -⌉ - - - - ƚ]/ - - - ⌈- -⌉ - [ ]

(Repetition of 87, omitted by F G P S_1 B_3 H_3 J_3)

94. é-šè máš-àm šu-gíd-dè

	é	šè	máš	àm	šu	gíd	dè
G	-	-	-	- [			]
P	-	-	-	-	-	⌈-⌉	[ ]
Y	-	-	- [				]
C_1	-	-	-	-	-	-	[ ]
D_1	[]	-	-	-	ši	[	]
N_1	-	-	-	-	ši	ǂ]	i
R_1	[						ǂ?
S_1	⌈-	-⌉	-	-	š[i		ǂ
W_2	-[						]
X_2	. . .						
Y_2	[	]	-	∅	-	-	-
H_3	[			ǂ	⌈ši	-	-⌉
J_3	[		ǂ	-	ši	[	]
B_4	. . .						
F_4	[		ǂ	- [			]

95. é dù-a máš-a nu-mu-un-dè-gál

G — — — — àm — †]

P — — ∅ — àm — — ni i[n]

Y — — ∅ — [ ]

D_1 — — ∅ — — — — †]

N_1 ⌈—⌉— — — — — — ∅ na —

S_1 ⌈— —⌉ ∅ — — — — [ ]

W_2 ⌈—⌉[ ]

X_2 ⌈—⌉— ∅ — — — — — — —

Y_2 ⌈— —⌉ ∅ — ∅ — — ni in —

H_3 ⌈— —⌉[ ]⌈x x⌉ — — —

96. mìn-kam-ma-šè é-šè máš-àm šu-gíd-dè

G — — — — — — —[ ]

P — — — — — — — — ⌈—⌉ †]

Y — — — ⌈—⌉ †]

D_1 [ ] — — — — — — ši — [ ]

N_1 [ ] — — — — — — ši — i

S_1 ⌈— —⌉ — — — — — — [‡

X_2 [‡ — — — — — — a — — i

Y_2 omits

H_3 — — — ⌈— — —⌉ — ⌈— ši⌉ — —

97. é-dù-a máš-a nu-mu-un-dè-gál

G - - - - àm - ƚ]

P - - - - àm - - n[i]

Y ⌈- -⌉ [ ]

D_1 ⌈-⌉- ∅ - - - - - - - [ ]

M_1 [ ]⌈- àm⌉[ ]

N_1 [ ] - - - - - - ∅ na -

S_1 ⌈- -⌉ ∅ - - - - - ni [ ]

X_2 - - ∅ - - - - - - - -

Y_2 omits

H_3 - - ∅ - ⌈- - -⌉ - - -

98. ì-sì-ga-na šu-a bal-e-dè

G - - - - ⌈- -⌉[ ]

P - - - - - - ƚ]

D_1 [ƚ - - - - ƚ]

M_1 [ ] - - - - ⌈-⌉[ ]

N_1 [ ]- né - - - - -

S_1 ⌈-⌉- - né - - - [ ]

X_2 ⌈- - -⌉ né - - - - -

Y_2 - - - né⌈šà⌉∅ - - -

R_3 [ ] - - - ∅ - -/⌈gim⌉ >

99. ᵈen-líl níg-du$_{11}$-ga-ni ba-en-dè-kúr

G - - - - -- ⌈- -⌉[ ]⌈-?⌉

P - - - - - - na - [ ]

D_1 [⫞ - [/ ⫞ - [ ]

M_1 [⫞ - - - - - ⫞*]   *x does not look like e[n]; possibly ⌈e⌉

N_1 [ ]- - - - - - - - - -

S_1 ⌈- - -⌉ - - - - - ⌈e⌉[ ]

X_2 - - - - - - - - - - gur

Y_2 - - - - - - - - è - ∅

R_3 omits

100. gú-gar-ra-né ság ba-an-da-ab-du$_{11}$

G - - - - ⫞ ⫞ - ⫞ ⫞ -

P - - - - ⫞]

D_1 . . .

M_1 [⫞ - - - - - - ⫞]

N_1 - - - - - - - - - -

S_1 ⌈- - -⌉ - - - [ ]

T_1 [ ] ⌈- - -⌉ ⫞]

H_2 [ ] - - - ⫞]

X_2 ⌈- - -⌉ - - - - - - -

Y_2 KA - ⫞] . . . - ∅ ∅ ∅ dù

R_3 < - - - - -/ mu ∅ na - -

101. erén-na-né zi-ga ba-ni-in-gar

	erén	na	né	zi	ga	ba	ni	in	gar
G	-	-	-	[				ǂ	-
P	-	-	-	-	gú	ǂ			]
M_1	-	-	-	-	gú	-	-	ǂ	]
N_1	[ ]	-	-	-	-	-	-	-	-
S_1	⸢-	a	-⸣	-	-	-	-	[	]
T_1	[	]	⸢-	-⸣	ǂ̶				]
H_2	[			ǂ	gú	-	-	- [	]
K_2	⸢-	a⸣[							]
X_2	-	a	-	-	gú	-	-	-	ǂ]
Y_2	[ǂ	a	-	[				ǂ	-
R_3	[ǂ	-	na	-	KA	-	-	∅	-

102. á tuk kisal-mah-šè ku$_4$-ku$_4$-gim

	á	tuk	kisal	mah	šè	ku$_4$	ku$_4$	gim
G	-	-	-	ǂ				]
P	-	-	-	-	ǂ			]
M_1	-	-	-	-	-	-	ǂ	]
N_1	-	-	-	-	-	-	-	-
S_1	-	⸢-⸣	-	-	-	-	[	]
T_1	[	]	⸢-	-	-⸣[			]
H_2	[			ǂ	-	-	-	ǂ]
K_2	-	-	⸢-⸣[					]
X_2	-	-	⸢-⸣	-	-	-	-	-
Y_2	[						ǂ	dè
R_3	-	-	-	-	a	- /	-	-

103. é-kur-šè šu-kéš ba-ši-in-ak

G	- - ⌈-⌉[ ]
P	- - - - - [ ]
M_1	- - - - - - - - [ ]
N_1	- - - - - - - - -
R_1	[ ]⌈- -⌉ - - [ ]
S_1	- ⸢ ⸣ - - - [ ]
T_1	omits
H_2	[⸣ - - - -
K_2	⌈- - -⌉[ ]
X_2	⌈- - -⌉ - - - - - -
Y_2	- - - - - [⸣
R_2	- - - - ⌈- - -⌉ ∅ -

104.	du$_{10}$	tuk	lirum		-šè	gam-	e-	gim	
G	- [							]	
P	-	-	-		ŧ			]	
V	[	ŧ	-		-	- [		]	
M_1	-	-	-		⸢-⸣	-!	*-?	ŧ?]	*NU for gam
N_1	-	-	ŧ]		⸢-⸣	[ ]	⸢-⸣	ŧ]	
R_1	[		ŧ		-	-	-	ŧ]	
S_1	- [		ŧ		-	- [		]	
T_1	omits								
H_2	[		ŧ		-	⸢-⸣	-	ŧ]	
X_2	[			]	-	-	-	ŧ]	
Y_2	-	-	lú kal		-	-	ŧ?	]	
R_2	-	-	lirum$_3$		-	-	-	-	

105.	gi-gun$_4$-na-aš eše gín ba-ši-in-ak
P	- - - ∅ - ŧ]
V	⌈-⌉ - - ∅ - - - - ŧ]
M_1	- - - ∅ - - - - - [ ]
N_1	- - - - - - - - - -
R_1	omits
S_1	ŧ] - bé - ⌈-⌉ - [ ]
T_1	[ƚ ∅ - - - [ƚ ŧ]
H_2	[ ] - - - - - - ŧ]
K_2	⌈- -⌉ [ ]
X_2	[ ]⌈- -⌉ ŧ]
Y_2	- - - ∅ - - - ŧ]
R_3	- - ∅ šè - - - - ∅ / -

106.	nita$_2$	lú-	la-	ga	uru	^{ki}	lah$_5$-	gim	
P	⌈-⌉	-	-	ŧ				]	
V	-	-	-	-	-	-	ŧ	]	
M_1	[ŧ	-	-	-	-	∅	-	[ ]	
N_1	-	-	-	-	-	∅	⌈-	-⌉	
O_1	[		]	-	-	∅	ŧ	]	
R_1	-	-	-	-	-	∅	-	-	
S_1	⌈-	-	-⌉	-	-	-	ŧ	]	
T_1	[		ŧ	⌈-	-	⌉∅	ŧ	]	
H_2	[		]	-	-	-	-	ŧ]	
K_2	-	-	ŧ					]	
Y_2	-	-	lu$_5$	-	-	-	-	-	
R_3	[ŧ	-	KÍD	∅	-	∅	ri	ri/	>

107. é-šè ^{giš}kun$_5$ gal-gal ba-ši-in-ri-ri

P -- - ŧ]

V -- - kun$_4$ - - - ŧ]

M$_1$ -- - kun$_4$ - - - - ŧ]

N$_1$ -- -- - - - ŧ] -

O$_1$ [ ]⸢ -- -⸣ ŧ] - - ⸢x x⸣* *x does not look like ri; possibly dé

R$_1$ -- -- - - - - - - -

S$_1$ ⸢-- -- - -⸣ - - [ ]

T$_1$ [ ] ⸢- -⸣ - ⸢-⸣[ ]⸢dé dé⸣

H$_2$ [ɟ - - - - [ ]

K$_2$ -- - ŧ]

Y$_2$ -- ∅ - - - - - - dé dé

R$_3$ <[ ] - - - - -/ ∅ ⸢lah$_4$⸣

108. é-kur ^{giš}má mah-gim gul-gul-lu-dè

D [ɟ - - ŧ ɟ

P [ ] - - ŧ]

V - - - - - - - [ ]

M$_1$ ⸢-⸣ - - - - - - [ ]

N$_1$ - - - - ⸢- - - -⸣ - -

O$_1$ [ ] - ŧ ɟ [ɟ - - -

R$_1$ - - - - - - - - - -

S$_1$ ⸢- - - - - -⸣ ŧ]

T$_1$ [ ] ⸢- - - -⸣ -

H$_2$ [ɟ - - [ ]

K$_2$ - - ∅ - - ŧ]

Y$_2$ - - ∅ ∅ - - - - ∅ -

109.	kur	kù	ba	al	gim	sahar	du_8	ù	dè
D	[	]	-	-	-	-	-	⌈-⌉	ɫ]
V	-	-	-	-	-	-	dù	ɫ	]
M_1	[	]	-	-	-	-	-	ɫ	]
O_1	[	ɟ	⌈-⌉	[	ɟ	-	-	-	-
R_1	-	-	-	-	-	-	-	-	-
S_1	⌈-	-	-	-⌉	-	-	dù	[	]
T_1	[					ɟ	⌈dù	-⌉	-
H_2	[						ɟ	-[	]
K_2	⌈-⌉	-	-	-	ɫ				]
Y_2	-	-	-	-	-	-	tu	-	-

110.	hur	sag	na4	za	gìn	na	gim	ku_5	re	dè
D	[	ɟ	-	-	-	-	-	-	-	⌈-⌉
I	-	-	ɫ							]
V	[ɟ	-	-	-	-	-	-	-	ɫ	]
M_1	[		ɟ	-	-	-	-	-	ɫ	]
O_1	[					ɟ	-	-	-	-
R_1	-	-	-	-	-	-	-	-	-	-
S_1	⌈-	-	-⌉	-	-	-	-	ɫ		]
T_1	[					]	⌈-	-	-	-⌉
H_2	[							]	⌈-⌉[	]
K_2	[				ɟ	ɫ				]
M_2	-	-	-	-	-	-	-	-	-	gim
Y_2	-	-	-	-	-	∅	gí	-	-	-
B_4	[	]	⌈-?⌉	[						]

111. uru^{ki} ^{d}iškur-re ba-an-dé-a-gim gú ki-šè gá-gá-dè

D [ ] - - - - - - - - / [ǂ - - - - - -

I - ∅ -[ ]e - - DU - - / - - - - - - -

V [ǂ - - - - - - - - - ǂ]

M_1 [ ]⌈ - - -⌉ - - - ǂ]

O_1 [ǂ? - ⌈- -⌉ - - - - - - - - -

R_1 - ∅ - - ⌈e?⌉- - DU - - / - - - ba an da ab lá

S_1 [ ]⌈x⌉ - - DU - ǂ -

T_1 [ ]⌈- - - - ba an⌉da ab lá

M_2 - ∅ - - - - - - - - - - - - - - - dam

Y_2 - - - - ∅ - - ∅ ∅ - KA - ∅ - - -

B_4 [ ] - - ra⌈- -⌉[ ]

112. é-e kur ^{giš}eren ku_5 nu-me-a

D [ǂ - - - - - - -

I ǂ ǂ - - - - - - -

T [ǂ - - - - - ǂ]⌈-⌉

V [ǂ - - - - - - [ ]

M_1 [ ] - - - - [ ]

O_1 [ ] - - - - - - -

R_1 - - - - - - - - - -

S_1 ⌈- -⌉ - - - - [ ]

M_2 - - - - - - - - - -

Y_2 - - - ∅ ku_5 eren - - -

B_4 [ ]- - - - ⌈-⌉[ ]

R_3 [ǂ - - ∅ - na - -/ -

113. ^{urudu}ha-zi-in gal-gal ba-ši-in-dé-dé

D [+ - - - - - - - x]

I [ ]- - - - - - - - DU DU

T [+ - - - - - +]⌈-?⌉

V [ ] - - - - - - - [ ]

O_1 [ ]⌈- - - -⌉ - - - - -

R_1 - - - - - - - - - - -

S_1 - ⌈-⌉ - - - - [ ]

M_2 - - - - - - - - - - -

Y_2 - - - - - - - - [ ]

B_4 ⌈-⌉ - - - - - +]

R_3 *- [+ - - - -/ ì ma ta - Ø *urudu follows ha-zi-in

114. ^{urudu}aga-silig-ga á-min-na- bi-da u_4-sar ba-an-ak

D [⫲ - ∅ - - - - ∅ - - -⌈-⌉ -

I - - - - - - a na - ta/- - - - -

T [⫲ - - ∅ - - a -[ ] - - [⫲

V [⫲ - -! - - a - ta [ ]

O_1 [[⌈- ∅ -⌉ - - - - [ù -] - - -

R_1 - - - ∅ ⌈- -⌉ a -[?]/⌈- -⌉ - - -

S_1 ∅ - - ∅ - - - - t[a]

M_2 - aga_3 - - - - a - - - - - - -

Y_2 - - ∅ ∅ - - ∅ da⌈bil⌉⫲]

B_4 ∅ - - ∅ - - a - t[a]

R_3 has 127f. here instead of 114

S_3 [⫲ -/mìn - - ∅ ù sa ar - ∅ -* *followed by 127f.

115. úr-bi-a ^{urudu}gí-dim ba-an-gar

D [ ] - - - - - - ⌈- -⌉

I - - - - - - - - - -

T [ǂ - - - - - ⌈- - -⌉

V [ǂ - - - - - [ ]

O_1 [ǂ - - - - - - - -

R_1 - - - Ø ⌈-$^?$⌉ - - - ƚ]

S_1 - - - Ø gi ƚ]

T_1 on edge of tablet, [a]n-gar possibly this line or 117

M_2 - - - - - - - - - -

Y_2 - - Ø Ø ⌈gi⌉[ ]

B_4 - - - - - - [ ]

R_3 - - - Ø - - - Ø -

116. suhuš kalam-ma-ka ki ba-e-lá

D [ǂ - - - - - - - -

I - - - - - - - - -

P ⌈- - -⌉[ ]

T - - - - ⌈-⌉ - - -

V [ ]. . . ⌈- -⌉[ ]

O_1 [ǂ - - - - - - -

S_1 - - - - ƚ]

M_2 - - - ke_4- - - -

Y_2 [ ]

B_4 - - - ke_4[ ]

117. pa-bi-a ^{urudu}ha-zi-in ba-an-gar

D [ǂ - - - - - - - - -

I - - - ∅ - - - [ ]⌈-⌉[ ]

P ⌈- -⌉ - - ⌈-⌉[ ]

T ⌈-⌉- ⌈-⌉ - - - - - - -

V [ǂ - - - - -

O_1 [ ] - - - - - - - -

S_1 - - - - - [ ]

M_2 - - - - - - - - - -

Y_2 [ ]

B_4 - - - - - - ƚ]

118. é-e guruš ug$_5$-ga-gim gú ki-šè ba-an-da-ab-lá

D [ǂ - - - - - - - - - ∅ - - -

I ⌈- -⌉ ƚ]

P ⌈-⌉- - - - ⌈- - -⌉ ƚ]

T [ǂ - - - - - - - - ∅ ∅ gá gá dè* *verb from 111

V [⌈- -⌉ ∅ ∅ gá gá⌈dè⌉*

O_1 [ǂ - ⌈- -⌉ - - - - ∅ - - -

S_1 - - - - ƚ]

M_2 - - - - - - - - - ƚ]

Y_2 [ ]

B_4 - - - - - - [ ]

119. gú kur-kur-ra ki-šè ba-an-da-ab-lá

D [+ - - - ke_4 - - - ∅ - - -

P ⌈-⌉ - - - - - - - +]

T - - - - ke_4 - - - - - - - - la

V [x* ⌈-⌉ - - - - - - *x=ke_4 or ra according to Wilcke Kollationen

O_1 [+ ⌈-⌉ke_4 - - - ∅ - - -

S_1 - - - - ⌈-⌉[ ]

T_1 [+ ⌈- - -⌉

M_2 - - - - - ⌈-⌉- - +]

Y_2 [ ] - +]

J_3 ⌈- - - - -⌉ +]

B_4 omits

120. {giš}alal -bi im-ma-ra-an-zil-zil

C ∅⌈ - - -⌉[ ]

D ∅[+ - - - - - - - -

P - - - - - - - +]

T [+ - - - - - - - -

V [+ - - - - - -

O_1 [ ]⌈- -⌉ - - -

S_1 ∅ - - [ ]

T_1 [ ] - -

M_2 ∅ - - - - - - +]

Y_2 [+ - ⌈-⌉ - +]

J_3 ∅ - - - [ ]

B_4 - -* - [ ] *adds -alal

121\. im šèg šèg an-na ba-e-e_{11}

	im	šèg	šèg	an	-na	ba	-e	$-e_{11}$
C	-	-	- [					]
D	[ ]	-	im šèg	-	-	-	-	x*
P	-	-	-	-	-	-	-	⌈x⌉
T	[ŧ	-	-	-	e	-	-	-
V	[		ŧ	-	-	-	-	-
O_1	[							ŧ
S_1	-	- [						]
T_1	[						]-	⌈-⌉
M_2	-	-	-	-	-	-	-	[ ]
Y_2	[	ŧ	-	-	-	ŧ		]
J_3	-	-	-	-	-	ŧ		]
B_4	-	-	-	-	ŧ			]

*x here compatible with P and O_1; ≠ šèg, sur or ús; possibly $gi_{(4)}$

122\. giš-ká-na-bi ba-ra-an-si-ig téš kalam-ma ba-kúr

	giš	-ká	-na	-bi	ba	-ra	-an	-si	-ig	téš	kalam	-ma	ba	-kúr
C	-	-	-	ke_4	-	[								]
D	[	ŧ	-	ke_4	-	-	-	-	-	-	-	-	-	BAD
P	-	-	-	-	-	-	-	-	⌈-	-	-⌉[			]
T	[ŧ	-	-	-	-	-	-	-	-	-	⌈-⌉	-	-	ŧ]
V	[			ŧ	-	-	-	-	-	-	-	-	-	-
S_1	-	ŧ												]
T_1	. . .													
M_2	-	-	∅	-	-	-	-	-	-	-	ŧ			]
Y_2	[		]	ke_4	-	-	-	-	[					]
J_3	-	-	-	ke_4	-	-	-	⌈-⌉	ŧ					]
B_4	-	-	-	-	-	-	ŧ							]

123. ká še nu-ku$_5$-da še i-ni-in-ku$_5$

C — — — — bi[ ]

D [⸸ — — — DU — — — ⸢— —⸣

J ⸢— —⸣[ ]

P — — — — — — —[ ]

T [⸸ — — — — — — — — —

V ⸢— — —⸣ — — — — — —

S_1 —[ ]

M_2 — — — — — — — — [ ]

Y_2 [⸸ — — — — — [ ]

J_3 — — — — — — — — ⸸]

B_4 — — — — — [ ]

124. šu kalam-ma-ta še ba-da-an-ku$_5$

C suhuš — — — [ ]

D [⸸ — — — ⸢—⸣ ⸸]

J — ⸸ ⸸ —

P — — — — — — ⸸]

T ⸢—⸣ — — — — — — — ⸢—⸣

V — — — — — — — — —

S_1 ⸸]

M_2 — — — — — — — [ ]

T_2 [⸸

Y_2 [⸸ — *— — ⸸] *preceded by nu

B_4 ⸢x — — —⸣[ ]

S_3 [/] — — ∅ —

```
125.    ká silim-ma-bé ᵍⁱˢal-e bí-in-ra
C         -   -   -  -  ƚ          ]
J         -   -  ƚ            ] -
P         -  ⌈-⌉  -  -    - -  - ƚ      ]
T         -   -   - ⌈-    - -⌉ - -  ƚ] ƚ]
V         -   -   -  -    - - - - -  -
M2       [   ɟ   -  -    - -  -[      ]
T2       [                          ɟ
Y2       [           ɟ   ∅ -  -[      ]
B4        -  ⌈-    -?  -   - -⌉[       ]

S3       [   ɟ   -  -    ∅ -  ∅/⊟?  ∅  RU

126.    kur-kur-re silim-silim-bi ba-kúr
C         -   -  -    ƚ              ]
J         -   -  -    ƚ              ]⌈-⌉
P         -   -  -    -     -   - [     ]
T         -   -  -    -    ⌈-   -⌉ -  [ɟ
V         -   -  -    -     -   -  -   -
G1       . . .
M2        -  ⌈-⌉[ ]   -     -   - [     ]
T2       [                          ɟ
W2       ⌈-   -  -    -     -   -⌉ ƚ    ]
Y2        ƚ      ɟ    -     -!  -  ƚ    ]
B4        -   -  -    ƚ              ]
D4       . . . (?)

S3       [       ǂ    -     -   -/[ ] gul
```

127.		a-gàr mah a-eštub^{ku_6} dagal-la-gim
C		- - - ⌈-? -? -?⌉[ ]
J		- ⌈- -⌉[ ] ⌈-?⌉
P	a-šà	- - - - ⌈-⌉ ∅ - ɫ]
T		- - - - ⌈-⌉ ∅ ɫ]
V	a-šà	- - - - - ∅ - - ke_4
G_1	a-šà	- - ⌈-⌉ - ɫ]
S_1	[ ]	⌈- - -⌉[ ]
M_2		- - ⌈-⌉ - - ɫ]
T_2		[ɫ?
W_2		- - - - - ɫ]
Y_2	a-šà	- ɫ] - - - ∅ - ɫ]
B_4		- - ⌈-⌉[ ]
D_4		- - -* - ɫ]**
R_3		$ugur_2$ - - - ∅ dugud a -***
S_3		$ugur_2$ - - - ∅ - ∅ / -****

*adds gim?

**skips to 173

***127f. between 113 and 115

****127f. follow 114

128. é-kur-ra [urudu]gí-dim gal-gal-bi kùš-kùš-a bí-in-sì-sì

C - - - - - ɫ]

J *⌜- - -⌝[x̶ dé dé

P - - - - ⌜- - - -⌝ ɫ]

T - - e - - - - - - [ ]

V - - - - - - - - - - - - - - - -

G_1 - - - ∅ gi - - ɫ]

S_1 - - - ∅ ⌜gil⌝[ ]

M_2 - - - ⌜-⌝ ɫ ɫ - [ ]

W_2 - - re - - - - - e ɫ ɫ - - - - - -

Y_2 - - - ∅ gi - - - x**]

B_4 - - - ⌜-⌝ha zi in - [ ]

R_3 ∅ ∅ ∅ ∅ - - - - - ⌜-⌝ ∅ -/- ∅ - -***

S_3 - - - a EDEN[urudu] / - - - - ∅ - -/ ∅ - -****

*preceded by U on edge

**x begins U + DIŠ

***line precedes 115

****line follows 114

129. itima é u_4 nu-zu-ba un- e igi i-ni-in-bar

C - ma - - - - [ ]

J [ƭ - - [ ]

P - - - - - - - - - - [ ]

T - - - - - - - - - ∅⌈- - -⌉* *i.e., verb interpreted ì-in-bar

V [ƭ ⌈-⌉- - - - - - - -⌈- ∅ -⌉

G_1 - - - - - - ƭ]

S_1 - - - ƭ]

M_2 - ma - - - - ⌈-⌉ ƭ]

W_2 - UD - - - - - [ƭ - - - - - -

Y_2 - - - - - bé - ma - ƭ]

B_4 - ma* -⌈- -⌉ - - - - ƭ] *adds -ba

130. urudu-šen kù dingir-re-e-ne-ke_4 uri^{ki} igi i-ni-in-bar

C - - - - - [ ]

J [ƭ - ƭ] - ⌈-⌉

P - - - - - -[ ] - ƭ]

T - - - - - - - - - - - ∅⌈- - -![1]⌉*

V [ ] ⌈-⌉∅ e - - - ∅ -

G_1 - - - - - - - ⌈-⌉[ ]

S_1 ⌈-⌉ - - - ƭ]

M_2 - - - - - - - ƭ]

W_2 - - - - ⌈- -⌉- - - ∅ - - - ∅ -

Y_2 - - - - - - ƭ]

B_4 - - - - - - - - ƭ]

*i.e., ì-in-bar!

131. la-ha-ma dub-lá gal é-e su_8-ga-bi

C - - - - ŧ]

J - - - [ӿ[ӿ⌈ - - -⌉

P - - - - - - ⌈-⌉-[ ]

T - - - - - - - - - - -

V ŧ ӿ ⌈- -⌉ - - -

G_1 - - - - - - - ŧ]

S_1 ⌈- -⌉ - - - [ ]

M_2 - - - - - - ŧ]

W_2 - - - [ ] - - a - - -

Y_2 - - - - ∅ - -[ ]

B_4 - - - - - [ŧ - a ŧ]

132. lú an-zil kú-a nu-me-eš̌-a

C - - - ŧ]

J - - - ŧ]-[ ]

P - - - - - - - a[ ]

T - - - - - - ∅ - àm

V - [ ] ⌈-⌉ - - - - -

G_1 - - - - - - - ŧ]

S_1 - - - [ ]

M_2 - - - - - - [ ]

W_2 - - ŧ ŧ - - - - -

Y_2 [ ]⌈-⌉ gu_4∅ - - [ ]

B_4 - - - - -⌈- - -⌉[ ]

133. ^{d}na-ra-am-^{d}sin šà izi-ka ba-an-sìg

C - - - - [ ]

J - - - - - - - - - ⌈-⌉ - ⌈-⌉[ ]

P - - - - - - ⌈-⌉ - - - ł]

T - - - ∅ - - - - - - - -

V - - - - - - - - - - - - -

G_1 ∅[ł - - - - - - ⌈-⌉[ ]

S_1 ⌈- -⌉- - -⌈-⌉[ ]

M_2 - - - - - - -!* - ke_4 bí in - *ŠU

W_2 - - - - - - - - - - - - -

Y_2 [ł - - - - - [ ]

B_4 ∅ - - - - - - - - - [ ]

134. ^{giš}eren ^{giš}šu-úr-mìn ^{giš}za-ba-lum ^{giš}taskarin

C - ⌈-⌉ - [ ]

J - - - - - ⌈-⌉ - - [ł - - -

P - - - - - - ∅ - - - - [ ]

T - - - - - - - - - - - -

V - - - - - - - - - - - -

G_1 [ ] - - - - - -[ ]

S_1 ⌈- - ∅ -⌉ - - ł]

M_2 - - - - - me - - - - - -

W_2 ⌈- -⌉ - - - - - - - - - -

Y_2 [ ]

B_4 - - -[ ]

135. giš gi-gun$_4$-na-bé-eš GUM ba-an-sur-sur

C	- - ŧ]
J	- - - - ŧ ŧ ⌈-⌉ - - - -
P	- - - - - éš - - - ŧ]
T	- - ∅ - - - - - - - -
V	- - - - - - - - - - -
G_1	[ ] - - - - - ŧ]
S_1	⌈- -⌉ - - - - [ ]
W_2	- - ∅ - - - - - - - -
Y_2	[ ]
B_4	- ŧ]

136. kù-GI-bi mi-si-IŠ-ra bí-in-ak

C	- - ŧ]	
J	⌈- - -⌉ - - [ ] - - -	
P	- - - *GIŠ MI ∅ - -* - - [ ]	*i.e., giššu sahar-ra
T	- - - [*] - - - - - - - -	*photo shows trace of possible G[IŠ], as P
V	- - - - - - - - - - -	
G_1	[ ]- - - ⌈-⌉ ŧ]	
S_1	- - - - - ⌈x⌉[ ]	
M_2	- - - - - ∅ - - - e_{11}	
W_2	- - - ⌈- -⌉ - - - - - -	
Y_2	[ ]	
B_4	⌈-⌉[ ]	

137. kù-babbar-bi KUŠ.LU.ÚB / KUŠ.LU.ÚB-šir-ra bí-in-ak

C - - [ ]

J [ŧ - - - - Ø Ø - - -

P - - - - - Ø - - - [ ]

T - - - - - Ø - - - - -

V - - - KUŠ - Ø - - - - -

G_1 - - - - - - - ŧ]

S_1 ⌈- -⌉ - - - - ŧ]

T_1 . . .

M_2 - - - - - - - - - - -

W_2 - - - - - - ŧ]⌈-⌉ - - -

Y_2 [ ]

138. urudu-bi še mah DU-a-gim kar-ra bí-in-si-si

C - [ ]

I [ŧ - ŧ /] - - - [ ]

J [ŧ - [ŧ - ŧ] - - - - ŧ ŧ

P - - ⌈-⌉ - - [ ]

T - - - - - - - - - - - - -

V - - - - - - - - - - - - -

G_1 - - - - te -* - [ ]

S_1 ⌈- -⌉ - - - - - ŧ]

T_1 [ŧ - - ⌈-⌉

M_2 - - - - - - - - re - - - -

W_2 - - - - - - - ⌈- -⌉ - - - ŧ]

Y_2 [ ]

*TE.A could also = kar

```
139.    kù-bi kù-dím-e im-dím-e

C        ƭ                      ]
I       [ɟ -  -   - [           ]
J       [  ɟ ⌈-   -  -⌉[ɟ  -  -
P        - - ⌈-⌉  -  - [        ]
T        - -  -   -  -  -  -  -
V        - -  -   -  -  -  -  -
G_1     [ɟ -  -   -  - iƭ       ]
S_1      -⌈-  -   -⌉ -  ƭ       ]
T_1      - ƭ]⌈-⌉[          ] -  -
M_2      - -  -   -  -  -  -  -
W_2      - -  -   -  -  ƭ       ]
Y_2     [                       ]
```

```
140.    za-bi za-dím-e    im-dím-e

C        ƭ                          ]
I       [ɟ -  -    -  - [           ]
J       [   ] -  ⌈-  -⌉[    ɟ  -  -
P        - -  -    - ⌈-⌉[           ]
T        - -  -    -  -     -  -  -
V        - -  -    -  -     -  -  -
G_1     [        di]m - i   ƭ       ]
S_1     ⌈- -  -⌉   -  -     ƭ       ]
T_1      - -  -   ⌈-⌉[      ɟ  -  -
M_2      -*-  -    -  -     -  -  -        *erased dím between za and bi
Y_2     [                   ]⌈-⌉[ ]
```

141.	urudu-	bi	simug	im-	tu_{11}-	bé
I	-	-	-	Ø	ŧ	]
J	[	]	⌈-	-⌉	-	-
P	-	-	-	[		]
T	-	-	-	-	-	e
V	-	-	-	-	-	-
G_1	[		]	-	ŧ	]
S_1	⌈-	-⌉	-	ŧ		]
T_1	omits					
M_2	-	-	-	-	-	-
Y_2	[			ɟ	-	-

142.	níg-	ga	uru	ki	hul-	a	nu-	me-	a
I	-	-	-	Ø	-	-	- [		]
J	[	]	⌈-	Ø	-⌉	-	-	-	-
P	-	-	ŧ						]
T	-	-	-	-	-	-	-	-	-
V	-	-	-	Ø	-	-	-	-	-
G_1	[						ɟ[		]
S_1	⌈-	-	-	Ø	-⌉	-	-	-	[ ]
T_1	-	-	-	Ø	-	-	-	-	-
M_2	-	-	-	Ø	-	-	-	-	-
Y_2	[ ]	⌈-	-⌉	Ø	-	-	-	-	-

143. é-e ^{giš}má gal-gal kar-ra ba-an-ús

I – – Ø – – – – re ɫ]

J [ɫ – – ⌈– – – –⌉ – –

P – – [ ]

T – – – – – – – – – – –

V [ɫ – – – – – – – – – –

S_1 ⌈– – – – –⌉ – ɫ]

T_1 – – – – – – – – – – –

M_2 – – Ø – – – – – – – –

Y_2 – – – – – – TE – – – –

144. é ^{d}en-líl-lá-šè ^{giš}má gal-gal kar-ra ba-an-ús

I – – – – – ke$_4$ Ø – ⌈– –⌉ – re – – –

J [ɫ – – – ⌈– – – – –⌉ – – – –

P – – ɫ]

T – – – – – – – – – – ⌈–⌉ – – – –

V [ ]– – – – – –⌈– – – –⌉ – – – ɫ]

S_1 – – – – – – – – – ɫ]

T_1 – – – – – – – – – – – – – – – –

M_2 – – – – – – Ø – – – – – – – –

Y_2 – – – – – – – – – – TE – – – –

145. níg-ga uru^{ki}-ta ba-ra-è

J [ ] - ∅ ⸢-⸣ - - -

P ⸢-⸣ ƚ]

T - - - - - - - - e_{11}

V . . .

J_1 [ǂ ƚ]

S_1 - - - ∅ - - ƚ]

T_1 - - - ∅ - ⸢- -⸣[ ]

M_2 - - - ∅ - - - -

Y_2 - - - ∅ - - - -

146. níg-ga uru^{ki}-ta è- da-ni

J [ ] ⸢- ∅ -⸣ - - -

T - - - - - e_{11}- -

J_1 [ǂ - - ⸢-⸣[ ]

S_1 ⸢- -⸣ - ∅ ⸢-⸣ - ƚ]

T_1 ⸢-⸣ - - ∅ - - [ ]

M_2 - - - ∅ - - - bi

Y_2 - - - ∅ - - - an-è

147. a-ga-dè^{ki} dím-ma-bi ba-ra-è

J [ǂ - - - - - - - -

T - - - - - - - - - - -

J_1 [ǂ - - - ƚ]

S_1 ⸢- - - - - -⸣ - ƚ]

T_1 [ǂ - - - ƚ]

M_2 - - - ∅ - ƚ ǂ - - -

Y_2 - - - - - - - - - - -

148. ^{giš}má-e kar íb-tuk$_4$-e umuš a-ga-dè^{ki} ba-kúr

G - ƚ]

J [ǂ - - - - ⌈- ∅ -⌉ - - - - -

T - - ∅ - - - - - - -⌈- -⌉ - -

J_1 - - ∅ - - - ƚ]

S_1 ⌈- - - - -⌉ kúr ∅ - [ ]

M_2 ∅ - - - - kúr [ ] - - - ∅ ⌈-⌉ -

Y_2 ⌈. . . -⌉ - kúr ∅ èš - - - - ⌈- -⌉

149. ud te-eš du$_{11}$-ga kalam téš-a gar-ra

G - - ƚ]

J [ ] - - - - [ǂ - -

N [ ] ƚ]

T - - - - - - - - - -

V [ ] ⌈-⌉ [ ]

J_1 - - - - - ƚ]

S_1 ⌈- - - - -⌉ - [ ]

M_2 - - - - ƚ] - - - - -

Y_2 [ ]⌈- - -⌉ - - ⌈-⌉

150. a-ma-ru zi-ga gaba-šu-gar nu-tuk

G - - - [ ]

J [ ] - - - ⌈-⌉ - - - [ ]

N [ ] - - [ ]

T - - ⌈-⌉ - - - - ⌈-⌉ - -

V [ ] - - [ ]

J_1 - - - - [ ]

S_1 ⌈- - - - -⌉ - [ ]

M_2 - - - - ŧ] - - - - -

Y_2 - - ⌈-⌉ - - - - - - -

151. ᵈen-líl-le nam-e-kur ki-ág-gá-ni ba-hul-a-šè a-na-àm im-gu-lu- -a-bi

G - - - - - [/]- - - ŧ]

J [ ] - - - [ŧ - - a - ⌈- -⌉ - - /[ŧ - ⌈- - - x x⌉ -

N [ŧ - - [/]⌈-⌉ - -⌈-⌉[ŧ - - -

S [ ]⌈- -⌉ ŧ /] - - - - ø - [ ]

T - - - - - - - - ⌈-⌉ - - - ŧ /]- - ⌈- -⌉ - - ul - ba

V [ŧ - - - [/] - - - - - ŧ]

J_1 ⌈- -⌉ - ŧ]

S_1 ⌈- - - - - - -⌉ - - [ ]

M_2 - - - - - [/]

Y_2 - - - - - - - á - - ø - - - - / - - ø bí - -! - ba

C_3 [ ] - - - - - ŧ /] - - -[//]- - ø - - - ⌈x (x) x⌉ -[ ]

152.	kur gú-bí -na-šè igi na-an-íl
J	[ǂ - ∅ - ni⸢bí?⸣[ ]
N	- - - - - ǂ]⸢- -⸣
S	[ǂ - - - - ǂ]
T	- - -[ki] - - - bi[ǂ - ⸢-⸣
W	⸢- - bi⸣ - - - - [ ]
S_1	⸢- - bi⸣ [ǂ - - [ ]
M_2	- - - [ ]
Y_2	⸢-⸣[ǂ - - - - - - -
C_3	- - - - - - b[i ǂ - -
Y_3	. . .

153.	hur-sag dagal téš-bi nam-ta-an-si-ig
J	[ ] - - - - - ǂ ǂ
N	- - - - - - - - [ǂ -
S	[ ] - - - - ǂ]
T	- - - - - [ǂ - [ ]
W	- - - - - - ǂ]
S_1	⸢- - -⸣ - - - ǂ]
M_2	- [ ]
Y_2	[ǂ - - - - da - - -
C_3	⸢- -⸣ - - - - - - - -
Y_3	⸢- -⸣ - - [ ]

154. un-gá nu-sì-ga kalam-ma nu-šid-da

J [ǂ - ⌈- -⌉ - ⌈-⌉ - ƚ ǂ

N ⌈- - - -⌉ - - - - - -

S [] - - - - - ƚ]

T - - - - ⌈- - -⌉ - - ƚ]

U [ǂ - - -

W - - ⌈-⌉ - - - - - [- x]

S_1 ⌈- - - - -⌉ - [ǂ

M_2 - - - ƚ]

Y_2 -[ǂ - - - - - - - e

C_3 [ ] - - - - - - - -

Y_3 - - - - ƚ]

155. gu-ti-um[ki] un kéš-da nu- zu

J [ǂ - - - ma - - - um -

N [ǂ ⌈-⌉ - - -

S [] - - - - - ⌈-⌉ [ ]

T - - -⌈- - -⌉ - - -

U [ ] - - -

W - - - - - - - - -

S_1 ⌈- - - ∅ - -⌉ ƚ ǂ um ∅

M_2 - - - - [ ]

Y_2 - - - ∅ - - - - -

C_3 [ǂ - - - - - ⌈-⌉ -

Y_3 - - - - ƚ]

156.	dím-ma lú-ulu$_3$^{lu} galga ur-ra SIG$_7$.ALAN ^{ugu}ugu$_4$-bi	
J	[ ] - - - - arhuš - ⌈e$^?$⌉ - - - - -	
N	[ ] ⌈x* -⌉ - - - /[⫲ -	*x can= GÁ x X
S	⌈-⌉ - - ⌈-⌉ ∅ ⌈-⌉ - [ ]	
T	- - - - - ⌈GÁxX - a -⌉ - ⫲]	
U	[⫲ - - - - -	
W	- - - - ∅ - - e - -/ ugu$_2$ - -	
S$_1$	⌈- - - - ∅ -⌉ - [⫲ ugu$_x$*- -	*=A.UGU
M$_2$	- - - [ ]	
Y$_2$	- - - - ∅ arhus ùr$^?$∅ - - - - -	
C$_3$	[⫲ - - ∅ - - e - ⌈- x (x) -⌉	
Y$_3$	[⫲ - - - ⫲*]	*x can=l[u] or G[Á(x X)]

157.	^{d}en-lil-le kur-ta nam-ta-an-è
J	[ ] - ⌈-⌉ - - - - - -
L	[⫲ - [ ]
N	[ ] - ⌈- -⌉
S	⌈- - -⌉ - - - - - - ⫲]
T	- - - - ⌈- -⌉ - - ∅ ⫲]
U	[⫲ - - -
W	- - - - - - - - - [⫲
S$_1$	⌈- - - -⌉ - - [ ] - -
M$_2$	- - - - - ⫲]
Y$_2$	- - ⫲] - - - - - - -
C$_3$	. . .
Y$_3$	[⫲ ⌈-⌉ ⫲]

158.	ŠID.ŠID buru$_5^{mušen}$-gim ki àm-ú-ús
J	[ ] ⌈ - - -⌉ - ⌈-⌉ - -
L	[ǂ - ⌈ - - ⌉ - - - [ ]
N	[ ]- - [ǂ
S	⌈- - - - ⌉ - - - - ŧ]
T	- - - - - - - [ ]
U	[ǂ - - - - -
W	- - - - - - - mi -
S_1	⌈- - - - ⌉ - [ǂ - -
M_2	- - - - [ ]
Y_2	⌈- -⌉ u_5 - ø - - mu -

159.	á-bi gu máš-anše-gim eden-na mu-un-na-an-lá
J	[ ] - - ⌈- - - -⌉ - - - - - -
L	- - - - - - ŧ]
N	[ǂ - - - - - - ŧ]
S	- - - - - - - - - ⌈- ø ø -⌉lá
T	- -⌈gu_4 - - -⌉ - - - ø ŧ]
U	[ǂ - - - - ø ⌈- -⌉ -
W	- - gu_4 - -! - - - ŧ ø? ǂ? ø -
S_1	⌈- - - - -⌉ ŧ ǂ - - - - - -
M_2	- - - - ŧ]
Y_2	⌈-⌉ - gu_4 - - ka - - - - - - ø -

160. níg-na-me á-bi la-ba-ra-è

J [⫟ - - ⌈-⌉ -⌈- -⌉ - -

L - - - - - - - - - ⫠]

N [⫟ - - - - - - -

S ⌈-⌉ - - - - - ⌈-⌉ - ⌈-⌉

T - - - ⌈-⌉ - - - ⫠]

U [⫟ - - - - - -

W - - - - - ⫠]

S_1 ⌈- - - - -⌉- [⫟ -

M_2 - - - - -[ ]

Y_2 [⫟ - - - - - - ⌈-⌉ -

161. lú-na-me á-bi la-ba-an-tag_4-tag_4

J ⌈- -⌉ - - - - - - - -

L - - - - - - - - ⌈-*⌉ ⫠*] *sign may be šub

N [⫟ - - - - - - - - - a

S - - - - - ⫠]⌈-⌉ -

T - - [⫟ - - - [ ]

U [ ] - - - - ∅* - - *erasure

W - - - - - ⫠]

S_1 ⌈- - - - - -⌉[ ] - - -

M_2 - - - - - [ ]

Y_2 [⫟ - - - - - - - - -

162. lú-kin-gi$_4$-a har-ra-an-na nu-mu-un-gin

J [ǂ - ⸢-⸣ - - - [ ]⸢- -⸣ -

L - - - - - - - - - - - - -

N [ǂ - - - - - - - - - - - -

S - - - - - - ǂ ǂ - - -

T - - ǂ ǂ - DA ǂ]

U [ ] - - - - - - ⸢-⸣ - ∅ um -

W - - - - - - - - - - - [ ]

S$_1$ ⸢- - - - - -⸣ - ǂ] - ∅ um -

M$_2$ - - - - - - - - - - ǂ]

Y$_2$ [ǂ - - - - - - - - - - - -

163. ^{giš}má ra-gaba íd-da nu-mu-un-dab$_5$-bé

J [ǂ[?]⸢- - -⸣ [ ] -

L - - - - - - - - - - - - -

N ∅ - - - - dè - - - - -

S ∅ - - - - - ⸢-⸣[ǂ dib -

T - - ǂ ǂ - ⸢- dib⸣[ ]

U [ǂ - - - - - - dib ⸢-⸣

W ∅ - - - - - [ ]⸢-⸣[ ]

S$_1$ ⸢- - - - - -⸣ - [ ] - - -

M$_2$ ∅ - - - - - - - - - -

Y$_2$ ∅ - - ∅ - - - - ∅ tag$_4$ tag$_4$

164. ùz-gi ^{d}en-líl-lá amaš-ta ba-ra-ra-aš na-gada-bi bí-in-ús-ú-ús

J [ǂ [ ]⌈- - - - -⌉/ ⌈x x⌉ [ ]

L - - - - - - - - - - - - - / - - - - - - - ∅ -

N - - - - - - - - - - - - - / - - - - - - - ù -

S ɫ ǂ - - ɫ ǂ ⌈- - - -⌉/ ɫ ǂ - - - -

T -[ǂ ⌈-⌉ ɫ]

U [ ] - - - - - - - - - - - - - ⌈-⌉ - - - - - ∅ ∅

S$_1$ - ⌈- - - - - - -⌉ - - - ⌈-⌉ - unu$_3$ - - - - - ∅ ∅

M$_2$ - - - - - - - - - - - - - - - / - ⌈-⌉ - - - - - - -

Y$_2$ - - - - ⌈-⌉ - ⌈-⌉ - - - - - - / ⌈-⌉ - - - - dab$_5$

165. šilam tùr-bi-ta ba-ra-ra-aš unu$_3$ -bi bí-in-ús-ú-ús

J ɫ] - - - - na-gada ⌈- - -⌉ -! ∅ ∅

L áb - - - - - - - - - - / - - - - - - ∅ -

N - - - - - - - - - - / - - - - - - ù -

S ⌈- -⌉ - - - - - - - / - - - - - - [?]-

T ɫ] na-gada [ ]

U [ǂ - - - - - - [ǂ [ǂ - - ∅ ∅

S$_1$ - - - - - - - - - - na-gada - - ⌈- -⌉ ∅ ∅

M$_2$ - - - - - - - ⌈-⌉ - - - - - - - -/-

Y$_2$ - - - - - - - ∅ - ⌈- -/ -⌉ -⌈dab$_5$⌉

166. giš-gú-ka en-nu-un ba-e-dù

J ká? [ ] - - - - - - -

L ⌈-⌉ - ⌈-⌉ -[ ]

N ⌈- -⌉[-] - - - - - -

S - - - - - - - - -

T -[*] - [ ] *x looks like k[á]

U [-] - - - - -⌈du⌉

S_1 ⌈-⌉ - ⌈-⌉ - - - - - - -

M_2 - - - - - - - - -

167. har-ra-an-na lú-sa-gaz ba-e-tuš

J - -[-] - - - - sìg

L ⌈- - -⌉ - - - - - - -

N [-] - - - - -

S - - - - - - ⌈-⌉ e - ⌈-⌉ -

T [ ]

U [ ]⌈-⌉ - - - - ⌈- -⌉

S_1 ⌈-⌉ - - - - [ ] - - - -

M_2 - - - - - - - - - -

Q_2 [-] -

Y_2 - - - - - - -[ ]

168. abul kalam-ma-ka ^{giš}ig im-ma ba-e-gub

J - ⌈ - -⌉ - ∅ - - - - - - -

L - - - - ∅ - - - - - ⌈-⌉

N [ǂ - ∅ - - - - - - -

S ⌈- ⌉ - - ke$_4$ ⌈-$^{?}$- - -$^{?}$ - -⌉ -

T [ ]⌈-⌉ - - dul

U [ǂ ⌈-⌉ - - - - ⌈- - - -⌉

S$_1$ ⌈- ⌉ - - ⌈-⌉[ǂ - - - - - -

M$_2$ -$^{!}$ - - - - - - - bí in -

Q$_2$ [ǂ ⌈-⌉[ǂ - - - ⌈-⌉ ǂ]

Y$_2$ - - - - - ǂ]

169. kur-kur-re bàd uru^{ki}-ne-ne-ka gù gig mi-ni-ib-bé-ne

L - - - - - - - - - - / - - - - - - - -

N [ ] ⌈-⌉∅ - - - /[ǂ - - - - - -

S [ ] - ⌈-⌉ ǂ] - - /[ǂ ⌈-⌉ - - ⌈-⌉ - -

T [ǂ - ga[ ]

U [ ] ⌈- -⌉∅ - - - - [ǂ ga im me ∅ ∅ ∅

S$_1$ - - - - - - - né ǂ ǂ - - - - ⌈- -⌉

M$_2$ - - - - - ∅ - - ke$_4$ - - - -/ íb - -

Q$_2$ - - - - - ∅ ⌈- - -⌉ - - - - - ⌈-⌉[ ]

Y$_2$ - - - - - ∅ - ǂ /] - - ǂ]

170. uru^{ki} šà eden bar dagal nu-me-a mú-sar mu-un-dè-gál

L - - - - - - - - -/- - - - - -

N [ ]⌈- -⌉ - - ⌈- -⌉

S [ ] - - - - - -/- ⌈-⌉ - - ni -

T [ǂ -⌈ra?⌉[b]i in mú

U [ǂ ⌈- -⌉ - - - - - - - ∅ - -

S_1 ⌈- . . . ⌉ - - - ǂ]⌈- -⌉ [ ]

Q_2 - ∅ - - ⌈- -⌉ - - - - - - ∅ - -

Y_2 - - - - - - - - ∅ - - nu ∅ ∅ -

171. u_4 uru^{ki} ba-dím-dím-ma- ba ba-sì-sì-ga- ba

G [ǂ ǂ]

L - - - bi - - - - a - / - - - - a -

S [ǂ ∅ - - - - - /[ǂ - - -

T ⌈- - ∅ - - - -⌉ a - - - - - a -

U [ ] - ⌈-⌉ - ⌈-⌉* - ∅ - - - a - *or ⌈ma-ba⌉

Z [ǂ ǂ]

P_1 - - ∅ - - - - - ∅ - - - [ ]

S_1 . . .

Q_2 - ⌈-⌉∅ ba - - - - - - - - ⌈-⌉ -

Y_2 - - ∅ - - - - - - - - a -

172.	a-gàr gal-gal-e še nu-um-túm	
G	[ ]⌈-⌉ - - tù[m]	
L	⌈- -⌉ - - - - - - - -	
S	[ǂ - - - - - -	
U	[ ]⌈- -⌉ - bé - - - tùm	
Z	*- - - [ ]- ⌈-⌉[ ]	*preceded by [a-šà]
P_1	*- - - - ∅ - - - ⌈-⌉	*preceded by a-šà
Q_2	- - - - - - - - - -	
Y_2	- - ⌈-⌉ - -⌈gú?⌉me e NE	

173.	a-gàr sù-sù-ge ku_6 nu-um-túm	
G	[g]a - - - tù[m]	
L	[]⌈-⌉ - - - - - - ǂ]	
S	[ǂ - - - - - -	
U	[ ]⌈- -⌉ - - - tùm	
Z	*[]⌈- gal - - - -⌉[ ]	*preceded by [a-šà]
P_1	*- - - - ga - - - [ ]	*preceded by a-šà
Q_2	- - - ⌈- gal⌉ - - ⌈-⌉ -	
Y_2	- - [ǂ ⌈- -⌉ [ǂ - - du_{11}	
D_4	- - - - ga [ ]	

174. pú-^{giš}kiri$_6$ làl geštin nu-um-túm

G [ ] - - tù[m]

L [ǂ - - - - ǂ]

S [ǂ - - - - -

U [ ] - - tùm

Z [ǂ - - - [ ]

P_1 - - - ⌈- -⌉ - - [ ]

Q_2 - - - ⌈- - - - -⌉

Y_2 - - [ ] - - du$_{11}$

D_4 - - - - - [ ]* *skips to 200

175. IM.UD sír-da la-ba-šèg ^{giš}maš-gurum la-ba- mú

G [ ] - - - - - -! - - [ ]

L [ ] - - - ǂ]/ - - NU - - šè[g]

S ⌈- -⌉ - - - - - / - - - - - -

U . . .

Z [ǂ - - - ǂ]

P_1 - - [ ] - - - -! - [ ]

Q_2 - - ⌈-⌉ - ⌈- - - - - - - - an -⌉

Y_2 ǂ ǂ - - ⌈-⌉ e Ø Ø

176. u$_4$-ba ì diš gín-e ba$_7$ sila$_3$-àm

G [ ] - - - - - ǂ]

L . . .

S - - - - - šè - - -

Z [ǂ - - - [ ]

P_1 - ǂ ǂ - - [ ]

Q_2 - - - - ⌈- (-) - - -⌉

Y_2 [ ]⌈- - Ø -⌉ ǂ]* *probably no àm

177. še diš gín-e ba$_7$ sila$_3$-àm

G [ ] - - ∅ - - ŧ]

S - - - šè - - -

Z [ ] - - [ ]

P$_1$ - [ǂ - - [ ]

Q$_2$ - - ŧ]⌈- -⌉ ŧ]

Y$_2$ [ ] - - ∅ - ŧ]* *probably no àm

V$_3$ [ ] ŧ]

178. síg diš gín-e ba$_7$ ma-na-àm

G [ ] - - ∅ - - - ŧ]

S - - - šè - - - -

Z [ ] - - ⌈-⌉ [ ]

P$_1$ [ǂ - - - [ ]

Q$_2$ - - - [ǂ* *x ≠ AN

Y$_2$ [ ] - - ∅ - ŧ]* *probably no àm

V$_3$ [ ] - ŧ]

179. ku$_6$ diš gín-e ^{giš}ba-an-e íb-si

G [ ] - - ∅ - - - - - -

S - - - šè - - - -⌈-⌉ -

P$_1$ [ǂ - ŧ]

Q$_2$ - - ŧ]x[ ] -

Y$_2$ [ǂ - - ∅ ∅ ⌈bán?⌉- ib -

C$_3$ [ǂ - - ⌈- - - - -⌉[ ]

V$_3$ - - ⌈- x⌉[ ]

180. ganba uru^{ki}-ba-ka ur$_5$-gim íb-sa$_{10}$-sa$_{10}$

G [ǂ ⸢ – – –?⸣ǂ ǂ hé – – –

S – ⸢ – – – – –⸣ – ⸢–⸣ ta ⸢–⸣

U . . .

E_1 [ ]⸢–?⸣[ ]

Q_2 ⸢–⸣[ ]⸢–⸣ – ǂ] hé⸢– – –⸣

Y_2 ⸢–⸣ – – – – – [ǂ – – – –

C_3 – – ∅ ⸢– – – – –? –? –?⸣

V_3 – – ∅ – ⸢– – –⸣ [ ]

181. ùr-ra nú-a ùr-ra ba-ug$_7$

G [ǂ – – ǂ ǂ – – –

S [ ]⸢– – –⸣

U [ǂ⸢– – –⸣ –

E_1 . . .

Q_2 –⸢– – – –⸣ – – –?

Y_2 – ∅ – – – – – ǂ]

C_3 ⸢– –⸣ – –⸢– – –⸣ –

V_3 – – – – ǂ]

182. é-a nú-a ki nu-um-túm

G – – – –⸢–⸣ – ∅ – mu

S [ǂ – –

U [ǂ – – – ∅ – mu

Z [m]u

E_1 . . .

Q_2 ⸢–⸣[ ] ⸢–⸣[ ]

Y_2 – ∅ – – – – – [ ]

C_3 ⸢– – – – – – x x⸣

V_3 – –⸢– –⸣[ ]

183. un šà-gar-bi-ta ní-bi-a šu im-dúb-dúb-ne

```
G       - -  -  -  -  -  -  -  ⌈-  -⌉  -   -  -
S      [                ]  -  te -/[        ]  -  -
U      [       ǂ  -  -  -  -  -  -  -  -   -  -  -
Z      [                         ]⌈-  -   -   -⌉[ ]
E1      . . .
Y2     ⌈-⌉-   -  -  ø  - ⌈ba⌉ø  AN ba [           ]
C3      . . .                       ⌈-    -⌉[     ]
V3      - -  -  ǂ                                 ]
```

184. ki-ùr ki-gal ^{d}en-líl-lá-ke$_{4}$

```
G      ⌈- -⌉ -  -  -  -  -  -  -
S      [             ]  -  -  -  -
U      [   ] -  -  -  -  -  -  -
Z      [              ǂ  -  -  -
E1     [             ] ǂ         ]
Y2      - -  -  -  -  -  [       ]
G3     [  ǂ  -  -  -  -  -  -  -
V3      - -  - [                 ]
J4     ⌈-⌉[                      ]
```

185. ur sila si-ga KA ba-ni-ib-kéš

G - - - - - - - ∅ -

S [ǂ - - - -

U [ ] - - ⌈-⌉ - in -

Z [ǂ* - *x can = n]i or i]n

E_1 [ǂ [ ]

G_1 [ǂ

Y_2 - - - - ǂ ǂ [ ]

G_3 [ǂ - - - - - - in -

V_3 - - - [ ]

J_4 - [ ]

186. šà-ba lú min DU téš-e ba-ni-ib-kú

G ⌈-⌉- - - [ ] - - - - - -

S [ ]⌈-⌉ - - - - - ⌈-⌉

U [ ] - - - - - - - - -

Z [ ]⌈- - - - -⌉

E_1 [ǂ - [ ]

G_1 [ ] -

Y_2 ⌈-⌉- - - [ ]

G_3 [ ] - - - - - - - in - e

V_3 - ∅ ∅ - - [ ]

C_4 [ǂ -

J_4 - - [ ]

187. lú eš$_5$ DU téš-e ba-ni-ib-kú

G ⌈-⌉ - - ƚ]⌈-⌉- - - -

S [ǂ ⌈-⌉- - - -

U [ ] - - - - - - -

Z [ǂ ⌈- - - -⌉ ƚ]

E$_1$ [ ]⌈-⌉ - - [ ]

Y$_2$ - - da - [ ]

G$_3$ [ ] -! - - - - - - -

V$_3$ - - [ ]

C$_4$ [ ]- ƚ]

J$_4$ - ƚ]

188. KA ba-dub-dub sag ba-dab$_5$-dab$_5$

G [ǂ - - ⌈-⌉ - - ⌈- -⌉

S ⌈-⌉ƚ] ⌈- - - -⌉

U [ ] - - - - - -

Z [ǂ ⌈- -⌉ - -

E$_1$ [ǂ - - [ ]

Y$_2$ - - - - ⌈- - TU TU⌉

G$_3$ [ǂ - - - - -

V$_3$ - - [ ]

C$_4$ [ ] -

J$_4$ - ƚ]

K$_4$ [a]n-dub-d[ub / a]n-TU-TU

189. KA ba-dub sag numun-e-eš̌ ba-ab-gar

G [ ]⌈- -⌉ - - - - ⌈- -⌉

S - - ⌈- x⌉ - - - - - -

U [ ] - - - ∅ - - - -

Z [ɟ - ∅ - - - -

E_1 [ɟ - - - ƚ]

X_2 [ ]⌈-⌉[ ]

Y_2 ⌈-⌉- ƚ ɟ ∅ - - - -

G_3 [ɟ - - - - - [ ]

V_3 - - [ ]

C_4 [ɟ? -

J_4 - - [ ]

K_4 - -* - - ƚ] *adds -an-

190. sag zi sag lul-la su-bal ba-ni-ib-ak

G [ ]⌈- -⌉ - - ⌈- - - - -⌉

S - ⌈-⌉ ⌈- -⌉ - - - - - - -

U [ ] - - - - - - - - -

Z [ ]⌈- - -⌉ - - - - - -

E_1 [ɟ - - ƚ]

X_2 [ɟ - ƚ]

Y_2 ƚ]⌈x⌉ [ɟ? - ∅ - ši in -

G_3 [ɟ - ⌈-⌉ [ ]

V_3 - - [ ]

C_4 [ɟ - -

J_4 - ƚ]

K_4 omits

191.	mèš mèš-e an-ta i-im-nú
G	[ ] - - [ ]
S	⸢- -⸣ -⸢-⸣ - - - -
U	[ ] - - - - - -
W	ɫ]
Z	[ ]⸢- -⸣ - - - -
E_1	[ ] - - - - [ ]
Q_2	⸢- -⸣ . . .
X_2	[ɫ ∅ - -
Y_2	ɫ] - -
G_3	[ ]⸢- -⸣[ ]
V_3	- ɫ]
C_4	[ɫ ɫ]
J_4	⸢-⸣ [ ]
K_4	- - a - - ba[ ]

192. úš lú lul-e úš lú zi-da-ke_4 an-ta na-mu-un-DU

G [ ] - - ⌈-⌉ [-]

S [- -] - ⌈- -⌉ - - ⌈- -⌉/[]⌈-⌉ - ⌈-⌉ - [ ]

U [l]a - - - - - - - - - - -

W - - ⌈- -?-⌉ [-]

Z [-] la - - ⌈- -⌉[-] - - - ⌈-⌉ -

C_1 [-] - - - - [-]

E_1 -[-] - - - [-]

Q_2 [-] - - - ⌈-⌉ [- -] - -! - ⌈-⌉ [-]

X_2 [-] - - - ⌈- - -⌉ -

Y_2 ⌈-⌉[ ] - - ∅ - - - - - -

G_3 [ ] - - - - [ ]

V_3 omits

C_4 [ ] - - ⌈-⌉

K_4 ù-rí-in lú lu[l /] lú zi-ra an-t[a /]-ma-[ ]

193. u_4-ba ᵈen-líl-le èš gal-gal-la-ni-ta

G	. . .
S	⌜-⌝[ ]- - - - - ⌜- - ø? -⌝
U	[ ]- - - - - - -
W	- - - - - - - - - - - - -!
Z	[ ]- - - - - [-] - -
C_1	[] - - - - - [-]
E_1	- - - - - - - - - - [ ]
Q_2	[ ] - - - - - ⌜-⌝ - - - - -
X_2	[ ]- - - - - -
Y_2	- - - - [-]- - - - - -
G_3	[ ]- - - - - - [ ]
V_3	- - - [-]
C_4	[ ] - -
J_4	⌜-⌝[ ]
K_4	ø ø - - - - é[ ]

194. èš gi TUR.TUR im-ma-ra-an-dù

O	. . .
S	- - - ⌈-⌉ - - - - -
U	[ ] - - - - -
W	- - - - - - - - -
Z	[ǂ - - - - - - -
C_1	[ǂ - - ∅ - - [ ]
E_1	- - - - - - [ ]
Q_2	[ ] - ƚ] - - - -
X_2	[ ] - - - - -
Y_2	- - - - [ ] - - - ƚ]
G_3	[ǂ - - - - - ⌈- -⌉
V_3	- - [ ]
C_4	[ǂ du_8
J_4	- - [ ]
K_4	- - - - [ ]

195.	utu	è-	ta	utu	šú-	uš	$erim_3$-	bi	ba-	tur	
D	[								]-	-	
O	-	ŧ								]	
S	-	-	-	-	-	-	⌈-⌉	ma	- -	-	
U	[					ŧ e	-		- -	-	
W	-	-	-	-	-	-	-	ma	- -	-	
Z	[			ŧ	-	-	-	-*	- -	-	*evas.?
C_1	[	ŧ	-	-	-	ŧ				]	
E_1	-	-	-	-	-	-	-	[		]	
Q_2	⌈-	-⌉	-	-	ŧ		ŧ*		- -	-	*or m]a
X_2	[					ŧ šè	-		- -	-	
Y_2	⌈-⌉-		-	-	[ ]	-	-		- -	ŧ]	
G_3	[	]	-	-	-	-	-	ma	-⌈-	-⌉	
V_3	-	-	ŧ							]	
C_4	[									]-	
J_4	-	-	- [							]	

K_4 [sig?]-ta igi-nim!(TÙM)-šè [ ]

196.	um-ma u$_4$-ta ba-ra-ab-tag$_4$-a
D	[⸣
O	- - [ ]
S	⌈- -⌉ - - - ⌈-⌉ - - -
U	[ ] - Ø - -
W	- - - - - - - - -
Z	[ ] - ⌈-⌉ - - -
C$_1$	[ ] - - - - - [ ]
E$_1$	- - - - - - ⌈-⌉[ ]
Q$_2$	- - - ⌈-⌉[⸣ - -
X$_2$	[⸣ - - - - -
Y$_2$	⌈-⌉- - - [⸣ - - - Ø
G$_3$	[ ] - - - - - - ⌈-⌉
V$_3$	[⸣ - ⸢]
C$_4$	[ ]-
J$_4$	- - - ⸢]

197. ab-ba u$_4$-ta ba-ra-ab-tag$_4$-a

	ab	ba	u$_4$	ta	ba	ra	ab	tag$_4$	a
D	[								ǂ
O	-	ŧ							]
S	-	-	-	-	-	⸢-⸣	-	-	-
U	[				]	-	∅	-	-
W	-	-	-	-	-	-	-	-	-
Z	[					ǂ	-	[ ]	⸢-⸣
C_1	[	ǂ	-	-	-	-	-	[	]
E_1	-	-	-	-	[				]
Q_2	-	-	-	⸢-⸣	[		ǂ	-	-
X_2	[			ǂ	-	-	-	-	-
Y_2	-	-	-	-	⸢-	-	-⸣	-	∅
G_3	[	]	-	-	-	-	-	-	-
V_3	[ǂ	-	ŧ						]
C_4	[							]	-
J_4	-	-	-	ŧ					]

198.	gala-	mah	mu-	ta	ba-	ra-	ab-	tag_4-	a
D	[			]	⌈-	-	-⌉	-	-
O	-	ŧ							]
S	⌈-⌉	-	-	-	-	-	-	-	-
U	[				]	-	∅	-	-
W	-	-	-	-	-	-	-	-	-
Z	. . .								
C_1	[ɟ	-	-	-	-	-	-	ŧ	]
E_1	-	-	- [						]
F_2	[					ɟ	ŧ		]
Q_2	-	ŧ					ɟ	-	-
X_2	[				ɟ	⌈-	-	-⌉[	]
Y_2	⌈-⌉	-	-	-	ŧ		ɟ	-	∅
G_3	[ ]	-	-	-	-	-	-	-	-
V_3	[ɟ	ŧ							]
C_4	[								]-
J_4	⌈-	-	-⌉[						]

199. u$_4$ imin gi$_6$ imin-šè

D [ǂ AN - -

O - - - A[N]

S - - - [(?)] - -

U [ ] - ⌈-⌉

W - - - - -

C$_1$ [ǂ - àm - [ ]

E$_1$ - - - ⌈-⌉[ ]

F$_2$ [ ] - [ ]

Q$_2$ - - [ǂ -

Y$_2$ - - - ⌈-⌉[ ]

G$_3$ [ǂ - AN - [ ]

C$_4$ [ ]e

200. balag imin-e an-úr gub-ba-gim ki mu-un-ši-ib- ús

D [ ] - - - - ⌈-⌉ - - - - ú -

O - - - - - [ ]

S ⌈-⌉ - ∅ - ⌈- -⌉ ǂ /] - - ǂ ǂ

U omits

W - - ∅ - - - - - ⌈-⌉ - ne⌈- -⌉ -

C$_1$ [ ] ⌈- ∅ -⌉ - - - - ⌈-⌉ - [ ]

E$_1$ - - - - - - - - - ǂ]

S$_1$ [ ] . . . -

F$_2$ [ ] - - ⌈- -⌉ ǂ*] *x ≠ ši; perhaps n[e]

Q$_2$ - - ∅ - ⌈-⌉[ǂ - ⌈- -⌉ ǂ] -

Y$_2$ - - - - - ǂ]

G$_3$ [ǂ* - - - - - - ǂ ǂ - *x can = [imi]n or [e]

C$_4$ [ǂ ǂ]

D$_4$ *-! - ∅ - - [ ] *follows 174

201. ùb me-zé li-li-ìs ᵈiškur-gim šà-ba mu-na-an-tuk

D [ǂ - - - - - - - ø ø ø ø ø ø

O - šèm - - - - [ ]

S ⌈-⌉ šèm ⌈- -⌉ ǂ /]⌈- -⌉ - - - [ ]

U [ǂ - - - ǂ]

W - šèm - - - - - - - - - - - ø -

C_1 [ ] - ⌈-⌉ - - - [ ]

E_1 - - - - - - - - - - ǂ]

S_1 [ ] - ⌈- x x x x⌉ -

F_2 [ ] - - - - - - un [ ]

Q_2 - - - - ⌈- - - -⌉[/] - - -

Y_2 ⌈-⌉- - - - ø - ǂ]⌈- - - ø -⌉

G_3 [ ]- -* - - - - - - -/ - - - - - - *adds èm

C_4 [ǂ [ ]

D_4 - šèm UD.KA.BAR- - -![ ]* *skips to 213

202. um-ma a urú-mu nu-gá-gá

D [ ] - - - - ⌈-⌉

K [ ]⌈- -⌉

O - - - ǂ ǂ - [ ]

S - - - - gá ǂ ǂ

U . . .

W [ǂ - - - - -* - - *adds um

E_1 - - - - - - - [ ]

S_1 [ ] - - -

F_2 [ǂ - -

Y_2 - - - - - ǂ] -

G_3 [ǂ - - - - - - - -

C_4 [ ]

203. ab-ba a lú-bi nu-gá-gá

D [ ] - - - ŧ]

K [ ] - - ⌈-⌉ - -

O - - - - - [ ]

S - - - - - - ŧ ɟ

E_1 - - - - - - - [ ]

S_1 [ ] - - -

F_2 [ɟ - -

Y_2 - - - - - [ ] -

G_3 [ɟ - - - - - - -

C_4 [ ] ŧ]

204. gala-e a é-kur nu-gá-gá

D [ ]⌈-⌉- - - - -

K [ ]⌈- - - -⌉ -

O - ∅ - - - ŧ]

S - - - - - - ŧ]

Z [ ]⌈- -⌉[ ]

E_1 - - - - - - - [ ]

S_1 [ ] - - -

F_2 [ɟ - -

Y_2 - ∅ - - - ŧ] -

G_3 [ɟ - - - - - - -

C_4 [ ] ŧ]

205. ki-sikil-bé SÍG.ŠAB-bi nu-gá-gá

D [ŧ - e - - -

K [ŧ - ⌜- e? - - -⌝

O - - ⌜-⌝ - - [ ]

S - - - - - ø - ⌜- -⌝

Z [ŧ - ⌜-⌝[ ]

E_1 - - - - - e - - [ ]

S_1 [ ] - - - -

F_2 [ŧ - - -

Y_2 - - ø GIŠ ZU ø ƚ ŧ -

G_3 [ ] - - - - - - -

C_4 [ŧ

206. guruš-bé gír-kin nu-gá-gá

D [ŧ e - - -

K [ ] - - ⌜-⌝[ ]⌜-⌝

O - - - kì [ ]

S - - - ⌜-⌝ - - -

Z [ ] - - [ ]

E_1 - - - - - - [ ]

S_1 [ ] - - -

F_2 [ ] - - -

Y_2 - - - - ƚ] -

G_3 [ ] - kì - - -

C_4 [ ] -

207. ír-bi ír ama a-a ^{d}en-líl-lá-ke_4

K [ ]⌈- - - -⌉- -[ ] - -

O ǂ]⌈- -⌉[ ]

S - - - - - - - - - - - ⌈-⌉

Z [ ] - - -[ ]

E_1 - - - - - - - - - - - [ ]

S_1 [ ]-⌈- - -⌉ - -

W_1 ⌈-⌉[ ]

F_2 [ ]- - ⌈-⌉ - -

Y_2 - - - - ǂ]- - - - -

G_3 [ǂ - - - - - - - - -

C_4 [ ] -

208. du_6-kù su-zi gùr-ru du_{10} kù ^{d}en-líl-lá-ke_4 i-im-gá-gá-ne

K [ ] . . . [ ] - - -

S - ⌈- - - x x -⌉ - - - - - - ∅ / - - - - - -

Z [ ] - - - ǂ]

E_1 - - - - - - - - - - - - ǂ ∅?/]- - - - [ ]

S_1 [ǂ - - -⌈- -⌉ - -

W_1 - - [ ]

F_2 [ ] - - - - - - - - - - ǂ]

Y_2 -? - - - - - - ǂ ǂ - - - ∅ - ǂ ǂ -

G_3 [ǂ ∅ - - - - ⌈- -⌉ - /[ ] - - -

C_4 [ǂ - -

209. nam-bé-éš ᵈen-líl itima kù ba-an-ku_4 šà ka tab-ba ba-an-nú

K [ ]⌈- - -⌉ . . .

S - - ⌈- -⌉- - - ka - - - / - - - - - - -

Z [ ] ⌈-?⌉ - - - - ŧ]

E_1 - - - - - - - - - - - ŧ]

S_1 [ ] ⌈- -⌉ ŧ ŧ - - - ⌈-⌉

W_1 [- -] - - ŧ]

F_2 [ŧ - - ⌈-⌉ - - - - - - ŧ]

Y_2 - - - - - - - ama_5 ŧ] - - mu - ŧ/] ∅ ∅ - - nu_5

G_3 [ŧ? ⌈-? -⌉ - - / [ŧ - - ŧ]

C_4 [ ]⌈x x⌉*

L_4 - - - - - - - [/] - - -! ⱡ]

*traces
do not look like
-an-nú

210. u$_4$-ba ^{d}sin ^{d}en-ki ^{d}inanna ^{d}ninurta ^{d}iškur ^{d}utu ^{d}nusku ^{d}nisaba dingir gal-gal-e-ne

K [ ] ⌈-⌉ ⸷ ⸸ ⌈- -⌉ - - - - / . . . -

S - - ⌈- -⌉ - - - - - - ⌈-⌉ - - / - - - - - - ⌈- hé$^{?}$elm$^{?}$ me eš

Z [ ]⌈- -⌉ - - [ ]

E_1 - - [⸸ - - - - - - ⸷ / ⸸ - - - - ⸷]

S_1 [ ] - - -⌈-⌉ ∅ ∅ - - - ⌈-$^{?}$ -$^{?}$ -$^{?}$ -⌉

W_1 - - - - - ⸷ /]- - - ⸷]

F_2 [⸸ ⌈- - - - - -⌉/[⸸ [ ]

Y_2 - - - - - - -[⸸ - - - -/ - - - - [⸸ - - - -

G_3 [⸸ - -[/ ⸸ - - [ ]

L_4 - - - - - - - ⸷ /] - - ⸷]

211. šà ^{d}en-líl-lá-ke$_4$ a-šed$_{10}$ im-šed$_{10}$ -e-ne a-ra-zu-ta ba-ab-bé-ne

K [‡ - - [ ]

S - - - - - - - - - ⌈ - -⌉ -/ -⌈- - -⌉ - - - -

Z [ ] - - - [/] . . .

E_1 [‡ - ø ø - - - - - ø - ŧ!]

F_1 [ ]- - - - - - - BU ø [‡/ - - - - - - - ⌈-⌉

S_1 [‡ - [ ] ⌈- - - -⌉

W_1 - - - - - - [ ]

Y_2 ⌈- - -⌉ - - ⌈- - - - su⌉ ø ø - - -/[‡

G_3 [ ] ⌈-⌉[ ]

L_3 [‡ - - [/ ‡ - -* - - ŧ] *could be ša

212. ^{d}en-líl uru uru-zu im-hul-a uru-zu-gim hé- dù

K [ǂ - ŧ]⸢- - - - - -⸣

S - - ⸢-⸣[ ] - - - - - - - - - -

Z . . .

E_1 [ǂ - - - - - - - [ ]

F_1 - - - - - - i- - -/ - - - - -

S_1 [ǂ ⸢- -⸣ - em du

W_1 - - - - - - [ ]

Y_2 [ ] - -

G_3 [ ]

L_3 [ǂ - - - - - ŧ]

213. gi-gun$_4$-na-zu šu bí-in-lá-lá nibru^{ki}-gim hé- dù

K [ǂ dù a [ ] - -

S - ŧ ǂ ⸢x⸣ ∅ - - ⸢dù⸣a / - - - - -

E_1 [ǂ ⸢- -⸣ - ∅ - ∅ ŧ]

F_1 - - - - - - - - - - / - - - - -

S_1 [ ] ⸢- - -⸣ - em⸢du⸣

W_1 - - - - ŧ]

Y_2 ŧ] - -

G_3 . . .

L_3 [ǂ - ⸢- -⸣ - - [ ]

D_4 *[ǂ - - - - ŧ] *follows 201

214. uru-zu sag PÚ -ba he-ni-ib-si-si

K . . . - -

S - - ⌈-⌉ - - - - - ⌈-⌉ -

E_1 [ ]⌈-⌉ ǂ]

F_1 [ǂ ∅ - ⌈-⌉[ ] - - - - - -

S_1 [ ]⌈- -⌉ - - -

W_1 - - - x [ ]

Y_2 [ ] -

D_3 - - - - - - - - - -

G_3 [ǂ - - -

L_3 [ǂ - - - - [ ]

D_4 [ǂ - - - - - - DI DI

215. lú lú ù-zu-dè na-an-ni-in-pà-dè

K [ǂ ⌈- - -⌉ ∅ - ⌈-⌉

S - - - - - - - - - - -

F_1 [ǂ ∅⌈- - -⌉ - - - - ⌈-⌉

S_1 [ ]⌈- - - x⌉[ ]⌈-⌉ -

W_1 - - ∅ - ǂ]

Y_2 [ǂ ∅

D_3 - - - - - - - - ∅ - [ ]

G_3 [ ] - - - ∅ - -

L_3 [ǂ - - - - [ ]

T_3 - ǂ]

216. šeš-e šeš-a-né giskim na-an-ni-in-è

K [ŧ ⌈-⌉ - na ne NE

S - - - - - ir - - - - - ⌈-⌉

F_1 [ ] ⌈- - -⌉ir - - - - - ⌈x⌉* *could be è or pà

P_1 [ ]⌈- - -⌉ŧ]

S_1 [ ] - - - - [N]E

V_1 Ø Ø - - n[e]

W_1 - Ø - - n[e]

I_2 ⌈-⌉ - - -⌈- ir[??]⌉ ŧ]

Y_2 [ӿ

D_3 **- - - - -** - - - - [ ]

G_3 [ŧ - - - - - - Ø ⌈x ⌉***

L_3 [ŧ - - - ŧ]

T_3 - - - - - [ ]

**These first five signs repeated in small characters on tablet top

***NE most likely; e less so; definitely not è

217. ki-sikil-bé ama_5-na giš hul hé-en-da-ab-ra

K [⁑ - - - - - -

S - - - - - - - - - - - -

F_1 [ǂ - - - - - - ⌜-⌝[ ]

P_1 ⌜- -⌝ - - - - - [ ]

S_1 [ǂ ⌜-⌝ - ⌜- - - - - -⌝

V_1 - - - - [ ]

I_2 - - - - - - [ ]

Y_2 [ǂ?eb? - - -

D_3 - - - - - - - - - [ ]

L_3 [ǂ ⌜-⌝ [ ]

T_3 - [ǂ - ⌜-⌝ - - ŧ]

218. ad-da-bé é dam ug_7-a-na gù gig-bi hé-em-me

K [ǂ? - - - - ⌜-⌝ -

S - - - - - - - -/ - - - - - -

F_1 [ǂ - - - - - - -/ - - - ∅ - -

P_1 - - - - - - - - [ ]

S_1 [ǂ ⌜-⌝ . . .

V_1 - - - - [ ]

I_2 - - - - - - - ŧ]

Y_2 [⁑ - ∅ ∅ - - ∅ - ∅ -

D_3 - - - - - - - ŧ/]- - - - - [ ]

T_3 - - - - - - - - [ ]

219. tu^{mušen}-bé ab-làl-ba še hé-ni-in-ša$_4$

K [ ] - - [ ]

S - - - - - - - - - - - -

F_1 [+ - - ⌈- - -⌉ - ⌈- -⌉[ ]

P_1 - - - - - - ⌈x*⌉[ ] *x not še or níg

S_1 [+ ⌈-⌉ - ⌈-⌉ . . . ⌈-⌉

V_1 - - - - [ ]

I_2 - - - - - - +*] *x begins similarly to P_1

Y_2 [+ - - - - - - ⌈-?⌉

D_3 - - - - - - - - - +]

T_3 - - - - - - níg +]

220. buru$_5$^{mušen}-bé á-búr-ba níg hé-ni-ib-ra

K [ ] - []

Q +]

S - - - - - - - - - ⌈-⌉ -

F_1 . . .

P_1 - - gim - - - - [ ]

S_1 [+ ⌈- - bé?⌉- ⌈-⌉[ ]⌈- -⌉

V_1 - - - +]

I_2 - - - ⌈- -⌉ - [ ]

Y_2 [ ] mu da ab SUR

D_3 - - gim - - - - - - +]

T_3 - - - ⌈- - -⌉ - +]

221.	tu^{mušen} ní-te-a-gim ur$_5$-da hé-ak-e
Q	⌈-⌉[ ]
S	- - - - - - - - - ⌈-⌉ -
F_1	[ ]⌈- - - -⌉[ ]
P_1	- - - - - - ŧ]
S_1	omits
V_1	⌈-⌉ - - ŧ]
I_2	- - - - - - - ŧ]
Y_2	[ŧ - - - e ke$_4$ Ø
D_3	- - - - - - - - - ŧ]
T_3	- - - - - ⌈-⌉ - - ŧ]

```
222.   mìn-kam-ma-šè ᵈsin ᵈen-ki ᵈinanna ᵈninurta ᵈiškur ᵈutu ᵈnusku ᵈnisaba dingir hé-em-me-eš
Q        -  ƚ                              /                                     ]
S        -  -  -  -  - -  - - -  -   -   - ⌜-⌝ / -  -  - -  -  -   -    -    -  - ƚ   ]-
P1       -  -  -  -  - -  - - -  -   ƚ                 /]-  -   -   -    ƚ              ]
S1       [                ]- -  ∅   ∅   -   -    -         .  .  .                ⌜-  -⌝
V1       [       ƚ  - [                                                              ]
I2       -  -  -  -  - -  - ƚ                    /]-  -   - -  -[                      ]
Y2       ƚ                ƚ -  -   -   -   -   -  /[         ƚ  -   -   -    -   gal?∅ -? ∅
D3       -  -  -  -  - -  - - -  -   -   -  ƚ /]-  -  - -  -  -   -    -    -  - [      ]
T3       -  -  -  -  - -  - - -  - [         //]-  -  - -  -  -   -    -    ƚ?          ]
```

223. uru^{ki}-šè igi-ne-ne i-im-gá-gá-ne

Q	- ∅ - [ ]
S	- ∅ - - - - - - - - - -
I_1	[ ] ⨍]
P_1	- - - - - - - -[ ]
S_1	[⨍ - - ⌜- - - - -⌝
V_1	[ ]⌜-⌝[ ]
I_2	- ∅ - ⨍]
Y_2	- [-] ⨍ í]l$^?$la ì - ⌜- - -⌝
D_3	- - - - - - - - - - ⨍]
T_3	- ∅ - - - - -⌜-⌝[ ]

224. a-ga-dè^{ki} áš hul-a im-ma-ab-bal-e-ne

G	-[ ]
Q	-⌜-⌝[ ]
S	- - - - - - - - - - - - ∅ -
I_1	[⨍ ⨍]
S_1	[⨍ - - ⌜- - - - - - -⌝
I_2	- - ⨍]
Y_2	- - - - ∅⌜tuk$_4$⌝e mu na ra r[a]
D_3	- - - - - - - - [⨍ - [ ]
T_3	- - - - - - -⌜-⌝[ ]

225. uru^{ki} é-kur-šè ba-e-a-ul$_4$-en ^{d}en-líl hé-àm

G ⸗]

Q - ∅ ⌈- - - -⌉[ ]

S - ∅ - - ra - - - - - - - - - - ⌈-⌉

I_1 [ ] - - ⌈x x⌉[ ]

S_1 [ ]∅ ⌈- - ra -⌉ - ∅ ⌈- -? - - - - ul$_4$?⌉

I_2 - ∅ ⸗]

Y_2 - - - - -! - - ∅ le ∅ - - - - [ ]

D_3 - - - - - - - - ⸗] x[ ]

F_3 [ ] - a e ⌈- ∅ - -⌉ - [ ]

T_3 - ∅ - - ⌈ra?⌉ - - - - - [ ]

I_4 [ ]⌈e⌉ - - - - ul$_4$ e

226. a-ga-dè^{ki} é-kur-šè ba-e-a-ul$_4$-en ^{d}en-líl hé-àm

G ⌈- -!⌉⸗]- - ⸗]

Q - - - - - - - [ ]

S - - - - - - ra - - - - - ⌈- -⌉ - - [ ]

I_1 - - - - - ⸗]

S_1 [ ]⌈-⌉- ⌈- -⌉[ ]⌈- - - - ul$_4$?⌉

Y_2 ⌈-⌉- - - - - - - - ∅ ∅ ul ∅ - - - - - [ ]

D_3 - - - - - - - - - ⌈- -⌉[/]- - - - [ ]

F_3 ⌈- - -⌉- - - - - - a e - ∅ - - - - - ⌈-⌉

T_3 [ ]- - - - - - ∅? ⌈-!? - - -? ∅ - - -⌉[ ]

I_4 [ ] - - ∅ - e - - - - - ul$_4$ e

227. bàd kù-zu en-na sukud-rá-bi a-nir hé-em-da-sá

G - ⌈- - - -⌉ ŧ]

Q - - - - - - [/]⌈- -⌉ - [ ]

S - - - - - - - - - - - - ⌈- - -⌉

I_1 - - - - ŧ]

S_1 [ǂ - - ⌈- - -?⌉[ ]⌈- eb - -⌉

X_1 - ⌈- - - -⌉ [ ]

Y_2 [ǂ - - e - da ∅ - - -/⌈-? x (x)⌉

D_3 - - - - ŧ /]

F_3 - - - - - - - - - / - - - eb - - a

T_3 ⌈- - -⌉ - nam - [ ]

I_4 [ ] - - - - - - - - - -

228. gi-gun$_4$-na-zu sahar-gim hé-dub

G - - - - ŧ]

K . . .

Q - ⌈-⌉ [ ]⌈-⌉[ ]

S - - - - - - - -

I_1 - - - ⌈bi⌉ ŧ]

S_1 [ ] - - - ⌈- - - -⌉

X_1 - - - - ŧ]

Y_2 [ǂ - bi - - - -

D_3 [ǂ ŧ]

F_3 - - - - - - - -

T_3 - - - - - - ŧ]

I_4 [ǂ - - -

229. dub-lá la-ha-ma su$_8$-su$_8$-ga-bi

G - - - - - [ ]

K [ǂ - - -

Q - - - [ ]

S - - - - - - - - zu

I_1 - - - - ǂ]

S_1 [ǂ - - - - - ⸢- - -⸣

X_1 - - - - - - ǂ]

D_2 [ ] - - - - - - -

Y_2 [ ] - - - - sù sù - -

F_3 - - - - - - - - -

T_3 - - - - - - [ ]

I_4 [ǂ - - - - -

230. guruš mah geštin nag-a -gim ki-šè hé-em-ta-gá-gá

G - - - - g[á]

K [ǂ - - - - - - -

Q - - [ ]

S - - - - - - - - - Ø gá - ⸢x⸣* *= gá or e

I_1 - - - ǂ]

S_1 [ǂ - - - - - ⸢- . . . - -⸣

X_1 [ǂ - - g[á]

D_2 [ǂ - - gá - - - - ǂ]

Y_2 [ ] - - - Ø - - - - eb Ø - -

F_3 [ǂ - - - Ø - -! Ø - eb - - -

T_3 - - - ⸢-⸣ - - ǂ]

I_4 [ǂ - - - ⸢- -⸣ - - - -

231. im-zu abzu-ba hé-eb-gi_4

G ⌈- bil - a ŧ]

K [e]m -

Q - - ŧ]

S - - - - - - -

I_1 ⌈- -⌉ ŧ]

S_1 - - ⌈- - - - -⌉

X_1 [ǂ - - - [ ]

D_2 [ǂ - a - - ŧ]

Y_2 [ǂ - - - - -

F_3 - - - - ŧ]

T_3 - - - - - e[m?]

I_4 [ ] - a ŧ]éb ŧ]

232. im ^{d}en-ki-ke_4 nam-kud-rá hé-a

G ⌈-⌉[ ]⌈- -⌉[ ]

K [ ] ⌈-⌉ - - - -

Q - - - ŧ]

S - - - - - - - - - -

I_1 [ǂ ŧ]

S_1 [ǂ - - - - ⌈- - - - -⌉

D_2 [ ]- - - - - da - [ ]

Y_2 [ ]- - - ∅ - - da - -

F_3 - - - - - - - ⌈- -⌉ -

T_3 ⌈-⌉- - - - - ⌈- x*⌉[ ] *for x, cf. 234

W_3 [ǂ ŧ]

I_4 [ ] - - - ŧ]

233.	še-zu ab-sín-ba hé-eb-gi$_4$	
G	⌈-⌉[ ] - [ ]	
K	[ ]⌈bé⌉ - em -	
Q	⌈-⌉- [ ]	
S	- - - - - - - -	
S_1	- - ⌈- - - - em? -⌉	
D_2	[ǂ - - - - - [ ]	
Y_2	[ǂ - - - - - gi	
F_3	omits	
T_3	- - - - - ǂ]	
W_3	[ǂ - - [ ]	
I_4	[ǂ be - Ø? ǂ]*	*one more sign following g[i$_4$]

234.	še ^{d}ezinu-e nam-kud-rá hé-a	
G	⌈-⌉[ ] ⌈-⌉[ ]	
K	[ ] - - ⌈-⌉ - - -	
S	- - - - - - - - -	
S_1	- - - ⌈- - - - - -⌉	
D_2	- - - ke$_4$ - - da - [ ]	
Y_2	[ ] - Ø - - da - -	
F_3	omits	
L_3	[ ] ǂ]	
T_3	- - - - - - ǂ*]	*da more likely than rá
W_3	[ ]⌈- -⌉ [ ]	
I_4	[ǂ - - - ǂ]*	*x ≠ A; followed by one more sign

235.	gis̆-	zu	tir-	bi-	a	hé-	eb-	gi_4
G	⌈-⌉	[			]	x[		]
K	[		ǂ	-	-	ǂ	e]m	-
S	-	-	-	-	-	-	-	⌈-⌉
F_1	[	ǂ	⌈-⌉[					]
S_1	-	-	gis̆⌈-	-	-	-	-	-⌉
D_2	-	-	-	-	-	-	-	-
Y_2	[	]	-	-	∅	-	-	gi
F_3	-	bi	gis̆ -	-	-	-	-	-
L_3	[	ǂ	-	-	-	[		]
T_3	-	-	-	-	⌈-⌉	ǂ		]
W_3	[	]	-	[				]
I_4	[			ǂ	-	-	-	[ ]

236.	gis̆	d	nin-	$ildu_2$	-ma-	ke_4	nam-	kud-	rá	hé-	a
K	[		ǂ	-	∅	-	-	-	-	-	-
S	-	-	-	-	-	-	-	-	-	-	-
F_1	-	-	-	-	[						]
S_1	-	-	-	ild⌈u_3	∅	-	-	-	-	-	-⌉
D_2	-	-	-	-	∅	-	-	-	da	-	-
Y_2	[	]	-	NÍG.NAGAR	∅	ka	-	-	da	-	[ǂ?*
D_3	-	-	[								]
F_3	-	-	-	$ildu_3$	-	-	-	-	-	⌈-	-⌉
L_3	[		ǂ	$ildu_3$	-	ǂ!					]
T_3	-	-	-	ǂ							]
W_3	[		]-	[							]
I_4	[					]	-	-	-	-	à[m]

*or ∅

237.	gu_4 gaz-gaz-e dam hé-en-gaz-e	
K	[ ] - - - ni - ∅ - -	
S	- - - - - - - - -	
F_1	- - - - - - ƚ]	
S_1	- - - - ⌈- - - - -⌉	
A_2	⌈-⌉ ƚ]	
D_2	- - - - - - ∅ - -	
Y_2	[ƚ - - - - ∅ - ⌈-⌉?*	*or ∅
D_3	- - - [ ]	
F_3	[ƚ - - - - ƚ]	
L_3	[ ] ⌈-⌉ - ƚ]	
T_3	- - - z[u]	
W_3	[ ] - ƚ]	
G_4	[x* - [ ]	*x more like [ga]z than ⌈e⌉ or [z]u
C_4	. . .	
I_4	[ƚ - ∅ - -	

238.	udu	šum-	šum-	zu	dumu		hé-	en-	šum-	e
K	[		⸣	⌈e	-	ni⌉	-	Ø	-	-
S	-	-	-	-	-		-	-	-	-
F_1	-	-	-	-	-		-	-	-	⌈-⌉
S_1	[	⸣	-	e	-	[		]	⌈-	-⌉
A_2	-	⸢								]
D_2	-	-	-	e	-	ni	-	ni	-	-
Y_2	[	⸣	-	-	-		⌈-	Ø	-	-⌉
D_3	-	-	-	⌈-⌉	[					]
E_3	-	-	-	[	⸣		-	Ø	⸢	]
F_3	[		⸣	-	-		-	Ø	⌈-⌉[	]
L_3	[			]	-		-	Ø	⸢	]
T_3	-	-	-	⸢						]
W_3	[ ]	-	-	⸢						]
G_4	[			]	-	ni	-	Ø	⸢	]
C_4	[	]	-	e [						]
I_4	[			]	-	ni	-	Ø	-	-

239. ukú-zu dumu kù-ge-eš pà-da-na a hé-em-ta-ab-ra-ra

K	[ ]⌈- - - -⌉[ ]⌈- -⌉
S	- - - - - - - - - - / - - - - ∅ - -
F_1	- - - - - - - - - - / - - en da - - -
S_1	[ ]⌈-⌉ - ∅ - ⌈- -⌉[⸸
A_2	- ⸸]
D_2	- - - - - ⌈èš - -⌉ - ⌈- - ∅ - ∅ - -⌉
Y_2	[ ] - ⌈- - - . . . ⌈-/ x (x) ∅⌉ - ⌈-⌉
D_3	- - - - - - [/]- - - m[i]
E_3	- - - - ⌈-⌉ - - [/]- - - - - ⸸]
L_3	[ ]⌈-⌉ - - ⸸ /]⌈x x⌉[ ]
W_3	[ ]⌈-⌉ ⸸]
T_3	[ ] - ⌈-⌉[ ]
G_4	[ ] èš - - - - ⸸]
C_4	[ ] - - - - - - ⌈- -⌉[ ]
I_4	[⸸ - - - - - en - - - ⌈-⌉

240. kar-kid-zu ká éš-dam-ma-na-ka ní ha-ba-ni-ib-lá-e

K	[ ] - - [ ]⌈-⌉ - -
S	- - ∅ - - - - - - / - - - - - - - -
F_1	- - - - - - - ∅ - / - - - - - - - -
S_1	[ ] - - ⌈x* - - - - - - - -⌉ *could be ka or ke$_4$
A_2	- ŧ]
D_2	- ∅ - - - - na - ⌈ke$_4$?⌉- [ ] - -
Y_2	[ ] - - - - ∅ ∅ - ⌈- ∅ - ib? -? -?⌉
D_3	- - - ∅ - - ∅ - ke$_4$ - - [ ]
E_3	- - - - - ⌈-⌉[/] - - - - [ ]
G_4	[ǂ - - - - - ŧ]
C_4	[ǂ ⌈- -⌉ - - - ∅ - - - [ ]
I_4	[ǂ ∅ - - - - - - íb - [ ]

241. ama nu-gig-zu ama nu-bar- zu dumu hé-en-gi$_4$-gi$_4$

K	[ǂ ⌈-⌉ - - - ∅ ŧ]
S	- - - - - - - - - - - ⌈- -⌉
F_1	- - - - - - - - / - - - - -
S_1	[ǂ - ⌈- - - - - -⌉
A_2	⌈-⌉ - [ ]
D_2	- - - ∅ - - - ra - - ni - [ ]
Y_2	[ ] - - ∅ - ⌈-⌉ - - ⌈- ⌉- ∅ - ∅
D_3	- - - - - - - - [ ]
E_3	- - ∅ - - - - - [ ]
P_3	ŧ]
G_4	[ǂ - - ra - - ni - ∅ - -
C_4	[ ] - - - - - - - - ni[ ]
I_4	[ǂ ⌈-⌉ - - - - - ∅ - ŧ]

242. kù-GI-zu kù-šè hé-sa_{10}-sa_{10}

K [ǂ - - ǂ]

S -[ǂ - - - - - -

F_1 ⌈- -⌉ - - - - - -

S_1 [ ] - ⌈- - -⌉

A_2 - - [ ]

D_2 ⌈-⌉- - - - - - ǂ]

Y_2 [ǂ ø - - [ǂ [ ]⌈-⌉

D_3 - - - - - - [ ]

E_3 - - - - - [ ]

P_3 - - x*] *x = b[i]? (cf. 243)

G_4 [ ] - -! ø -! -

C_4 - - - -* - - [ ] *adds babbar

I_4 [ǂ - ǂ]

243. kù-babbar-zu níg za-ha-am-šè hé-sa_{10}-sa_{10}

S ǂ ǂ ⌈-⌉ - - - - - - ⌈-⌉ - -

F_1 ǂ] - - ⌈-⌉ - - - - - - ⌈-⌉

S_1 [ǂ ⌈- - -⌉

A_2 - - ǂ]

D_2 - - - - - - an - - - -

Y_2 [ ] - - - - ǂ] ⌈-⌉

D_3 - - - - - - - - ǂ]

E_3 - - - - - - - - [ ]

P_3 - - bi ǂ]

G_4 [ ]⌈-⌉ - - an - - - -

C_4 ⌈-⌉ - - - zahan$_2$ ⌈- -⌉ - ǂ]

I_4 . . .

244. urudu-zu a-gar$_5$-šè hé-sa$_{10}$-sa$_{10}$

S [ ] - - - - - - - -

C_1 [ ]⌈-⌉ [ ]

F_1 [ ] - - - - - - - -

S_1 [ɟ - ⌈- -⌉

A_2 - ŧ]

D_2 - - - - - - - - -

Y_2 [ ] bi a kara$_4^?$za - [ ] -

D_3 omits

E_3 - - - - - - [ ]

P_3 - bi - ŧ]

G_4 [ɟ - - - ŧ]

C_4 omits

245. a-ga-dè[ki] á-tuk-zu á-ni hé-eb-ta- ku$_5$

S [ɟ - - - - - - - - - - - -

C_1 [ɟ x* - *x does not look like an

S_1 [ ]⌈- -? an? -⌉

A_2 - - - [ ]

D_2 - - - - - - - - - - - - -

Y_2 [ɟ - -! - - [ ]- ⌈- Ø Ø -?⌉

D_3 - - - - - - - - - - ŧ]

E_3 - - - - - - Ø - - ŧ]

P_3 - - - - ŧ]

G_4]⌈- - -⌉[ ]

C_4 - - - - - - - - - - - [ ]

246. ^{kuš}lu-úb dag-si-né na- an- íl-íl-e

O	[ ] -
S	[ǂ - - ǂ] nam ∅ - - -
X	⌈- - - - x⌉[ ]
C_1	[ǂ i
L_1	[ǂ - - ∅ - - ni - - -
S_1	[⌈x - - ∅⌉
A_2	- - [ ]
D_2	- - - - sa?- - - - - -
Y_2	[ǂ - - - - ǂ]⌈-⌉ ∅
D_3	- - - - - - - - ⌈-⌉ - -
E_3	- - - - - - - - [ǂ i
P_3	- - - - -![ ]
C_4	- - ⌈- - -⌉ - nam ∅ ǂ]

247.	anše ni-is-kum-zu á-ni na-an-húl-e u_4 šúš-a hé-nú
O	[ ] - - -/ [] -
S	[ ] PIRIG - - - - - - - la/- šú ⌈úš⌉- -
X	⌈- - - . . . - . . .⌉
C_1	[ ] - - x]
L_1	x] - - - - - - - - - - -/⌈-⌉ - - - -
S_1	[x - - ⌈-? -? -⌉ -
W_1	[x - [ ]
A_2	- x]
D_2	- - - - - - - - - ø - le - - - - -
Y_2	[x - - - ⌈ . . . - -⌉
D_3	- - - - ⌈- -⌉[/] - - ⌈- x⌉[ ]
E_3	- - - - - - - - - - x /] - - - - x]
P_3	- - - - [/] - [ ]
C_4	- x*] - ⌈-⌉- - - ⌈NE.NE⌉[ ]

*x more like PI[RIG] than n[i]

248. uru^{ki}-bi šà-gar-ra hé-ni-ib-ug$_7$-e

O [ ]⌈- -⌉ -

S [ǂ ∅ - - ǂ ǂ - ǂ ǂ -

X omits

C_1 [ǂ -

L_1 - - - [ǂ - - - - -

S_1 [ǂ ⌈-⌉ -

W_1 [ǂ ⌈-⌉ - [ ]

A_2 . . .

D_2 omits

Y_2 [ǂ ⌈- - x - - -$^?$⌉ - -

D_3 - ∅ - - - ⌈-⌉ - - ǂ$^?$]

E_3 [ ] - - - - - - íb - -

P_3 - ǂ]

C_4 omits

249. dumu-gi$_7$ ninda ša$_6$-ga kú-kú-zu ú-šim-e ha-ba-nú

O [ ] - - ∅ - -$^!$ /-

S [ǂ - ǂ] - ∅ - ⌈- -⌉ ∅ - - -

X ⌈- - - - - - a -⌉ ǂ]⌈x x -⌉

C_1 [ ] - - -

L_1 - - - - ⌈-$^?$ - a ∅⌉ - - ⌈- -⌉[ ]

S_1 [ ] - - - -

W_1 [ ] - - - - [ ]

D_2 ⌈- - - -⌉ - - a - - ⌈- -$^?$- -$^?$ -⌉

Y_2 [ǂ ⌈-⌉ - - - - [∅$^?$ ǂ - ∅ - ab$^?$/⌈-⌉

D_3 - - ⌈-⌉ - - - ⌈-⌉ [/]- -$^!$ - - - [ ]

E_3 [ǂ - - - - - - -/ - ⌈-⌉ - - - -

P_3 - ⌈-⌉ [ ]

C_4 - - [ ] - - - - ǂ]

250. lú sag$_5$ -e ba-zi-ga-zu

O [ɟ -

S [ɟ - -

X ⸢- - - - - - -⸣

C_1 [ ]⸢-⸣

L_1 - - - - - - -

S_1 [ ] - ƚ ɟ -

W_1 [ɟ gá - ƚ]

D_2 [ ]⸢x x⸣[ ] -

O_2 [ ] - - - - - ƚ]

Y_2 [ ] ⸢- gá⸣- - - -

D_3 - ⸢-⸣ - - - - [ ]

E_3 ⸢-⸣ - - ⸢-⸣ - - -

P_3 ⸢-⸣[ ]

C_4 - ⸢ x (x)x⸣ - [ ]

251. tag-tag ^{giš}ùr-ra-na hé-kú-e

O [ ] x (x) x

S [ ] - - -

X - - -⸢x x* ni -⸣ - - *ùr-ra unlikely

L_1 - - -⸢-? -⸣ - - - -

S_1 [ɟ [ɟ - ⸢x x⸣

W_1 [ɟ - - - - [ ]

D_2 [ ] - - -

O_2 [ɟ - - - ni - ƚ]

Y_2 [ɟ - - - - - - - ∅

E_3 ⸢- - -⸣[ ] - - - - -

C_4 - - - - - - ƚ]

252. ^{giš}ig gal ^{kuš}gur$_{21}$ é ad-da-na-ka

	giš	ig	gal	kuš	gur$_{21}$	é	ad	da	na	ka	
O	[									ǂ	
S	-	-	a	-	-	-	-	-	-	-	
X	-	-	⌈-⌉	-	⌈x x*⌉	-	-	-	⌈-?	-⌉	*does not look like E.ÉB
L_1	-	-	-	⌈-	-⌉	-	-	-	-	-	
S_1	[				ǂ	-	-	[ǂ	-	-	
W_1	[		ǂ	-	-	-	ǂ			]	
D_2	[						]	⌈-⌉	-	-	
O_2	[	ǂ	⌈-⌉	-	-	-	-	ǂ		]	
Y_2	[	ǂ	Ø	Ø	-	-	-	-	-	-	
E_3	⌈-	-	-	-?	-?⌉	-	-	-	-	HAR*	*scribe skipped to end of next line
C_4	-	-	Ø	-	-	-	ǂ			]	

253. ^{kuš}gur$_{21}$-bi KA-ni-ta hé-HAR-re

	kuš	gur$_{21}$	bi	KA	ni	ta	hé	HAR	re
O	[							ǂ	⌈-?⌉
S	-	-	-	-	-	-	-	-	-
X	-	-	-	⌈-	-	-	-⌉	-	-
L_1	-	⌈-	-⌉	-	-	ǂ	ǂ	-	-
S_1	[					ǂ	-	-	-
W_1	[		ǂ	-	-	-	ǂ		]
D_2	[						]	⌈-	-⌉
O_2	[	ǂ	-	-	-	-	-	[	]
Y_2	[	]	-	-	ne	-	-	a	-
E_3	omits (see the preceding line)								
C_4	-	-	-	-	-	-	[		]

254. é-gal šà húl-la dù -a-za šà-sìg hé-en-šub

S - - - - - - - - - - - - - -

X - ⌈ . . . - - x⌉ - - ∅ -

L_1 - ⌈- - - - gál la⌉- - - - - -

S_1 [ ] - - zu - - [ǂ - ⌈-⌉

W_1 [ǂ - - - ∅ - - - ǂ]

D_2 ǂ]⌈- -⌉ -

O_2 [ǂ ⌈-⌉ - - - zu - - ǂ]

Y_2 [ ] - - - - - ∅ - - ⌈- ⌉∅ zi

E_3 ⌈- - - - -⌉ - - zu - - - - [ ]

C_4 - - - - - - - zu ǂ]

255. lú hul eden ki-si- ga-ke$_4$ gù hu-mu-ra-ra-ra

S - - - - - - - - - - - - -

X - - gál ⌈- x x x⌉- - - - - - - - -

L_1 *- -[s]i - ig - -/[ǂ ǂ ǂ - *follows 262

S_1 [ ] - - - - -[ǂ - ǂ]

W_1 *[ǂ - - - *follows 262

D_2 ⌈- - x⌉[ǂ ⌈-⌉ - - - - - -

O_2 [ǂ gál - si - - - ǂ]

P_2 . . .

Y_2 [ ] - - - - ∅ - - ⌈-⌉gi$_4$ ∅ ∅

E_3 - - ⌈-⌉ ∅ - - ka/⌈- - -⌉ - - -

C^4_4 - ⌈-⌉ - - - - -! ǂ]

256. ki-us-ga šu-luḫ-ha gar-ra-zu

S — - - - - - e - - -

X — - - - - - e - - -

L_1 — - - - - - - [ ] - -

S_1 — [ǂ - - [ǂ ŧ]

W_1 — [ ] e - - -

D_2 — -⸢-⸣ - ŧ ǂ -

O_2 — [ǂ ⸢-⸣ - ⸢-?⸣[ ]

P_2 — [] ŧ ǂ ⸢- - - - - -⸣

Y_2 — [ǂ ge$_4$ ∅ - - - - -

E_3 — ⸢- - - - - - - -⸣ -

C_4 — [ǂ ŧ]⸢- -⸣ ŧ?]

L_4 — [ ] - -

257. ka$_5$ du$_6$ gul gul -la-ke$_4$ kun hé-ni-ib-ùr-ùr-re

S — - - - - - - - - - - - - - -

X — - - - - - - - - - - - - - -

A_1 — - - [ ]

L_1 — - zu ki du$_6$ ul du$_6$ ul - - / - - - - - - - ra

S_1 — [ǂ - - ⸢- -⸣ ŧ]

W_1 — [ǂ - - ŧ]

D_2 — ⸢-⸣[ǂ - - - ⸢- -⸣ e

P_2 — [ǂ ŧ]⸢- - - -⸣/ - ŧ]⸢- - x*⸣

Y_2 — [ ] - - - - ∅ - ⸢-⸣/∅ ∅ - - ⸢-⸣

E_3 — ⸢- - - du$_6$ - -⸣ - / - ⸢- - - -⸣ - e

C_4 — - ⸢- - -⸣ - ⸢ka⸣[ ]

L_4 — [ ] -/[ ] - -

*x = ⸢ra⸣ or ⸢e⸣

258.	abul		kalam	ma	gar	ra	zu
S	-		-	-	-	-	-
X	-	la	-	-	-	-	-
A_1	-		-	- [			]
L_1	-		-	-	-	-	-
S_1	[		ǂ	-	-	ɫ	]
W_1	. . .						
D_2	⸢-⸣ [					]	-
P_2	-		ɫ				]
Y_2	[ǂ		-	me	-	-	-
E_3	-		⸢-⸣	[ǂ	⸢-	-	-⸣
X_3	[					ǂ	⸢-⸣
C_4	⸢-⸣		⸢-	-⸣[			]

259.	ù	ku	ku	mušen (sup.)	mušen	šà	sìg	ga	ke₄	gùd	hé	em	ma	an	ús	
S	-	-	-	-	-	-	-	-	-	-	-	-	-	-	-	
X	⸢-	-	-	-	-	-	-	-	-	-⸣	-	-	-	-	⸢-	e⸣
A_1	-	-	-	-	[					/					]	
L_1	-	-	-	-	∅	-	-	-	-	-	-	-	-	-	-	
S_1	[					]	-	∅	-	-	-	ɫ			]	
W_1	[						]	-	-	ɫ]	-	x	x	[	]	
D_2	⸢-	-	-	-⸣	[			ǂ	-	/ [ǂ	-	-	-	-	-	e
P_2	-	-	-	ɫ					]	/ ɫ					]	
Y_2	[ ]-	-	-		∅	-	-	∅	-	-/	im	ma	ni	ib	-	
X_3	[									ǂ	*	-	-	-	ɫ]	*GIŠ.AK
C_4	[ǂ	-	-	-	-	-	- [		]	⸢-⸣[					]	

Line 259 as printed: ù-ku-ku[mušen] mušen šà-sìg-ga-ke₄ gùd hé-em-ma-an-ús

260. uru^{ki} tigi-da ù nu-ku-ku-za

S - ∅ ŧ] - - - - - - -

X ⌈- ∅ - -⌉ -⌈-⌉ - - da

A_1 - - ŧ]

L_1 - - - - - - - - - -

S_1 [ ] - - - - [ ]

W_1 [ ]⌈-⌉- - - -

D_2 - [ǂ ⌈- -⌉ - - da

P_2 - ∅ ŧ]

Y_2 [ ] - za - - - - -

X_3 [ ]- - - -

C_4 [ ] - - -[ ]

261. š̌à húl-la-da nu-nú- za

S - - - - - - -

X [] ⌈- - -⌉ - - ù da

A_1 - - [ ]

L_1 - ⌈-⌉ - - nú - -

S_1 [ ] - - n[ú]

W_1 [ǂ -

D_2 - ⌈- - - - -⌉ ù da

P_2 - ⌈-⌉[ ]

Y_2 [ǂ - - dù* - - - *adds -a

X_3 [ ] -

C_4 [ǂ ⌈- -⌉ - ŧ]

262.	tùr-e si gu_4 ^{d}nanna-ke_4	
S	- - - - - - -	
X	[ ]⌜-⌝[ǂ gim?	
A_1	- ǂ]	
L_1	- -⌜-⌝ - - - -	
S_1	[ǂ* - - - [ ]	*poss. = i]g (cf. C_4)
W_1	[ ]⌜-⌝ -	
D_2	⌜- - - -⌝ - - -	
P_2	⌜-⌝[ ]	
Y_2	- - - - - - -	
X_3	[ ]⌜-⌝	
C_4	[ǂ* ǂ?]	*adds -si-ig

263.	eden ki-si-ga-ke_4 $nigin_2$-na -gim	$še_{26}$	hu-mu-un-gi_4-gi_4-gi_4
S	- - - - - - - -	$še_{25}$	- - - - / - -
X	[		] ⌜- - -⌝
A_1	ǂ		]
L_1	* - ⌜si - - - ∅ x -	KA x X⌝	- - - - - -
S_1	[ ] ⌜-? -?⌝ -	⌜-⌝	- - - [ ]
W_1	**[ǂ ⌜-⌝ - ∅ ∅ ∅	⌜-⌝	- - - - [ ]
P_2	- - ǂ -]/		-[ ]
Y_2	[ǂ - - - - x (x) -	KA	- - ∅ / - - ǂ]
X_3	omits		
C_4	[ǂ - ⌜-⌝ -? gá ∅ ǂ		]

*follows 254

**follows 254

264. gú ^{giš}má gíd-da íd-da-zu ú gíd-da hé-em-mú

S - ∅ - ⌈-⌉ - - - - - - - - - - -

L_1 [ł ƚ ł - - - - - - ⌈- -⌉

S_1 [ ] - - - - - - - [ ]

W_1 [ ] - - -

I_2 [ł

P_2 - ∅ -! - - ⌈-⌉ ƚ]

Y_2 [ł ∅ - - ∅ - - - - - - ⌈-⌉[ ]

X_3 [ł - - - - - - -

C_4 [ł - - ⌈- - - -⌉ - ƚ]

265. har-ra-an ^{giš}gigir-ra ba-gar-ra-zu ú a-nir hé-em-mú

S - - - - - - - - - - - - - - - -

L_1 [ł - - - - - - ⌈-⌉

S_1 [ł? - - - - - - - - - [ ]

W_1 [ ] ⌈- -⌉[ ] -

I_2 [ ] -

P_2 - - - - - ∅ - - - - [ ]

Y_2 [ł - - - - ∅ ∅ ∅ ∅ - - ⌈-⌉[ ]

X_3 [ ] - -/[ ] -

C_4 [ł - - - ⌈-⌉ e -* ⌈- -⌉ - - ƚ] *inserts -ab-

266. mìn-kam-ma-šè gú má gíd-da ki a-lá íd-da-zu

Q [ ]⌈-⌉[ ]

S - - - - - - - - - - - - - -

L_1 ⌈-⌉[ǂ Ø - - - -

S_1 [ǂ - - - - - - - - [ ]

W_1 [ ]⌈- -⌉ ŧ ǂ

I_2 [ ] -

P_2 - - - - - - - - - [ ]

X_3 [ǂ - - - - - -

C_4 [ǂ - - ⌈- - - -⌉ - ŧ]

G_4 [ǂ ⌈- - -⌉ - - -

267. šeg$_9$-bar mul muš-ul$_4$ kur-ra-ke$_4$ lú na-an-ni-ib-dib-bé

Q - - - ⌈- - - -⌉ Ø - ǂ]

S - - ⌈-⌉ - - - - ka/ - - - - - - - -

A_1 - - ŧ /]- [ ]

L_1 - - ŧ ǂ - - - Ø - -

S_1 [ ] - - - - - - - - - Ø - [ ]

W_1 [ ] ⌈- -⌉[ ]

X_1 [/] - [´]

I_2 [k]a /[ǂ

P_2 - - mú ul$_4$ anše - - ka - [ ]

X_3 [ ] - - - Ø Ø - -

C_4 [ǂ - - - ŧ ǂ -[ ]

G_4 [ǂ - - - - - - - Ø Ø - -

268. eden šà ú ša$_6$-ga mú-a-zu gi ír-ra hé-em-mú

Q ⌈-⌉ - - - ∅ - ∅ bi gi$_4$ - ∅ ⌈-⌉[ ]

S - - [ ]⌈-⌉ - - - - - - - - - -

A_1 - - - ŧ /]- ŧ]

L_1 - - - - ŧ] ŧ] - - - ∅ -

S_1 [ ]⌈-⌉ - - bi - - - - [ ]

W_1 [ ] - ŧ]

X_1 [ǂ - - b[i]

I_2 [ǂ -

P_2 - - ∅ - - - - - - - -[/]- ŧ]

X_3 [ ]- - - ∅ DI - -

G_4 [ ]x - za gú a - - -$^!$ -

C_4 - - - - - - - - - - - [ ]

269. a-ga-dè^{ki} a du$_{10}$-ga dé-a-zu a mun-na hé-em-dé

Q -⌈- - -⌉ - - - da ∅ bi - - ∅ ba [ ]

S -⌈- -⌉- - - - - - - - - ⌈-⌉ - - en -

A_1 íd da ∅ ∅ - ŧ /]- ŧ]

L_1 - - - - - ŧ D]U - - - - ∅ - - DU

S_1 [ ] - DU - - - - - - - en []

W_1 [ ] - - ⌈-⌉[ ]

X_1 [ǂ - - bi[ ]

I_2 [ǂ$^!$

P_2 - - - - - - - - -⌈-/-⌉ [ǂ - - en -

X_3 [ǂ - - en DU$^?$* *over eras.

C_4 - - - - - - - - - - - [ ]

G_4 [ ]bi - - -$^!$ - - -* *line repeated, omitting na

270. uru^{ki}-bi-a ga-tuš bí-in-du$_{11}$-ga ki-tuš na-an-ni-du$_{10}$-ge

Q	- ø - - - - - - - ⌈- - - - -⌉ ø ŧ]
S	- ø - - - - - - - - - - - - na - -
L_1	- - - - - [ɟ - ⌈- -⌉ - - - - ø - -
S_1	[ɟ - - ø - ⌈-⌉ - - - - - ŧ]
W_1	[ɟ ⌈- -⌉ ø ŧ]
X_1	[ ] - - tuš [ ]
I_2	[ɟ /[ɟ*
P_2	ŧ ɟ - - - - - /[ɟ - na - -
A_4	⌈- ø - -⌉[ ]
C_4	- ø - - - - - - - - - - - [ ]
G_4	[- ɟ - - ⌈-⌉ ŧ]

*or d]u$_{10}$

271. a-ga-dè^{ki}-a ga-nú bí-in-du$_{11}$-ga ki-nú na-an-ni-du$_{10}$-ge

Q	- - - - ø - - - ø - ⌈-⌉ - ø - - ø - ø
S	- - - - - - - - - - - /- - - - na - -
L_1	- - - - -⌈- - -⌉ - - - /- - - - - - -
S_1	[ ]⌈- - - ø -⌉ - - - - - ŧ]
W_1	[ ]⌈- - -⌉[ ]
X_1	[ ] - - ŧ]
I_2	[ɟ/[ɟ*
P_2	[ɟ - - - -/[ɟ [ɟ - -
A_4	- - - - [ ]
C_4	ŧ]- - - - - - - - - ŧ]

*or d]u$_{10}$

272. ì-ne-éš ^{d}utu u_4 -dè-e-a ur_5 hé-en-na-nam-ma-àm

Q -- ∅ --- e ⌈-⌉ ∅ ∅ - - ∅ - - ∅ ∅

S -- - --- - - - - - - - - - -!

L_1 -- - --- - - - - - - ∅ - - - ∅

S_1 [ ] - - ƚ]

W_1 [ ]⌈-⌉ - - - [ ]

X_1 [ ] - ƚ]

X_3 [ƚ* - ∅ ∅ - *or n]a?

A_4 -- - - [ ]

C_4 [ƚ - - --- - - - - -? ƚ]

273. gú ^{giš}má gíd-da íd-da-ba ú gíd-da ba-an-mú

Q - - - ∅ ∅ - ⌈- - ^{ù}⌉- - ∅ - ∅ -

S - ∅ - [ ] - - - - ⌈-⌉ - - - - - -

L_1 - - - - ∅ - - zu - - - - - - -

W_1 [ ]⌈- - -⌉[ ]

X_1 . . .

X_3 [ƚ - ⌈-⌉ -! -

A_4 - - - ƚ]

C_4 [ ]- - - - - - - [ ]

274. har-ra-an ^{giš}gigir-ra ba-gar-ra-ba ú a-nir ba-an-mú

Q - - - - - ∅ - - - - - - ∅ - - ∅ -

S - - - [ ] - - - - - ƚ] - - - -

W [ ]⌈-⌉[ ]

L_1 - - - - - - - - - zu - - - - - - -

X_1 [ ] ⌈-⌉ ∅ - ⌈-⌉[ ]

X_3 [ ] - hé ∅ -

A_4 - - - -[ ]

C_4 [ƚ - ∅ - e -* -[ ] *adds -ab-

275. mìn-kam-ma-šè gú ^{giš}má gíd-da ki a-lá íd-da-ba

G [ǂ ⌈-⌉

Q - - - - - - - ∅ ∅ ∅ ∅ ∅ - - ∅

S - - - - ɫ] -/ - - - ɫ]-

L_1 - - - - - - - - ∅ - ∅ - - - zu

X_3 [ ] - - - - zu

A_4 - - ∅ - - [ ]

C_4 [ ] - - ⌈-⌉ ∅ - - - [ ]

276. šeg$_9$-bar mul muš-ul$_4$ kur-ra-ke$_4$ lú nu-mu-ni-in-dib-bé

G [ ] - -

Q - - - - - - - ∅ - - ∅ ∅ ∅ - ∅

S - - - - - - - ka /- - - - - - -

L_1 - - - - - - - - - - - - ∅ -! -

X_1 [ǂ ɫ /]⌈- -⌉ - [ǂ ⌈- -⌉

X_3 [ǂ - na ∅ ∅ ⌈an⌉ - -

A_4 - - ɫ]

C_4 [ǂ - - - [ ]

277. eden šà ú ša$_6$-ga mú-a-bé gi ír-ra ba-an-mú

G [ ] - - -

Q - - - - ∅ - ∅ - - - ∅ - ∅ -

S ɫ ǂ - - - - - ba/- - - - - -

L_1 - - - - - - - - /- - - - - -

X_1 [ǂ - ⌈-⌉ - - ɫ ǂ ∅ - ∅ ⌈-⌉

X_3 [ǂ - - - - -

A_4 *- ∅ - - - - -⌈∅ -⌉? ɫ?] *line written on edge

C_4 [ ]⌈-⌉[ ]

278. a-ga-dè[ki] a du_{10}-ga dé-a-bi a mun-na ba-an-dé

G [ ] - - -

Q - - - - - ⌈- -⌉ da Ø⌈- -⌉ - Ø - Ø -

S - - - - - - - - - ba/- - - - - - -

L_1 - - - - - - - DU[!] - - /- - Ø - - DU* *over eras.

Y_2 [ ]⌈- -⌉[ ]

X_3 [ ] - - -

A_4 - - ŧ]

279. uru[ki]-bi-a ga-tuš bí-in-du_{11}-ga ki-tuš nu-um-ma-an-na-du_{10}

G [ǂ - Ø - -

Q - Ø - - - [ ] ŧ] - na Ø Ø Ø ni -

S - Ø - - - - - - - - -/ - - - - - - - -

L_1 - - - - - - - - - - -/ - ŧ]⌈-⌉ - Ø Ø - ge

X_1 [ ]⌈- - - - -⌉ - - ŧ ǂ

Y_2 [ǂ - ǂ]

X_3 [ ] ⌈- -⌉ [ ]⌈-⌉ - Ø - - -

A_4 - [ ]

280. a-ga-dè[ki]-a ga-nú bí-in-du_{11}-ga ki-nú nu-um-ma-an-na-du_{10}

G [ǂ - - ⌈-⌉/[ǂ -

Q - - - - Ø - [ ]⌈- Ø -⌉ - Ø Ø Ø Ø Ø Ø Ø Ø

S - - - - - - - - - - - /- - - - - - - ⌈-⌉

L_1 [ ]⌈-⌉[ǂ ⌈-⌉ - - /[ǂ - - ⌈- Ø Ø - ge⌉

X_1 [ ] - - ⌈-⌉ - - [/ ǂ - ŧ]

Y_2 [ǂ - ⌈-⌉[ ]

X_3 [ ] - - - /[ ]⌈-⌉ - - - du_{10}

I_4 [ǂ [ǂ [ ]

281.	a-ga-dè^{ki} hul-a ^{d}inanna zà-mí
G	[ǂ -
Q	- - - - - [ ]⌈- -⌉ - -
S	- - - - [/]- - - [ ]
L_1	[ǂ - - - - -
X_1	[ǂ - - - ŧ]
O_2	. . . (?)
A_2	⌈-⌉[/]- [ ]
Y_2	[ǂ ∅ - - [ ]
X_3	[ǂ -
I_4	[ǂ ⌈-⌉

CHAPTER VIII

PHILOLOGICAL COMMENTARY[1]

1. The incipit (sag-ki gíd-da) is entered in the catalogues UET 6 123: 17 (Kramer, RA 55 171), TRS 28:12 (Kramer, BASOR 88 17), and UM 29-15-155:18 (Kramer, BASOR 88 15). In the Ur catalogue, it is bracketed by the great hymn to Enlil and the debate between Hoe and Plow, in the Louvre and Philadelphia catalogues by the debate between Ewe and Grain, and the otherwise unknown eden i-lu gar-ù.

For sag-ki—gíd used to signal the downfall of dynasties, see Chap. III.[2] The phrase always denotes divine (or royal) displeasure directed toward a city, land, or people:

(^{d}en-líl-le . . .) kur-da sag-ki um-ma-da-an-gíd
ki-bal-da nam im-ma-da-an-ku$_5$
ki-bal kur sag-ki gíd-da-ni-šè
a-a-mu ^{d}en-líl-le im-ma-ši-in-gi$_4$-gi$_4$
After Enlil frowned upon the foreign land,
He cursed the rebellious land,
To the rebellious foreign land, upon which he frowned,
My father Enlil sent me.
(AOAT 1 298:106ff.)
(uru . . .) ^{d}en-líl-le sag-ki gíd-da-gim gú-bi na-an-zi-zi
Like a city frowned upon by Enlil, may it never raise its head.
(In Eb 50 = 109)
en-né ki-bal kur sag-ki-ni ù-ma-da-gíd-da
When the lord (Ningirsu) frowned upon the rebellious foreign land (Gudea Cyl. B viii 4)

sag-ki gíd-da-ni un-bi saḫar-e-eš ri-ga
When he (Ninazu) frowns, its people are thrown to the dust (TCS 3 42:438)

^{d}girra-gim sag-ki gíd-da-mu gù téš-a bí-sì
Like the fire-god, my (Urnammu's) frown instills obedience (ZA 53 119 ii 39)

^{d}en-líl-le ma-da sag-ki ba-da-gíd-da-ba
When Enlil frowned on the country (AOAT 5 63 [*Hoe and Plow*])

uru ^{d}inanna sag-ki ba-gíd-i . . .
The city upon which Inanna frowns . . . (Inninšagura 33)

See also TCL 15 1:27, and the *Tukultininurta Epic* iii 46 (AAA 20 pl. 104) *nekelmânni* *^{d}aššur šar kiš[ūti]* "Aššur, king of the world, has frowned upon me."

2f. For the killing of the bull of heaven by Gilgamesh and Enkidu, see Falkenstein, RLA 3 361; Borger, RLA 4 413f. The translation of these lines by CAD s.v. *alû* B must be rejected, for the reasons given by Durand.

Kish and Uruk were the two dominant powers of an earlier, semilegendary period of Sumerian history, the period of the heroic rulers of Uruk (Enmerkar, Lugalbanda, Gilgamesh), when the prominence of Kish in northern Babylonia led to the use of the title "King of Kish" by any king who could claim hegemony over that region.[3] These same cities were also the dominant powers in Babylonia at the end of the Early Dynastic period, and Sargon's displacement of his patron, Urzababa of Kish, and his conquest of Lugalzagesi of Uruk, all, as in this text, with divine sanction, are the subject of a Sumerian historical tale (see Chap. III). An Akkadian literary-historical text[4] portrays Sargon's victory over Lugalzagesi —a feat attested on Sargon's own monuments[5]—as a liberation for Kish. However, there is no contemporary evidence that Uruk's hegemony extended as far north as Kish.

Interestingly, Inanna was the patron goddess of both Kish and Uruk, as well as Agade. Her establishment of her cult-center in Agade (lines 7ff.) and her subsequent abandonment of the city (60ff.) represent the earthly manifestations of decisions by Enlil (1-6; 57) regarding the transferral of sovereignty. Cf. Chap. III and the comm. to lines 55f. and 57.

4. KI.UD is used to introduce Sargon in a similar context in the Sumerian Sargon Legend TRS 73:10 KI.UD-bi šar-ru-um-ki-in uru-ni u[ru?] (Chap. III).

5. Compare Shulgi D 60 sig-ta igi-nim-šè kalam-[ma] ^{d}en-líl lugal kur-kur-[ra-ke$_4$] nam-sipa-bi ma-ra-[an-sum] "From south to north, Enlil, king of all the lands, gave me the shepherdhood of the homeland." Nam-en and nam-lugal reflect claims to legitimacy in Uruk and Kish (or south and north; cf. Falkenstein and Durand) respectively, but the pair had also become nearly synonymous terms for the ruler's function, as in l. 67, or Shulgi D 287 nam-en nam-lugal-la u$_4$ sù-da nam-šè gú-mu-rí-íb-tar^{ar} "I shall declare long-lasting sovereignty and kingship as your fate!"

7f. All references support the understanding of ama$_5$ as a part of a house or a special building reserved for women. It can be extended metaphorically to apply to the entire temple or even city (as here) of a female deity, but this is no reason to translate "storehouse" (Krecher Kultlyrik 112, ZA 60 202).[6] Durand p. 179 would connect the ama$_5$ (É x MÍ) of Inanna with the é-mí, estate of the ruler's wife, known from Pre-Sargonic Girsu.[7]

9. The interpretation of the crucial lines 56f. (see the comm. thereto) depends partly on understanding the absence of é "house, temple" before Ulmaš here as indicating that Inanna, according to this composition, did not have a proper temple in Agade.

10f. Contrary to Falkenstein, there is no reason to assign inherent feminine semantic content to bàn-da, which here means "young," as in nin$_9$ bàn-da, šeš bàn-da, lú bàn-da[8] or ^{d}en-líl-bàn-da.[9] Here, dumu bàn-da is translated "young girl" because the ama$_5$ is an area restricted to females (see the comm. to 8). One of Inanna's powers, according to Inninšagura 138, is the ability to construct an é and an ama$_5$.

12. é-níg-ga-ra is not from *é-níg-gar-ra "building where things are put" (so Falkenstein), but is to be understood as "building for goods," as in níg-ga(r) (GA = gar$_9$ or gur$_{11}$) = *makkūru*. Cf. Kraus Viehhaltung 10ff.

14f. For the pair ú nir-gál—a nir-gál, cf. Römer Königshymnen 216.

16f. Limet, RAI 17 66 suggests that the ablutions here are those performed preliminary to specific monthly festivals.

18. For téš—kú, see Green, JCS 30 153f. Here, it means "to eat together," whereas in 186f. it means "to be eaten together."

19-28. Cf. Pettinato, Mesopotamia 7 135f.

19. Durand's equation of lú bar-ra with *ubarum,* and the connection of the latter with uru bar (-ra), which would then be equivalent to *wabartum,*[10] appear too specific, at least for this passage. The simile with "unusual birds" suggests that exotic-looking foreigners are meant here, with no more specific status implied.

20. Civil's interpretation of this line (JAOS 92 271), understanding le-um as a loan from Akk. *lē'um* "writing board, document," and GUD.AN.NA in W_1 as a play on the homonymity of Akk. *lium* (= GUD.AN.NA) "bull" and *lē'um,* must be correct, because of the parallel in the Lugalannemundu text ZA 42 40:5f. (cf. Chap. III):

> PA ⌈x x x⌉ *a-na le-im ú-te-er* le-um-ma gur[11]-ru-dam
> gú-un kur-kur-ra-ke₄ mi-ni-in-gi-na[12]
> (The one who) in order to re-enter . . .[13] on the roll (of tribute payers)
> Established the tribute to be paid by foreign countries

In that text, the ruler of Marḫaši leads the list of rebellious subjects (l. 11), and Marḫaši is the subject of the fragmentary first part of A ii (op. cit. 41). Elsewhere there (A iii 29′f., iv 10′f., and 27′f.), Marḫaši occurs as part of a list of lands intended to represent the known world beyond Babylonia: Cedar Mountains, Elam, Marḫaši, Gutium, Subir, Amurru, and Sutium. Marḫaši also appears in the rebel coalition against Naramsin in the fictional inscription RA 70 112:33 and 115:14′. In the Agade period, Marḫaši was known as Baraḫšum (RGTC I 25). According to Sargonic inscriptions, it was conquered by Sargon, rebelled, and was reconquered by his successor Rimush.[14]

It is possible, upon collation, that the ⌈ki⌉ of Y_1 is really a giš (i.e., ^gišle-um-ma), but the omission of the ki would be peculiar in that ms., which writes ki in l. 48 after Meluḫḫa, when it is omitted by six other mss. The -šè in U_2 cannot be giš.

21. Boehmer, ZA 64 1ff., equates the áb-za-za with the water buffalo, which first appears in Mesopotamian iconography in the Sargonic period, and disappears soon after. The animal would be an import from the Indus Valley (= Meluḫḫa, cf. l. 48), along with the "mighty elephant"; Boehmer says that a Syrian elephant would not have been exotic enough to merit mention in this context (ibid. 11f.).

The topos of exotic animals as booty and tribute in later sources and iconography is mentioned by Boehmer, loc. cit. 5. Add, e.g., Aššurnaṣirpal's zoo (Ir 14 34:95ff.). For the orthography and reading of the word for "monkey," cf. Powell, ZA 68 178, and Klein, JCS 31 149ff.

23. Cf. Durand's alternative suggestion for the first two animals here. The reading $dara_3$ has been preferred to kušu (U.PIRIG), which otherwise never occurs alone outside lexical texts (Civil AS 20 134ff. with the author's privately distributed additions). $dara_3$ kur-ra is found only in Kramer, Essays Finkelstein 140:11. $dara_3$/kušu kur-ra > anše-kur-ra "horse" in Y_1 and U_3 is a scribal simplification of a lexically difficult phrase.

The end of the line follows A and U_3 for want of a clear Nippur variant. Whether to understand síg gíd "long wool" (cf. Waetzoldt Textilindustrie 47 n. 46) or SÍG.SUD_4 as in

$^{(udu/túg)}$SÍG.SUD/SUD_4(suluḫu), a special kind of sheep and garments made from its fleece (see AHW s.v. *suluḫḫû*, ELA 416, Lugalbanda-Hurrum 329), is likewise unclear.

24. Sleeplessness can be an affliction or annoyance, as in Atraḫasis, or a sign of eager industriousness, as here and 260f., and the Gudea passages quoted by Falkenstein p. 83.

25f. The reading é-ÁŠ is paleographically certain in both lines, but no meaning or parallels suggest themselves. Wilcke (written comm.) suggests simply é-zíz-a and é-zíz-babbar-ra, as storage buildings for wheat, parallel to the $araḫ_4$-še in l. 27; Sjöberg suggests áš = *ḫišiḫtu* "need, necessity."

28. Careful collation supports the reading im/um *ba-* for all mss. except X, which seems to read the line's beginning differently. Y_2, an especially faulty ms. (See Chap. V), understood im to be part of the prefix chain. Otherwise, the mss. support Durand's connection with še bal-a gur_7-a im-ùr-ra "bringing barley and hauling it to the granary" (So Maeda, ASJ 1 20). However, the variants um for im are difficult to explain if one accepts Durand's etymology of im = "clay."

29ff. Inanna bestows similar attributes on the various age grades of Uruk's population in *Inanna and Enki* (St Po 10 50:33ff.). For the double repetition of these age grades in 196ff., see Chap. IV.

30. In *Inanna and Enki* (St Po 10 50:33) the elders are given šà-kúš-ù "discussion," parallel to the ad-gi_4-gi_4 given the bur-šu-ma there and the um-ma here. For this reason, the translation of inim-inim-ma in this line is based on Lu 3:34 (MSL 12 122) inim-inim du_{11}-du_{11} = *muštāmû* "one who takes counsel." This quality (counsel) is withdrawn from the city by Utu in 70, where it has a more specific legal connotation.

34. UM+ME is not perfectly preserved in any ms., but is fairly certain in S_1 and V_3 and possible in G I and Y_2. A and U_3 have nearly identical signs that begin with a single horizontal; were it double, both could be sparse UM+ME, but it is single in both mss. A reading of GÌR.$NITA_2$ close to šagin(a) is confirmed by the evidence assembled by Lieberman, HSS 22 447 (see also the variant GÌR.$NITA_2$ for sanga in l. 51 of this composition). However, the writing GÌR.$NITA_2$-ma in H_1 and U_2 (> alim?-ma in Y_2) suggests that some scribes read the compound as Akk. *šakkanakkum*-ma. What the word means here is a mystery, and the syntactic and semantic difficulties of the whole line are reflected in the unusually large number of manuscript variants.

35f. Music in the city can signal prosperity, as here, in l. 260, and, e.g., in LW 12:16f., or can indicate just the opposite when accompanying laments, as in 199ff., below.

38f. Both ú-sal-la nú and ki $ša_6$-ga igi-du_8 are found together in the Lugalzagesi inscription BE 1 87 iii 22ff.:

kur ú-sal-la/ḫa-mu-da-nú
nam-lú-ulu_3/ú-šim-gim/šu-dagal ḫa-mu-da-du_{11}
. . . (2 lines)
un-e/ki $ša_6$-ga/igi ḫa-mu-da-du_8
Under me, may the lands rest contentedly,
May the populace become as widespread as grass . . .
May the people experience happiness!

Cf. TCL 15 12:51 kalam-ma ki ur_5 $ša_6$-ge-bi gá-e-me-en "I (Urnammu) am the agent of happiness for the land" (Castellino, ZA 53 119, 122, 128; Wilcke, RAI 19 212). The unambiguously positive meaning of ki $ša_6$-ga in these passages suggests that the variants ki-sì-ga in l. 39 for ki šá$_6$-ga, and the variants ki šá$_6$-ga for ki-sì-ga in Ninmešara 69 (YNER 3 22), are due purely to phonetic similarity, and not because ki šá$_6$-ga is a euphemism for ki-sì-ga (Hallo, YNER 3 55).

40f. For these lines, see Chap. III.

42. For the plene writing -ú-ús in A, see the comm. to 158.

43. For KÁ.GAL = abul, see Lieberman, HSS 72 133f., Steinkeller, RA 72 73f. The image is of a flood of commerce passing through the city's gates.

45. The choice of ní-ba-ke$_4$ over ní-ba/bi-ta was made on the basis of the most difficult reading.

46. For this line, see Chap. III. Is the V$_3$ variant to be restored lú ki nu-[túm], after the passage from the *Marriage of Martu* quoted there?

47. Nothing in the references cited by Falkenstein makes it necessary to interpret du$_7$ here (and in other passages with gu$_4$ and máš) as šu-du$_7$ "perfect, unblemished." A millennium or more later, NB texts do refer to oxen brought as offerings as *šuklulu* (= šu-du$_7$) "ungelded" (CAD A/1 369), but there is no reason to apply this to our line, nor is there any evidence that bucks (he-goats) were ever gelded.

51f. Because the ensi$_2$ was the highest provincial official in the Sargonic as well as the Ur III period, and the temple economies were directed by a sanga in both periods also, the administrative hierarchy reflected in line 51 fits either period. Why the sa$_{12}$-du$_5$, an official subordinate to the sanga and a sort of land registrar and inspector (cf. M. Lambert, Or An 13 7), should appear in 52 in connection with the supply of offerings, is a mystery. Likewise mysterious is the coupling of these land registrars with the Gu'edena, a fertile region divided between Lagash and Umma. Both Durand and Wilcke reject gú-eden-na here as referring to that specific region, and translate it literally as "edge of the plains," but this does nothing to enhance the line's intelligibility.

The variant GÌR.NITA$_2$ for sanga in ms. B indicates that the suggested readings for that compound are close to the truth. See most recently Lieberman, HSS 22 447 (sağğena), and Powell, JCS 25 182 (šağğana).

Van Dijk's suggestion (Syncrétisme 191) that the regular provision of offerings (l. 53) by the provincial administrators to Inanna of Agade in some way supplanted the supply of offerings by these officials to the Enlil temple at Nippur, is very plausible in light of l. 57 (but see the comm. thereto).

54. This line probably concludes the preceding section, but no satisfactory solution for the variant-laden second half of the line suggests itself. Note that G is the only Nippur text preserved there. Oelsner reports that the sign is not KA, DÙL, or SAG, and the sign he draws looks more like the preceding GIM than anything else, but judging from the photo, it is not really that either.

The scribes of S$_1$ Y$_1$ omit this and the following lines because they (or someone dictating to them) skipped from the sign below the nidba beginning 53 to the sign below the nidba beginning 55.

55ff. Lines 55-57 represent a turning point in the narrative, but are unfortunately highly elliptical. What *is* clear, is Inanna's abandonment of Agade in 60-65, followed by the withdrawal of favor by other important deities in 66-76, and Naramsin's dream of his dynasty's fall in 83ff. The similarity of these events with the topos of divine abandonment in the city laments (see Chap. III) suggests that this abandonment should be precipitated by a decision of Enlil, a suggestion which provides the basis of interpretation for 57.

55f. The reason Inanna cannot accept the offerings is to be found, with Durand, in the absence of a real temple fit to accommodate all that is being presented to her, which offends her aristocratic sensibilities. Lines 8 and 9 state that the city of Agade was her "woman's domain," and her throne was in Ulmaš, but the text nowhere speaks of an actual temple built for her. In our lines then, she cannot accept the offerings brought to her until a temple is founded (ki-gar).[15] This dissatisfaction accords well with the image of Inanna in other compositions, such as *Inanna and Enki,* and *Enki and the World Order.*

Line 56, admittedly, does not read smoothly. The majority of Nippur texts read di, not dù, and because dù "to build" is the easier reading in the presence of é "house, temple," I have read di (*marû* nonfinite form of du_{11}). That dumu-gi_7 cannot mean "Sumerian" (as argued for most recently by Alster Shuruppak 103f.) is proved by line 249, where dumu-gi_7 is applied to prosperous citizens of Agade. For the meaning "aristocrat" cf. Wilcke, RAI 19 230 ("von edler Abkunft").

57. Here, again with Durand, Enlil (in his temple Ekur) has refused a favorable oracle to build a temple for Inanna, the very temple which, according to the preceding lines, would enable her to accept the offerings flowing in to her from the various provinces of the empire. If the offerings brought to Agade in l. 53 are indeed supplanting those that should be brought to Nippur, then Enlil's refusal is understandable. Yet, Enlil frequently needs, or gives, no reason for passing negatively against a city or dynasty (see Chap. III), and Enlil's initial hostility here may be simply capricious, or, for humans, incomprehensible divine will.

The inim é-kur-ra here is the oracle that so depresses Naramsin in 88 (nam-é-kur-ra-šè), which he attempts to reverse by extispicy in 94ff., and is the negative pronouncement (níg-du_{11}-ga) that he tries to counter with force in 98ff. For the "silence" here cf. the same phrase used in connection with Enlil's hostility in the passage LSU 58ff. cited in Chap. III.

Seeking Enlil's sanction for a major new temple is known from "divine journey" texts,[16] but more relevant here is the introduction to Gudea's Cylinder A, where Enlil is implicitly granting approval for Ningirsu's commission to Gudea to build the Eninnu. The figurative and elliptical language there can be interpreted, through the phrase ^{d}en-líl-e en ^{d}nin-gír-su-šè igi-zi mu-ši-bar "Enlil looked approvingly at lord Ningirsu" (Cyl. A i 3), by means of Enlil's gaze in the introductions to Samsuiluna bilinguals B and C, which instigates the building of the walls of Sippar and Kish respectively:

u_4 ^{d}en-líl-le/lugal dingir-re-e-ne
en gal kur-kur-ra-ke_4
^{d}utu-ra igi $ša_6$-ga-na
mu-un-ši-in-bar-ra-àm
Zimbir^{ki}/uru ul ki-šu-peš-a-ni
bàd-bi dù-ù-dè . . . bí-in-du_{11}-ga-a
When Enlil, king of the gods
Great lord of all the lands,
Looked benevolently at Utu, and
Commanded . . . the building of the wall
Of Sippar, the eternal city,[17] his cult place
(RA 39 6f.)[18]

^{d}en-l[íl] . . . sipa nam- [tar-re]
^{d}za-ba_4-ba_4 ^{d}in[anna] . . .
[igi kù-g]a-na nam-mu/-un-ne-ši-in-du_8
[uru] kiš^{ki} /[ki-šu-p]eš sag-gá
[ki-tuš] maḫ-a-ne-ne

[bàd]-bi dù-ù-dè . . .
[šà-ga]- ni zi-dè-eš [na]m-mu-un-túm
Enlil . . . shepherd who determines destinies,
Looked radiantly at Zababa and Inanna . . .
He sincerely desired . . .
The building of the wall of the city of Kish,
The chief cult-place, their august residence. (Sollberger RA 63 31ff.)

In all three cases, the chain of authority is Enlil—City god(s)—ruler, and in our line, it is Enlil refusing Inanna, city god of Agade, and thereby refusing Naramsin, permission to build a temple.

For Enlil's decision precipitating the abandonment of a city by its god (as Inanna is about to do here), see Chaps. I and III, and the study of Green cited there.

The verb ki—gar in 56, used for founding a temple, is found in an Early Dynastic context which also suggests that Enlil's cooperation was needed for such an enterprise:

^{d}en-líl a-nun
ki mu-gar-gar
dingir gal-gal
Enlil, princely progeny,
The founder for
The great gods
(OIP 99 46:11ff.)[19]

58. The line is difficult. The use of tuk_4 with lá is unique, and, whereas tuk_4 is a good parallel to ní—te of the following line, the subject here cannot be Inanna, as it is in 59, unless the infix -na- refers to Enlil (= Ekur of 57), which is possible, but less probable than Inanna. Cf. the variants uru mu-un-da-tuk_4-e(n) to Ninmešara 79.

60ff. See Chap. III. The parallels cited there indicate that the variants -šè in J_2O_3 for 60 are erroneous. The point is that Inanna is abandoning Agade, not moving to another residence (e.g., Uruk, as Durand).

63ff. In these three lines, the theme of Inanna's abandonment of Agade is developed with the image of the warrior goddess leaving the city on a military expedition from which, in this context, she would not return. There is no question of Inanna fighting Agade here, as one variant only (B in 64) would have it, only of a militant march out of the city.

63. Cf. LW 1d:6f.:

⌈x⌉-gim ^{giš}šukur mi-ni-in-te-te [ ]
kal-ga ^{giš}tukul-e sag ba-an-sum-ma mè [ ]
Like a . . ., he approached the lances . . .,
A mighty one rushing to arms, battle . . . .

For the Nippur mss.'s ^{giš}tukul-(l)a vs. ^{giš}tukul-e in other mss., cf. Angim 124 me-lám an-gim dugud-da-a sag nu-mu-u[n-gá-gá] (ms. P′. Note -a also in the variants of mss. E and N′.)

64. The Nippur mss. è is preferred over the non-Nippur ri, which probably was influenced by the following line.

65. Despite the variant of E, the reading gaba-ba ì-in-ri is rejected here. The only instances of a prolonged *i* prefix in this text are 38 and 191 (i-im-nú), and 208 and 223 (i-im-gá-gá-ne). Only one definite variant ì-im for i-im- is attested (Y_2 in 223), whereas here in one

line there would be six mss. reading ì-in-. For gaba—ri with the dative suffix -ra, cf. TRS 70:26, and see Jacobsen, JANES 5 206.

66. In addition to Falkenstein's references to similar passages of time, cf. the Sargon Legend 3NT 296 (see Chap. III) 8 and r. 19 u_4 iá-àm u_4 u-àm ba-zal-la-ta "when five or ten days had passed."

67ff. See Chap. III.

67. sa here = *šukuttu* "ornament, insignia." Cf. Erra I 127 *šukuttu sīmat bēlūtika* "insignia appropriate to your sovereignty," parallel there to *agê bēlūtika* (128) "your sovereign crown," as sa is parallel to aga "crown" here.

68. With Hallo (YNER 3 97f.) and Durand, ma-an-si-um is to be compared with (giš)ma-(an-)si-ú/um in *Inanna and Ebiḫ,* parallel there, as here to gišgu-za "throne."[20] The word clearly designates a symbol of royalty which cannot be more specifically identified (cf. CAD *maššû* B [*massû, mansû*] "a symbol or signal"). Durand translates "corbeille," apparently connecting it with *maššû* A, but if it were the symbolic basket carried by the king, one would expect gidusu = *tupšikku.* Alster Shuruppak 82 says that it is the same as gima-an-sim "sieve," and is "an astral sign," but doesn't explain himself further.

The identification of ma-an-si-um with a king named in an "historical" omen[21] is highly dubious, and any attempt to see a person here[22] should be abandoned in view of the *Inanna and Ebiḫ* parallel.[23]

69. That Ninurta should be responsible for bestowing and withdrawing the symbols of royalty is somewhat of a mystery. The importance of Nippur in Ur III and OB coronation ceremonies is well known,[24] but it is Enlil and Ekur, not Ninurta and Ešumeša, that are mentioned in such contexts. Possibly Enlil's overall responsibility for the decision to abandon Agade prevents his inclusion here, where he is, instead, represented by his son, Ninurta.

70. See the comm. to l. 30.

72f. Cf. Angim 70 ní me-lám an-na an-šà-ta sag-gá-eš mu-un-rig$_7$-ga "Who (Ninurta), in heaven's midst, was presented with An's awesome radiance," and 124 me-lám an-gim dugud-da "radiance heavy as heaven." This association of an and me-lám, and the frequent descriptions of me-lám and other things reaching (ús) heaven,[25] support the reading of B, H_3, and S_3 against E, U_2, V_2, and Y_2, which read me-lám-(m)a-ni "his radiant aura," which, in any case, would make no sense here.

74f. For the various writings of /targul/ "mooring pole," see Lieberman, HSS 22 198f. The writing (giš)tár-GAG in H_3 and the Ur III exemplar is unique, and can be compared only to the Ur III PNN ur-(giš)tár-GAG (SL 115.38; UET 3 1297:1). dù here = *retû* "to drive in (a peg, nail or post), make fast," which probably refers to the firmness of the mooring pole itself, but which could refer to the function of the pole. Note STT 179:51f.:

> dgu-nu-ra targul gal-bi ḫu-mu-un-da
> dMIN *ina ter$_4$-ku[l-li]rabê lirtīšu*
> May Gunura pin him (the demon) down with her great mooring pole![26]

The opposite of dù = *retû,* is bu = *nasāḫu* "to tear out," likewise used of pegs, nails, posts, and mooring poles.

The references (Salonen Wasserfahrzeuge 112f.; Sjöberg, TCS 3 67) reveal the mooring pole as a metaphor for temples, cities and gods holding in place heaven, earth, or particular locations. Gods can wield mooring poles as well. Van Dijk, Syncrétisme 174f., would connect the image of a cosmic mooring pole to that of the cosmic tree and the conjuror's wand, but his thesis remains undeveloped. Whether the "holy" mooring pole of Agade was an actual symbol in the city, or the passage is entirely figurative, is uncertain. The meaning however is clear enough: Agade lost its cohesion.

For Enki and Abzu here, cf. EWO 10 [é-z]u maḫ abzu-ta si-ga DIM.GAL an ki-a "your lofty temple, set in the Abzu, mooring pole of heaven and earth," and the targul in EWO 168, mentioned in connection with Enki's emblem.[27] There is also the god ᵈDIM.GAL-abzu, known from Gudea and Pre-Sargonic Lagash (An Or 30 67). But the reason why *Enki* should pull out Agade's mooring pole is not clear, especially since he is already implicated in the abandonment in 71. It may have to do not with some special function of Enki, but rather with the attraction of Enki and Abzu ("the depths") to An and heaven in 72f., a contrasting pair which occurs also in Angim 69f.

77. See Chap. III. zi—til (cf. *napišta qatû*) "to end life" is the opposite of zi—túm "to save life" in the LSU examples quoted there. Cf. Wilcke Lugalbanda 1.408 zi aratta ᵏⁱ-ka engur-ra ḫé-ni-in-til "He will finish off that which is Aratta's life (like a fish) in the watery depths." For the simile of fish caught in the engur, see Heimpel Tierbilder 462, and for fish boiled alive in the engur, Kutscher, YNER 6 129. The suḫur^{ku_6} tur is discussed by Salonen Fischerei 220f. The prolongation of tur by -ra (preserved in C only) is unexpected; is ra here "to strike" (cf. Salonen Fischerei 270)?

78. Here igi—gál does not mean "to see," but is part of the description of Agade's anguished throes: raising the face or eyes (78), bending its neck down (79), then raising its head again (80), only to slide it back once more along the ground (81).

79. See Chap. III.

81. Preserved in C only, zé(r) is understood here as *neḫelṣû* "to slip, slide," a good description of reptilian locomotion.

82. The translation is only a guess, based on the assumption that Agade is the subject of the verb, as in the preceding lines.

83. Cf. LSU 17 nam-lugal-ka ki-tuš-bi kúr-ru-dè "in order to alienate the royal residence."

85. For the sequence é—erim$_3$, cf. 193ff., where èš is followed by erim$_3$.

J$_3$'s ság! is actually ÁŠ.GAN, suggesting that the scribe read erim$_3$-ma-áš, which would explain the erim$_3$ maš of Y$_2$.

86. Naramsin's dream is possibly alluded to in a Sumerian "proverb" that was used, in an Akkadian version, as the introduction to the *Assyrian Dream Book.* See Gordon, BiOr 17 129f. n. 57, and the forthcoming discussion by R. Falkowitz.

87. For this line in the Sumerian Sargon legend, in similar contexts, see Chap. III. Cf. ki lú-da nu-di "the secret/private place," discussed by Alster Dumuzi 121. The contrasting pair šà-ge—du$_{11}$ and eme—gar "to say to oneself" and "to say aloud, articulate," is discussed by Steible Rimsin 97f. A striking parallel can be found in a Mari letter, ARM 13 112 r. 5f. Kibridagan is reporting an ominous dream, in which a god warns against building a temple. The unfavorable dream was so upsetting that *ina ūmim ša šuttam šâti ittulu* [*ana*] *mamman ul iqbi* "on the day he saw that dream, he told no one about it."

This line is repeated after 93 by half the extant mss., because of the similarity of the verbs ending lines 86 and 93 (igi ba-ni-in-du$_8$-a and igi im-mi-in-du$_8$-a respectively). B$_4$ also inserts here 94f., the lines which follow this line when it reappears as 93a.

88. nam-é-kur-ra-šè refers back to the inim é-kur-ra of 57 (see the comm. thereto). For the second half of the line, see Chap. III. Michalowski, Essays Finkelstein 156, interprets both the Amarsin passage and this line as an attempt to pacify the gods. In both cases, it is more a sign of despair, and, perhaps, an attempt to elicit pity.

89f. See Civil, RA 61 64ff. Covering his chariot and uncovering his boat render both unfit for service. For [gi]kid-má-šà-ga and [gi]kid-má-šú-a in other than nautical contexts, see Civil, op. cit. 68.

For si-ig with ablative "to remove, tear/bring down," see lines 122 and 153; TCS 3 45:487 un-e zag-šè mu-na-ra-si-ig "The people have stepped aside for him"; AOAT 25 89:124 [giš]apin kù-zu . . . [giš]dal-ta um-ta-si-ig "Once you have taken down your sacred plow . . . from the beam"; Alster Dumuzi 58:56 an-za-am kù . . . [giš]kak-ta ba-ra-an-si-ig "The pure cup . . . was taken down from the peg."

Is bar-ra in Y_2 a misreading of šú-a, or, since Y_2 here has the verb si of the following line, is it a verbal prefix bar-ra-si, for ba-ra-an-si?

92f. See Chap. III. For šu sag-gá du_{11}-ga = *izbu* "anomaly," *uzzubu* "anomalous," see Sjöberg, JCS 25 136f.

93a. See the comm. to 87.

94-97. For parallels in other compositions, see Chap. III. In the commentary to 55ff., it is asserted that the temple for which divination is being performed is not the Ekur, but a temple for Inanna in Agade. As the abandonment of Agade by her goddess was a necessary preliminary to the destruction of the city (see the city-lament parallels cited in Chap. III), so the attempt to gain a favorable oracle for building her a temple from Enlil, who originally ordered Inanna's departure, can be seen as an attempt to encourage her return and thus avoid the city's preordained destruction. The alternative possibility, that Naramsin wants to rebuild Ekur itself, is less probable in terms of the abandonment-destruction pattern which has been used here to interpret the composition.

Sumerian divination in general, and máš šu—gíd in particular, are discussed by Falkenstein, RAI 14 46ff. For repeated divination in archaic Sumerian texts, see Alster, JCS 28 115.

The edition assumes a nonfinite verbal form here, with a variant tradition ši-gíd-dè, possibly from šu ì-gíd-dè (with Falkenstein), or vowel assimilation The strength of the variant tradition is problematic, because the form is unique, and both of the possible explanations offered would be probable explanations of a single idiosyncratic reading, but are unsatisfying when the reading is represented in so many mss.

98f. See Chap. III. The translation follows Falkenstein's reference to ì-sì-ga = *epištum,* but "in his rejection" may be equally possible. The Ur III ms., which skips 99, is perhaps to be translated "As if he could change his treatment." Despite the absence of an expected -lá after [d]en-líl in 99, it must be Enlil's pronouncement, not Naramsin's that is the object of kúr; cf. the parallels cited in Chap. III. This pronouncement is the inim é-kur-ra of 56, reinforced by the negative omens of the preceding lines. The form ba-en-dè-kúr may be from an original *ba-an-da-e-kúr, with -an- > -en- on the analogy of second person forms (nam-) ba-e-dè-$\sqrt{}$ (See Gragg, AOATS 5 45f.).

These two lines introduce Naramsin's actions in the following section of the composition as an attempt to force Enlil to change his refusal of permission to build a temple in Agade.

100f. Samsu-iluna D ii 22f. (RA 63 42) un ság-du_{11}-ga-bi gú-ba nam-mu-un-ne-gar-ra = [*nišīšunu saphātim*] *upahhiruma* "who gathered together their dispersed peoples" suggests that Gragg, AOATS 5 65 is correct translating l. 100 "What he had collected, he scattered." But what was it that he collected? Building materials, perhaps, or construction workers, as opposed to the soldiers mustered in 101; but one expects that the personnel would be pretty much the same for both public works and military expeditions.

Four mss. have read an otherwise unattested zi gú—gar in 101, for the expected zi-ga—gar known already from archaic Sumerian (Alster, JCS 28 124). This conflation of zi-ga—gar and gú—gar is due to the presence of gú-gar in the preceding line. However, note the Ur III version zi-KA—gar, for which the reading zi gù—gar seems more probable than zi-ga_{14}—gar. Similarly, zi-KA ba-ni-gar in Lugalbanda-Ḫurrum 23 (Wilcke Lugalbanda 196) seems unlikely to be read zi-ga_{14} etc., because zi-*ga* occurs, written normally, four times in the very same passage.

102-5. See Reiner, JAOS 88 186ff. For the kisal-maḫ as the site of athletic events, see Castellino Shulgi 291. The translation of šu-kéš—ak is only a guess; cf. the remarks of Durand. For the Ur III writing $lirum_3$ (KIB) for OB lirum (ŠU.KAL), note the following passages from Shulgi C:[28]

130. gešpu$_2$ lirum$_3$-ma [ ]-me-èn
131. kisal-maḫ-a ki-mè-gim ⌈a⌉-[ba?b]a?-ni-gi$_4$
In wrestling and athletics I am . . . ,
In the great courtyard, as on the battlefield, *who can oppose me*?
138. lirum$_3$-ta ù-su-tuk ì-me-nam
139. gešpu$_2$ ⌈x⌉-ta á-gál ì-me-nam
I am the one who is strongest at athletics,
I am the one who is most skilled in wrestling

The expression in 105 has been treated at length by Reiner, loc. cit., and further discussed by Durand. However the number 30 originally may have come to have been used, in this line, in the parallel LSU 244 (see Chap. III), and in GEN 137 ninnu-àm eše-gín ba-ši-in-ak "He treated the 50 (*mana's*) as 30 shekels," the 30 shekels are being compared to things of immensely greater value (the Giguna and Ekishnugal) or weight (the 50 mana garment[29] of Gilgamesh).[30]

106f. For lú-la-ga see Sjöberg, JCS 25 134; AOAT 25 146:37 (Ḫendursaga), preceded, as here, by nita; Sollberger, AOAT 25 447 (Ur III). For lú-LUL-ga in Y_2, cf. Sjöberg, loc. cit. For uru-laḫ$_{4\text{-}6}$, see An Or 52 118. The use of ladders in burglaries is discussed by Alster Šuruppak 110. The variants of T_1 and Y_2 to 107 do not suggest that RI be read de$_5$, but rather are influenced by line 113 ^{urudu}ḫa-zi-in gal-gal ba-ši-in-dé-dé. Note the similar error of T_1 in 111.

111. For the variant DU for dé in I R S_1 cf. I's DU.DU for dé-dé in 113. R_1 and T_1 have erroneously substituted the verb form of 118, which, as here, is preceeded by gú ki-šè. (Note the similar error of T_1 in 107.) In 118, the same similarity caused T and V to use the verb of 111. Because of the erroneous verb substitution, T_1 actually skips from here to 119, but the remnant of either 115 or 117 on T_1's edge indicates that the omitted lines were inserted there when the scribe discovered his error.[31] Is the variant KA for gú in Y_2 to be read phonetically as gù, or was it meant to be KA (= kir$_4$?), as in KA ki—su-ub, KA ki-šè—te, etc.?

112. See Chap. III.

113. See Chap. III. For the variant in I, cf. 111.

114. See LSU 382 in Chap. III. Closer to our line is InEb 140 gír á-min-a-bi ù/u$_4$-sar ba-an-ak "She sharpened both edges of her dagger."[32] Other references are:

gír-ùr-ra ù[33]-sar-ak(-a)-me-en
I am the one who sharpens the dagger
(Lipitištar hymn; Römer Königshymnen 35:73 = Krecher, ZA 60 209)

$^{\text{na4}}$ú-ru-tum mi-tum-gim ù-sar ḫé-ak-ne (OB)
$^{\text{na4}}$ú-ru-tum [-g]im ù-s[ar ḫ]é-e[n-d]a-a[b-k]e$_4$-ne =

$^{\text{na4}}$*ú-ru-*[*tum ki*]*-m*[*a m*]*i-i*[*ṭ-ṭ*]*i l*[*i-i*]*z-q*[*u-t*]*u-*[*k*]*a* (late)
O u.-stone, may they make you pointed like a mace!
(Lugale 579 = XIII 24)

^{d}nin-in-si-na-ke$_4$ gír-gag-e ù-sar im-ma-ak-e
Nininsina sharpens the scalpel (SRT 6:11; Römer, AOAT 1 284)

The Akkadian translation in the Lugale reference would seem to support Sjöberg's translation "sharpen" for ù/u$_4$-sar (Or 35 293; 37 233), but the tablet is so damaged that Van Dijk's restorations must be considered conjectural. This same reference seems also to lend support to Wilcke Lugalbanda 192 w.n. 471, who translates "to swing in an arc," from u$_4$-SAR = "crescent," since a pointed or sharpened stone mace is difficult to imagine.[34] However, it should be noted that except for *Curse of Agade* mss., most OB sources write *ù*-sar, not *u$_4$*-sar, and the Ur III ms. S$_3$ of *Curse of Agade* writes *ù*-sa-ar. In the Ur III period and earlier, u$_4$-SAR, when it means "crescent, new moon" is always written with u$_4$, as it is in unambiguous OB references, and I know of no writings sa-ar. Indeed, if u$_4$-SAR is to be read u$_4$-sakar (Civil, RA 60 92), then sa-ar would be unexpected.

For these reasons, Sjöberg's connection of ù/u$_4$-sar with the late bil. equations of sar with *zaqtu* "pointed, sharp" can be tentatively accepted and perhaps strengthened. The equation is made[35] in reference to a barbed whip, horns[36] and a dagger.[37] This last, Akk. *paṭru* = Sum. gír, occurs in the In Eb citation above, and varieties of gír occur in the Lipitištar and Nininsina passages.[38] In the *Instructions of Shuruppak* 159, the listener is warned against hiring prostitutes, which is ka u$_4$-sar-ra-kam.[39] In the Abu Salabikh version ii 3, it appears as ka *ù*-sar-ra-kam$_4$,[40] indicating that this is the same ù/u$_4$-sar under discussion here, and not u$_4$-SAR "crescent." What is "the mouth of a sharp thing"?[41] Sjöberg, TCS 3 75 w.n. 38, discusses ka gír-kin = Akk. *pî patrim zaqtim* "mouth(edge?) of a sharp dagger," which occurs together with ka nir-da "mouth of punishment," ka garaš$_2$ "mouth of catastrophe," and (ka) nam-tag "(mouth of) sin," and is used to characterize the awesomeness of a holy place, or some danger from which a deity saves a human.[42] ka gír-kin clearly indicates a dangerous place or situation, and this is probably the implication of ka ù/u$_4$-sar-ra as well. [See now simply *Materiali Epigrafici di Ebla* 4 322: 1135 ù-sar—ak = *śa'ālum* (> *šêlum*) "to sharpen."]

In the Old Babylonian period, then, there is an orthographic overlap of ù-sar/sa-ar, "sharp, to sharpen," and u$_4$-SAR "crescent," probably due to the dropping of the intervocalic /k/ in u$_4$-sakar (SAR),[43] resulting in the occasional writing of ù-sar as u$_4$-sar, but never the other way around, because of the close association of the UD sign with luminous phenomena.[44]

R$_3$ inserts 127f. here instead of 114, and S$_3$ inserts those lines here after 114. This is probably a secondary recensional development caused by the attraction of gí-dim in 128 to gí-dim in 115.

115. The phonetic variant orthographies *gi*-dim in this line and 128, where KID-dim recurs, provide both the reading gí-dim and its identification with Akk. *gidimmu* "spade" (Salonen Agricultura 132). Note also the interesting writing EDEN in S$_3$ (Ur III) to 118. ^{urudu}gí-dim occurs in the OB forerunner to Hh XI (MSL 7 225:178), not far from ^{urudu}aga-silig (see 114 here), and in Ur III contexts[45] together with ^{urudu}ḫa-zi-in (see 113 and 117 here).

For úr "roots" said of a building, cf. LN 98, cited in Chap. III.

118f. Cf. LSU 54 cited in Chap. III. For the verbs of T and V in 118, see the comm. to 111.

122. See Chap. III. giš-ká-na has been discussed by Hallo and Van Dijk, YNER 3 76.

123f. The name of this gate of Ekur known also from other texts[46] is problematic. As Falkenstein remarked, how does one "cut" (ku_5) grain in a gate? Also, if actual harvesting was intended, then one would expect še-gur_{10} (-ku_5) rather than še-ku_5 (cf. Salonen Agricultura 415). Understanding ku_5 in the sense of "to divert (offerings)" (for which, see Durand, RA 70 134), the gate's name then suggests an unending supply of grain for the temple, and Naramsin's destructive activities have resulted in this supply being cut off or diverted. šu kalam-ma-ta is also difficult. Because of the context, some kind of deprivation must be meant, rather than instrumentality.[47] In the parallel distich 125f., destruction in the "Gate of Well-Being" leads to the destruction of well-being in the foreign lands. Here, then, diverting grain from the "Gate from Which Grain Is Never Diverted," should result in the diversion of grain from the land (Sumer). Thus, šu is taken in the sense of "control, authority, possession," as in šu-PN(-ak).[48]

125. See Chap. III.

126. This line cannot mean that "the foreign lands turned their friendship into hostility," or "friendship (for Agade) was alienated in the foreign lands," because line 38 shows that Agade's prosperity caused contentment in the foreign lands, and Naramsin's impious acts in Nippur are now bringing that happy state to an end. If the foreign lands were turning against Agade here, rather than being adversely affected by Agade's actions, then the "bitter cries" uttered in the foreign lands when the Guti ravage Babylonia (169) would make little sense.

127f. As in 112ff., tools are being manufactured to destroy the Ekur, in this case, to excavate in the Ekur precinct as if to make the water-filled depressions in riverside fields, in which fish have been trapped by the receding waters. a-eštub$^{(ku_6)}$ means here, and in many other texts, carp-filled waters, and not simply spring flood-waters; for bibliography see Cohen Enmerkar 150; Römer Königshymnen 257. Later in this composition, the absence of fish in the inundated a-gàr is used as one example of the land's barrenness after the Gutian invasions (l. 173). The carp-flood in agricultural tracts is also found in Lugale 359 a-eštub$^{(ku_6)}$ a-gàr-ra mi-ni-in-dé-dé "He (Ninurta) inundated the agricultural tracts with the carp-flood." For an instance of actual fishing activity in the flooded a-gàr, see AbB 2 62.

A minority of mss. here and in 173 read a-šà a-gàr, probably under the influence of the OB technical term a-šà a-gàr (CAD E 250). For $ugur_2$ (SIG_7) in the Ur III mss., cf. Steible Rimsin 114; Lieberman, HSS 22 No. 683; and Civil apud Steinkeller, JESHO 24 129 n. 49. Ms. D_4 skips from 127 to 173 because both lines deal with fish in the a-gàr.

Line 128 has close parallels in the Sumerian Sargon Legend:[49]

é-[sikil-l]a é nam-tar-ra-ka alan-gim kùš-kùš-a sì-bí-íb
Cast it in moulds?, as if for figurines, in the Esikil, the temple of destinies! (3N T296:34)
é-sikil-la é-nam-tar-ra-ka kùš-kùš-a si mu-un-sá*uš-ta-sí-iq*
He prepared moulds? in the Esikil, the temple of destinies (3N T296:36)
PN gal-simug . . . alan-gim kùš-kùš-a ba-da-ab-sì-ga-bi
After PN, the master smith . . . had cast it in moulds?, as if for figurines (3N T296:45)

See the discussion by Cooper and Heimpel, JAOS 103.1. Note that in the OB forerunner to Hh XI (MSL 7 225:177), ^{urudu}kùš-kùš-e-dím immediately precedes the tool being made here in l. 128, ^{urudu}gí-dim (for which, see the comm. to 115).

129f. See Chap. III and Wilcke, ZA 62 59. For itima, see the comm. to 209. Edzard, RAI 20, suggests that the ^{urudu}šen may be the divine bathtub; more likely, however, it is the vessel used to pour water over the body when bathing (Salonen Hausgeräte I 92f.; Van Dijk,

Studien Falkenstein 247), but Edzard's point about the penetration of the most intimate parts of the temple is well taken (bedroom in 129, bathroom in 130).

The reading un-e rather than kalam-e has been adopted, despite the variant kalam-ma-e in the generally faulty ms. Y_2. If kalam-e is the correct reading, then kalam "the land (of Sumer)" and uri$^{(ki)}$ "Akkad" could simply be a *per merismum* for "everybody," and the anti-Akkadian force of 130 would be considerably reduced (see Chap. I, and now Jacobsen, AfO 26 10 n. 36).

131. The *laḫama*-figures, guardians of the temple, go back to the water-monsters who served Enki in the *abzu* (Green Eridu 108f.), and are known in later Akk. texts to have been set up in gateways as apotropaic figures (CAD s.v. *laḫmu*). Because of the association of *laḫama*-figures with the dub-lá here, in l. 229, and in Gudea Cyl. A xxiv 26ff., dub-lá is better understood as "gateway," with Heimpel Tierbilder 323ff., rather than "foundation platform" (Sjöberg, TCS 3 57; AfO 24 38 n. 6). The meaning "gateway" also accords much better with the existence of multiple dub-lá for a single temple (Falkenstein, An Or 30 124 n. 3). See also Edzard, RAI 20 156f.

132f. For the association of sacrilege and burning, cf. CT 6 2 (between second and third horizontal rulings, on left) *ēntum asakka ištanarriq i*[*ṣabba*]*tušima iqallûši* "The en-priestess will repeatedly steal what is taboo; when they catch her, they shall burn her."[50] Of only three attestations of execution by fire in the Code of Hammurabi, one involves the case of clergywomen found in a tavern, a place of ill repute off-limits to such personnel (CH § 110).

136f. The theme of plundered metals and precious stones is found already in the Uru-'inimgina Lament (Sollberger Corpus Ukg 16) i 6f., ii 4f., etc., kù za-gìn-bi/ba-ta-kéš-kéš "He looted its silver and lapis." For the reading of kù-GI, see Civil, JCS 28 183f. The containers in these lines have been discussed most recently by Cohen Enmerkar 191 and Wilcke, ZA 68 229f. Since the mi-si-IŠ(-r) was used as a container for precious metals, the two lines in the *Instructions of Shuruppak* in which it occurs can be rendered as follows:

33. é na-an-ni-bùr-e-en mi-si-IŠ al nam-me
Do not break into a house! Do not demand the *strongbox!*

250. mi-si-IŠ-ra lag nam-ba-e-šub-bé-en . . .
Do not put a clod in a *strongbox!*

143. See Chap. III.

149. For ud te-eš du_{11}-ga, see LEr 1:5 and Green's comment thereto. Note that te-eš in this expression only rarely appears as téš. kalam téš-a gar-ra is very close to the Hammurabi epithet kalam téš-a sì-ke (ZA 54 51:4). Cf. also gù téš-a gar (CT 15 11:19; said of Sin).

151. Inanna's revenge, after her rape, is similarly introduced in *Inanna and Šukalletuda* 129f., 168f., etc.:

u_4-ba munus-e nam-gal_4-la-na-šè a-na im-gu-lu-u_8-a-bi
kù ^{d}inanna-ke_4 nam-gal_4-la-na-šè a-na im-ak-a-bi
Then, the woman, because of her vulva, what should she destroy (in revenge) for it?
Holy Inanna, because of her vulva, what should she do (in revenge) for it?

Likewise Shulgi avenging Sumer (Shulgi D 218f., 238f.):

lugal-me-èn šu uru-gá ga-àm-gi_4
níg ke-en-gi-ra ba-a-gu-la kur-ra ga-àm-mi-íb-gu-ul
. . .

[ur]-sag-e [š]u uru-na mu-gi$_4$
níg ke-en-gi-ra ba-a-gu-ul-la kur-ra ì-mi-in-gu-ul
I, the king, will avenge my city!
Whatever has been destroyed in Sumer, I will destroy in the foreign lands!

. . .

The hero avenged his city.
Whatever had been destroyed in Sumer, he destroyed in the foreign lands.

152. The location of gú-bí-(in)^{ki} in the Persian Gulf area rested only on its association with Magan, Meluḫḫa and Dilmun in one Gudea inscription, and the importation from there of *ḫalub*-wood, also imported from Magan, in another (bibliography in RGTC 1 62). Wilcke Kollationen 29 now suggests the Zagros area, because of this line.

153. The verb si-ig with ablative infix is usually used for removing objects from structures (lines 90 and 122 here) or stripping off clothes (TCS 3 139f.; MSL 13 216). Cf., perhaps, TCS 3 45:487 un-e zag-šè mu-na-ra-si-ig "the people stepped aside (?) for him." The translation "scour(?)" here is based on si-si-ig = *zukkû.*

154-57. See Chap. III, Excursus B.

155. For kéš-da "inhibitions", see Alster Shuruppak 79 and Alster Studies 140.

156. For dím-ma (= Akk. *ṭēmu*) paired with galga (and umuš), see Sjöberg, ZA 54 58; for its use in insults, see Sjöberg, JCS 24 110, which also treats the use of dogs and monkeys in insults. For the variants galga ur-*e,* cf. Michalowski Royal Correspondence, Letter 22:34 galga ur-re (2mss.).

158. The orthography -ú-ús occurs also in lines 42, 164, and 165 (note the var. ù-ús in ms. N of 164 and 165). There are always variant mss. that omit the plene writing, as is often the case when it occurs in other compositions (e.g., Wilcke Lugalbanda l. 251; *Emeš and Enten* 53 [AOATS 5 75]; In Eb 162).

159f. See the passages cited by Falkenstein, ZA 57 79; Wilcke Lugalbanda p. 167; Salonen Vögel 33.

162. See Chap. III.

162f. Note the sequence ra-gaba, lú-kin-gi$_4$-a attested in MSL 12 33f.:23ff. (OB Proto-LU) and 97: 131ff.

164f. See Chap. III. The LU citation there is preceded by two lines (265f.) which make it clear that the animals driven from their pens are metaphors for the city's people.[51] One variant ms. for LU 266 actually reads ùz-zi, similar to *Curse of Agade* 164, for the other mss.' u$_8$-zi.[52] The goats and cows here, then, are the people of Babylonia.

These lines are an inversion of the passage beginning in Gudea Statue F iii 16:

áb zi-da amar zi mu-ni-šár-šár
unu$_3$-bi bí-ús
u$_8$ zi-da sila$_4$ zi mu-ni-šár-šár
sipa-bi im-mi-ús
ùz zi-da máš zi mu-ni-šár-šár
sipa-bi im-mi-ús
anše AMA.GAN-a dùr kaš$_4$-bi šu im-ma-ba
na-gada-bi bí-ús
He provided special cows and special calves in large numbers,
And had their cowherds follow,

He provided special ewes and special lambs in large numbers,
And had their shepherds follow,
He provided special goats and special kids in large numbers,
And had their shepherds follow,
He presented female asses and swift male asses,
And had their herdsmen follow.

There, Gudea is *providing* livestock for the newly built temple of Gatumdug, and providing personnel to tend them. Here, the Guti are *dispersing* the flocks and husbandmen (metaphors for the people and officials) of Babylonia.

For the reading of ÁB.KU, see Bauer Wirtschaftsurkunden 100. The later reading utul and Akk. equivalent *utullum* must have been due to a blurring of distinctions between the cowherd (unu) and chief herdsman (/utul/).[53] For ra "to drive animals," see Sjöberg, ZA 64 162. For the orthography -ú-ús, see the comm. to 158.

166. giš-gú-ka is understood as "(one deserving) of the neck-stock," and translated as a synonym to lú-sa-gaz in the next line. giš-gú occurs together with giš-šu "handcuff" in *Dumuzi's Dream* 81f., *Ewe and Grain* 87f.,[54] TuM NF III 42 viii 20, and MSL 6 158: 249f. (Hh forerunner); and with ^{giš}és-ad "snare" in UET 6 11:15. The neck-stock underlies the idiom of gú-giš—gar "to submit" < "to put the wood(en stock) on one's neck." A ladderlike neck-stock constraining a series of prisoners is represented on a Sargonic stele fragment in the Iraq Museum.[55]

168. All well-preserved mss. show im-*ma,* the MA being easily distinguishable from the following BA. It is tempting to read the difficult LSU 293, cited by Wilcke Kollationen, ^{d}en-líl-le [ab]ul-la kalam$^{!?}$-ma ^{giš}ig im-ma bí-[ ]. The interpretation of the line was suggested by M. Civil, who refers to BWL 272: 11 ^{giš}al im zal-la$^{!}$-a gar-ra = *allum ša ina ṭiṭṭim na*[*dû*] "Hoe that is set in the mud," and to im-ma—zal "to spend time in the mud," in his forthcoming edition of *Hoe and Plow.* The image is of a wide-open, insecure city.

For gub meaning to remove a door, see Sjöberg, JCS 24 112 to 107:12, and Green, JCS 30 146. Note especially the following for this line:

abul-a-ba ^{giš}si-gar su$_{13}$-dè ^{giš}ig-bi bí-ib-gub-bé
"The bolt on its city-gate is removed, she dislodges its door" (In Eb 78)
abul-la-bé ^{giš}si-gar bí-in-du$_{8}$-du$_{8}$-uš ^{giš}ig-bi u$_{4}$-dè gub-bu
"They loose the bolt from its city-gate, the storm (?) dislodges the door" (LSU 407)
[abul-la-bé ^{giš}s]i-gar bí-in-ku$_{5}$ ^{giš}ig-bi u$_{4}$-dè im-ma-gub
"It cuts the bolt from its city-gate, the storm (?) dislodges its door, into the dirt" (LEr 2:4)
^{d}en-líl-le [ab]ul-la maḫ$^{?}$-ba ^{giš}ig im-ma bí[-ib-gub][56]
"Enlil dislodges the door of its lofty (?) city-gate into the dirt" (LSU 293)

169. See the curse in l. 227, and Green Eridu 313, for laments at or on city walls.

170. Note the contrast of uru šà and uru bar ("urban" and "rural") in *Instructions of Shuruppak* 264 (Alster Studies 137). The image is of a depopulated city, with enough vacant land for widespread planting of vegetable gardens.

172-74. See Chap. III, and the comm. to 127.

176-79. The prices here represent a gross inflation, typical of periods of economic chaos, whether caused by invasions or other factors[57] and closely associated with the famine described in the following lines.[58] For commodity prices and their fluctuation, see now H. Farber, JESHO 21 1ff.

181. For the Shulgi D parallel cited by Falkenstein, see Klein Shulgi D 72:211 and 123f.

183. With Wilcke Kollationen, šu—dúb = *napāsu* Gtn. For the hunger topos, see Chap. III and the study cited in n. 56.

184f. The ur here is a metaphor for the Gutians (cf. Chap. III, Excursus B, and l. 156), as well as a pun on ki-ùr.

186f. For téš—kú, see the comm. to 18. The translation assumes that the men here are not consuming one another from hunger, but are being consumed by the Gutian "dogs." The scenes of massacre in the following lines support this interpretation.

188f. See Chap. III. The juxtaposition of dub and dab_5 is found also in dub-dab_5—za, one of the onomatopoeic compound verbs with u/a alternation discussed by Civil, JCS 20 119ff., and these lines have been translated as if the verbs were chosen for their onomatopoeic effect, and not for any intrinsic semantic value. Parallelism requires that KA here be a bodily part, whether ka "mouth," kir_4 "nose," or zú "teeth." Compare with the last half of 199. EWO 440[59] dinanna sag sa̮har-re-eš ḫé-mu-e-dub sag numun-e-eš ḫé-mu-e-gar "Inanna, you pile up heads like dust, you sow heads like seed!" Cf. also Krecher Kultlyrik 61 viii 10 with late parallels cited on p. 206, where "black heads" (= Sumerians) are sown as seed.

The writing TU.TU for dab_5-dab_5 in Y_2 and K_4 probably originated in the erroneous reading of dab_5 as ku, which was then written ku_4 (TU). Despite their relative antiquity, the Ur III mss. (R_3 S_3 K_4) are full of demonstrable errors, and Y_2 is perhaps the most error-laden of the OB mss.

190-92. See Chap. III. The image is of piles of corpses, the good and the evil alike slain indiscriminately.[60] For 190, see Civil, JCS 28 76:25 a-a dmu-ul-líl sag zi sag lul-la šu-bal ba-ni-ib-ak "Father Enlil, the loyal ones are taken in trade for the traitors," and his remarks, ibid. 79f. Did K_4 omit 190 because the preceding line begins with a similar sign, or was this line a post-Ur III addition to the text, attracted by 192?

Lines 191f. are to be further compared with Krecher Kultlyrik 55 iii 1-3 = 59 vi 12-14:

mèš mèš-e an-ta àm-nú
an-eden-na uri_3 uri_3-na an-ta na-mu-un-DU
uri_3 mu-lu lul-la mu-lu zi-ra an-ta na-mu-un-DU
Young men lay upon young men,
Blood ran upon blood in the high plain,
The blood of liars ran upon the blood of honest men

See the comments of Krecher, ibid. 157ff.

For /urin/ "blood," usually written ŠEŠ = uri_3, see Krecher, loc. cit. The Ur III ms.'s ù-rí-in here raises the question of the possible reading uri_4 for BAD = blood, despite the OB lexical equation uš = BAD = *dāmu* (MSL 14 93 103:2). Cf. uri_3 in the LSU parallel cited in Chap. III and in the passage from Krecher Kultlyrik above. Note also that Ur III zi-ra in 192 conforms to these parallels.

194f. For the sequence èš—$erim_3$, cf. é—$erim_3$ in l. 85. Note Ur III "south to north" for OB "east to west."

196-206. These lines depict the survivors of the Gutian devastation performing a seven-day[61] lamentation ceremony in Nippur to pacify Enlil (cf. Durand p. 181). For the cultic setting of city-laments, see Green Eridu 310ff., and of the *balag*-laments, Krecher Kultlyrik 34ff. and M. Cohen, SANE 1/2 13ff. The classes of individuals participating in the laments (196-198, 202-206), with the exception of the gala, who officiates at the ceremony, all occur in a happier context near the poem's beginning (see Chap. IV). The gala (204) and gala-maḫ (198), have been treated extensively by Renger, ZA 59 187ff., and see also Gelb, St Or 46 65ff. The um-ma and ab-ba here do not refer to age groups only (as in 29f.), but must be compared to the um-ma and AB x AŠ.IGI who participated in lamentation rituals in the Pre-Sargonic period (Deimel AnOr 2 37; Sollberger Corpus Ukg. 4f. ix 34, 38). Lines 196-98 occur verbatim (u_4 and mu followed by -da, not -ta) in BM 120011:16-18 (Kramer, *From the Poetry of Sumer* 35), said of survivors of the Deluge.

The vars. gi_6-AN in mss. D, O, and G_3 in 199 may be related to the attested orthographies gi_6-a-na and gi_6-an-na for gi_6-ù-na (M. Cohen, JCS 28 85).

Despite the harp-shaped archaic form of the sign BALAG, balag in Sum. literary texts is a large drum; cf. Hartmann Musik 52ff., CAD s.v. *balaggu,* M. Cohen, SANE 1/2 31. The seven balags here bring to mind tigi imin-e discussed by Kilmer, PAPS 115 147f. Because balag imin-e here clearly refers to actual drums, perhaps tigi imin-e does also, and is not the musicological term proposed by Kilmer. The "base of heaven," or "horizon," is usually the resting place of astral bodies or storms. Here, in l. 200, the *balag*-drums are being likened to thunderstorms on the horizon,[62] but also, the comparison to placement on the horizon suggests a circular arrangement of the *balag*-drums. This is what must be envisaged in 201, where the other drums are said to be played "within" or "among" the *balags*. All of these drums are known to have been used in ritual lamentation (see Hartmann Musik).

The cries which are being uttered in 202-4 are typical of lamentations (see Chap. III). To the treatment of nu-gá-gá "did not restain, suppress" by Krecher Kultlyrik 35 n. 97, add the equation nu-un-gá-gá = *ul ikalla* in CAD s.v. *kalû,*[63] also in contexts of lamentation. One reference there, [ ] SÍG.ŠAB nu-un-ma-ma = [ ] *baqāmu ul ikalla,* was cited by Sjöberg, Or 39 93 as a parallel to l. 205. Apparent proof of the reading ḫamanzer for SÍG.ŠAB is offered by Wilcke, AfO 24 13. The male equivalent here to the young women's tearing of hair is gír-kin "sharp daggers."[64] In LEr 5:3ff. Damgalnuna reacts to Eridu's destruction by lamenting, during which šu min-a-n[a gír b]a-da-ra šu bí-in-du_8 . . . síg-ni $^{ú}numun_2$-bur-gim ì-zé-e "she held dagger and sword in her two hands . . . and tore out her hair like rushes." Do these weapons suggest some sort of self-mutilation or ritual combat as part of the lamentation ceremony? Note the *kurgarra*[65] with bloody daggers (gír) parading before Inanna in the *Iddindagan Sacred Marriage* 74ff.,[66] which may be connected with Inanna's statement that she is a paranymph wearing a "sharp dagger" (me-ri-kin = *paṭri zaqtu*) in the late bilingual SBH 56:58f.[67]

A less formal lament performed by the survivors of destroyed Nippur is found in LN 38ff.:

> $^{kuš}ub_5$ ^{kuš}á-lá mu-un-tuk-a-ri
> i-lu gig-ga-àm a-na-šè u_4 mi-ni-íb-zal
> balag-di sig_4-ba e-ne ba-dúr-ru-ne-eš
> kúš-a gar-ra-bi ír-šè ba-ab-bé-ne
> lú dam šub-ba dumu šub-ba-ne
> a uru_2 ḫul-a-mu šìr-re-eš ba-ab-bé-ne
> uru_2-bi è-a ki-tuš-bi kar-ra
> še-eb uru_2 zé-ba-šè im-ši-šìr-šìr-e-dè-eš
> The players of *ub* and *ala* instruments—
> Why do they spend their days in bitter wailing?
> The *balag*-performers who lived within its masonry . . . recite as laments,

The abandoned wives and children
Recite, chanting "Alas, my destroyed city!"
Those who left their city, fled their residence,
Chant for the masonry of the fine city.

207f. Enlil's ancestors are discussed by Civil, AfO 25 66f. The du_6-kù ("holy mound") here is either the du_6-kù in Nippur or its heavenly counterpart (cf. Sjöberg, TCS 3 50f. with bibl.; Green Eridu 209). The du_{10} kù "holy lap" is certainly a pun on du_6-kù "holy mound." The phrase is attested in Sjöberg Mondgott 14:28, and Sjöberg, JCS 29 6:3. In both instances, it occurs in descriptions of gods "growing up" ($peš_{(11)}$) on their fathers' laps, which is hardly the context here. Perhaps there is a play on the euphemistic use of du_{10} (and its Akk. counterpart *birku*) for sexual organs, since the du_6-kù is known as the fertile source of husbandry and agriculture in *Ewe and Grain.*[68]

209. See the close parallel from the *Eridu Lament* cited in Chap. III, and also, from the same composition (5:1f.) nam-bé-éš ^{d}en-ki lugal-abzu-ke_4/uru-ni uru kúr-gim bar-ta ba-da-gub gú ki-šè ba-an-lá "Because of this, Enki, king of Abzu, went outside his city, as if it were an enemy city, and lay down prostrate." References for itima are:

(1) nam-bé-éš itima!-a-ka ba-an-ku_4 šà ka-tab-ba ba-an-nú (ELA 390)[69]
(2) ^{d}nu-dím-[mud] ⸢itima⸣^{ma}(var. -a for ma)-ka ba-an-ku_4 šà ka-tab-ba ba-an-nú (*Ur-Nammu's Death* 12)[70]
(3) itima kù ki-tuš kù-ga-ni-a im-ma-da-an-nú (3N T296:3)[71]
(4) itima-ka ki-tuš kù-ga-ni-a ^{d}ur-^{d}za-ba_4-ba_4 mi-ni-ib-ḫu-luḫ (3N T296 r.24)
(5) itima-ka ki-tuš kù-ga-ni-a ní im-kár-kár-ka (ELA 442)[72]
(6) kur sig itima kù ki ní-te-en-te-en-zu (*Enlilsudra* 76)[73]
(7) itima[74] é u_4 nu-zu-ba un-e igi i-ni-in-bar (*Curse of Agade* 129)
(8) ⸢itima⸣ kù u_4 nu-zu-ba un-e igi ḫé-ni-in-bar (LEr 6:12)
(9) é-itima^{ma} kur-rá àm-gal/é u_4 nu-zu kur-ra àm-gal (*Ekur Hymn* 4f.)[75]
(10) itima[76] ki ḫuš šà-túm-ma ri-a (*Temple Hymns* 188)[77]
(11) èš é-an-na-ra $^{i-di}$itima kù-ga-na ba-ra-an-na-an-kéš . . . èš é-an-na-ra itima kù-ga-na sag-giš mu-un-rig_7-eš = *bīt Eanna ellu kiṣṣašu la iklūši . . . bit Eanna ellu kiṣṣašu ana šeriktu išrukši* (*Exaltation of Inanna* 3:75f.,79f.)[78]
(12) ki-nú-a itima ^{d}nammu-àm = *kiṣṣušu majālu ša Nammu* (CT 16 46:191f.)[79]

A meaning "bedchamber" is supported by the fact that one lies down there (1, 2, 3, this line), finds refreshment there (6), and that it is a dark place (7, 8, 9). The late bilingual incantation (12) actually calls the itima a bedroom (see also the comm. to 129, for the parallelism "bedroom-bathroom"). In references (8) and (11) the itima is a metaphor for the entire temple (synechdoche). The variant ama_5 (É x MÍ) for itima (É x MI) in Y_2 is also found in a variant to (9). The variant ka for kù in S raises the question of itima($^{ma/}$a)-ka in references 1, 2, 4, 5). Rather than assuming the var. in S to be a simple auditory error ka < kù, it is preferable, in view of (1, 2, 4, 5), to postulate a form /itimak/, which then greatly enhances the likelihood of kù > ka. The possibility that kù is an error for ka is ruled out by great frequency of -kù as a modifier of itima (3, 6, 8, 11). In any case, the interpretation of S. Cohen, AOAT 25 108f. n. 85, which assumes a hypothetical compound verb *ka—ku_4, must be rejected. But his interpretation of šà ka-tab-ba there as "fasting" is convincing.

210ff. For the analogue to the divine curse in the city-laments, see Chap. III.

210. The choice of this specific set of deities in this order remains mysterious. The assertions of Van Dijk, Syncrétisme 205, and Durand 181, that these are the gods of the Sumerian south are unconvincing. On the one hand, not all important southern cities are mentioned; on the other, several of the deities could be associated with northern cities as well. The line's ending is poorly preserved on all mss., as is the ending of l. 222, with the exception of Y_2. On the basis of what is preserved, it appears that there were two traditions for the line ending:

(1) dingir gal-gal-e-ne
(2) dingir ḫé-em-me-eš

Ms. S_1 seems to use (1) in 210, and (2) in 222; S uses (1) in both lines; and the frequently untrustworthy Y_2 uses (1) in 210, and seems to conflate (1) and (2) in 222. If more mss. were preserved for both lines, it might turn out that most used (1) or (2) consistently in both, but the evidence at present justifies reading (1) in 210 and (2) in 222.

211. For prayer accompanied by soothing libations of cool water, see Angim 190f., with An Or 52 p. 138.

213. For šu—lá "to pollute, desecrate, defile," see CAD s.v. *lu'û*. The variant šu-dù in K and S is influenced by the dù at line's end. For šu—dù "to slander, denounce," see Sjöberg, JCS 24 111.

214. The image of heads (or people) in wells is unique in descriptions of destruction. Cf. the OB letter defectively cited by Durand: *šumma aḫi purattim gulgullātim la umalli* "if I do not fill the Euphrates' bank with skulls" (AbB 2 88:11). Otherwise, there is only the legal topos of the foundling abandoned in a well (CAD s.v. *būrtu* A bil.).

215-18. For disruptions of friendships and family relations, cf., e.g., LU 232ff., LSU 12ff., LW 3:22, and below, 237ff.

220. Cf. LEr 4:15 $buru_5$ ^mušen^-gim ⌈á⌉-[búr-bi sar-sar-r]a ba-e-re_7-eš "They went like birds chased from their nooks."

221. The translation is based on ur_5-da—ak = *nuppuqu* "to harden, become constipated."

222. See the comm. to 210.

224. For the var. of Y_2, cf. l. 58.

225f. Edzard, WO 8 166 n. 16 suggests that the /e/ in the prefix chain ba-e- need not be second person, but can be an alternant of ba-ni-. If /e/ here *is* second person, the -e(n) suffix in the majority of mss. is inexplicable. The /a/ following ba-e- is explained as a glide by Gragg, AOATS 5 85. The final verb looks like ⌈àm⌉ in both S and F_3, but could also be ⌈a-ul_4⌉, thereby agreeing with I_4 and probably S_1.

227. See Chap. III, l. 169, and Green Eridu 313 for lamentation on walls. The reading sá for DI is confirmed by the plene writing DI-a in F_3. For sá with the comitative infix, see Gragg, AOATS 5 58.

229. See the comm. to 131.

231-36. For the phrase X DN-e nam-kud-rá ḫé-a in the second line of each couplet, cf. LSU 131 íd ^d^en-ki-ke_4 nam-kud-rá-gim "Like a river cursed by Enki"; LEr 1:25 uru an-né nam-kud-rá-gim "Like a city cursed by An"; and the two similar references cited by Green in her commentary thereto.

231. Abzu as a source of clay is discussed by Green Eridu 170ff. For this line, see p. 172 there.

236. For the orthography ildu$_3$ (NAGAR.BU) rather than ildu$_2$ (IGI.NAGAR.BU) in the DN, see Farber, WO 8 120 n. 7.

237f. Mss. S, F$_1$, Y$_2$, and F$_3$ all read gaz-gaz-*e* in 237 and šum-šum-*zu* in 238. Since the use of an identical suffix in the two lines would be the expected, this division must be original.

239. Cf. M. Lambert, RA 64 190.

243. The translation follows suggestions of Farber-Flügge Inanna 255, where, because of the use of the verb za-ḫa-am in her text I i 19 in a long series describing Inanna's make-up and self-adornment, she suggests that níg za-ḫa-am here is literally "shiney substance," i.e., a common but flashy mineral such as pyrite. C$_4$, first read by Wilcke, and possibly D$_2$ and G$_4$, confuse za-ḫa-am with the foodstuff zaḫan, perhaps reading níg as ninda.[80]

246. The ^{kuš}lu-úb was a sort of haversack carried by soldiers and workmen, and used especially for provisions (Civil, AOAT 25 91 w.n. 32) The athlete would use it for his gear. dag-si appears to be some sort of stand;[81] the most revealing reference is Hh 7 A 146 (MSL 6 96) ^{giš}dag-si ^{kuš}ummu$_3$ = (*dakšû*) *ša nādi* ". . . for a water skin."[82] In the *Keš Temple Hymn* 25 (TCS 3), the temple is likened to má-gur$_8$ kù-gim dag-si ri-a "a holy cargo ship, equipped with a . . ."[83]

247. For the *niskum*-ass, literally, "choice ass," see Heimpel Tierbilder 273ff., who thinks it could have referred to a horse, and Zarins, JCS 30 15, who suggests onager or onager-ass hybrid. Cf. Klein Shulgi 66:31 anše-ni-is-ku-gim . . . ^{d}en-líl ḫúl-le-me-èn "Like a *nisku*-ass . . . you bring joy to Enlil"; Castellino Shulgi 32:22f. anše-PIRIG (var. ni-is-kum)-gim . . . šà an-na-ke$_4$ húl-la ma-ab-túm "Like a *niskum*-ass . . . An's heart rejoiced because of me." The writing anše-PIRIG also occurs here in ms. S and probably C$_4$. Cf. OECT 4 152 viii 42 (proto-diri) anše-PIRIG = *nisqum*; MSL 8/1 88:254 (Hh forerunner) anše-PIRIG (immediately preceding anše-kur-ra "horse").

248. See Chap. III.

249. See Chap. III. The use of dumu-gi$_7$ here for the prosperous citizens of Agade proves that it cannot mean "Sumerian"; cf. the comm. to 55f. Unlike ú-sal-la nú "to rest contentedly," which developed from an image of animals in a pasture, ú-šim-e nú has the negative connotation of animals lying down rather than grazing. Both here and in LSU 313 (cited Chap. III), there is a contrast between "lying in the grass" and eating good food, supporting the late bil. translations of ú-šim(-e)—nú = *biriš nīl* "Lying hungry" (ref. pointed out by T. Jacobsen). For conflicting evidence on whether to read ú-šim or ^{ú}šim, cf. Falkenstein, ZA 55 46 n.136; Civil, JAOS 92 271.

Compare Lamentations 4:5 "Those who once fed on delicacies are destitute in the streets."[84]

250. For LAK 157-9, see Van Dijk, JCS 19 18ff. The sign has a broken final vertical (LAK 157-8) in X and L$_1$, and a solid vertical (LAK 159) in W$_1$ O$_2$ Y$_2$ D$_3$ $^{?}$E$_3$. For the translation lú-sag$_5$ "noble," cf. JCS 19 9:206ff. šu-nir gal kù-GI sag$_5$-gá ^{d}nanna lugal-a-ni-ir hu-mu-na-dím "He made a large standard of the finest gold for Nanna his lord"; uru sag$_5$ "capital," ^{giš}gu-za sag$_5$-gá "first-class throne" (cited by Van Dijk, loc. cit.).

253. ḪAR can be done to or with the nose (kir$_4$), voice (gù), eyes (i-bí, igi), lips (nundum), cheeks (te); cf. Sjöberg, TCS 3 84f.; Alster Dumuzi 101; Wilcke, ZA 68 232,[85] MSL 13 247 sec. 9:2′. Can zú "teeth" be added to these and so read here (and perhaps in the passage cited by Alster Shuruppak 111), or is the sense here, which must have to do with an attempt to eat the hinges, an extension of kir$_4$—ḪAR in the meaning "to sniff at"?

254. Cf. LSU 110 é-nam-ti-la šà ḫúl-la-ka-na ír-gig mu-un-še$_8$ "In his joyful 'House of Life' he wept bitterly."

255. The "evil one" is understood as one of the numerous demons whose favorite haunt is the silent open countryside. For ḫul and ḫul-gál modifying demons, see CAD s.v. *lemnu* bil.; for demons in the eden, ibid. Ṣ 145f.; for the silent eden, ibid. 141. The alternative of taking ki-si-ga as a phonetic writing for ki-sì-ga "funerary offering" was rejected because, of the many mss. preserved for the phrase here and in 263, none shows sì, and there is no instance in other compositions where ki-sì-ga is written with si. However, this line and 263 are certainly puns on the ki-sì-ga eden-na, literally, a "funerary ceremony in the 'plains.'"[86]

ki-si-ga occurs outside this composition in *Fish and Bird,* where it definitely means "quiet place" (cited by Van Dijk, Studien Falkenstein 242) and in UET 6 11:71 ki-si-ga mu-ni-in-dúb!?-eš, where it is probably for gi-sig-ga "reed hut."[87]

Triplication of verbal roots has been discussed by Yoshikawa, *Hiroshima University Studies,* Literature Department 32 225ff. He points out, in the English summary, that it occurs mainly with verbs of the reduplication group, verbs that, as here and in 263, would be reduplicated in any case in the *marû* conjugation. Looking at his examples, it is striking that three have to do, as here and in 263, with noise making,[88] and others recur where there is falling or beating. Perhaps the additional repetition is an attempt to represent reverberation.

Mss. L_1 and W_1 exchange this line with the similar 263.

256. For recent discussions of the (ki-/é-) us-ga, see Falkenstein, AnOr 30 142f.; Sjöberg, TCS 3 120f.; Steible Haja 44ff.; Green Eridu 205f. No one has yet adequately explained the seeming contradiction between the us-ga as a fattening pen for animals on the one hand, and a place frequented by linen-clad priests[89] performing purification ceremonies[90] on the other.

257. There is a figurative pun here between the image of a fox sweeping his tail over a city's ruins, and the word šu-luḫ-ḫa in the preceding line, which can refer to cleaning or sweeping (see Salonen Hausgeräte I 76).

259. Cf. LEr 4:5 ù-ku-ku ^{mušen}mušen šà sìg-ga-ke$_4$ IGI [ ], Green's comm. thereto, and add InEb 165 (Limet, Or 40 18) bar-bi-a mušen šà-sìg-ga-ke$_4$ gùd ki im-ma-ni-ús "On its outskirts, the bird of depression established a nest."

260. See the comm. to 24.

263. See the comm. to 255. For KA x ŠID/DÚB (BALAG)—gi$_4$-gi$_4$, see Farber-Flügge Inanna 250f.; Landsberger, JAOS 88 145.

264f. See Chap. III and cf. Utuḫegal's description of the effects of Gutian occupation: kaskal kalam-ma-ka/ke$_4$ ú gíd-da bí-in-mú "Long grass grew on the land's highways" (RA 9 111 ii 14f. // RA 10 99:3). Note the pun here on má gíd and ú gíd, and the alliteration in 265. The ú a-nir "mourning grass" in 265 and gi ír-ra "lamentation reeds" in 268 are part of an expanded repertory of pejorative floral designations found in LSU: ú a-nir (11), ú ḫul (38), gi sag-ḫul (50) gi ír-ra (361f.). Cf. also, e.g., ú lipiš-gig-ga in Alster Shuruppak 160.

267. For šeg$_9$-bar "mountain sheep," see AnOr 52 157f.[91] mul is probably for si-mul, referring to the animals' horns (see Heimpel Tierbilder 83ff.). The late equation mul = *bibbu* "wild sheep" derives from the use of ^{mul}udu-idim = *bibbu* as a general word for star or planet, and cannot be used here. For muš-GÍR, Durand cites VAS 17 10, a collection of incantations against muš-GÍR and scorpions (gír-tab), which has a summary line in which all the incantations are called "incantations against scorpions." He would thus see the muš-GÍR as a variety of gír-tab "scorpion." Heimpel Tierbilder 471 points out that the Lugalbanda passage in which the muš-GÍR kur-ra (as this line) smells blood and fat would be inappropriate to a scorpion. Also, snakes and scorpions are literally at opposite ends of Hh 14 (MSL 8/2),

and gír-tab is never modified by muš. The VAS 17 10 summary can be explained by the fact that only the first two incantations are against the muš-GÍR, and after writing 19 more against the scorpion, the scribe simply overlooked the muš-GÍR in his summary. The reading of GÍR is once more uncertain, now that NA_4.MUŠ.GÍR is no longer read **mušgarru,* but *muššaru* (CAD s.v.).

268f. See the comm. to 264f., and Chap. III. Note the pun on a-ga-dè and a du_{10}-ga dé.

272. u_4-dè-e-a remains difficult; the derivation from u_4-è (Falkenstein, Kramer, Durand) is followed here. Less likely suggestions are offered by Van Dijk, Syncrétisme 205 n. 1, and M. Cohen WO 8 33.

273-80. See the comm. to 264-271.

281. *Inanna and Ebih* has a similar, but slightly expanded, doxology: ebiḫ[ki] ḫul-a dumu gal [d]sin-na ki-sikil [d]inanna zà-mí. According to Van Dijk Syncrétisme 206, the doxology is praising the Sumerian Inanna who has defeated the Akkadian Ištar, and Wilcke, Voix de l'opposition 63f. sees the doxology as praising a reformed Akkadian Inanna, who has become pro-Sumerian by destroying Agade. For these interpretations, see Chap. I.

Notes

1. In order to keep the commentary as brief as possible, no attempt has been made to treat all lexemes comprehensively. This task can now be left to the Pennsylvania Sumerian Dictionary project. But certain words and phrases that have not yet been adequately treated are discussed at length, and full justification is given for all interpretations that would not be obvious to the specialist. For reasons of economy, material already present in the commentaries of Falkenstein and Durand is not repeated, nor are interpretations adopted from their work credited to them in every instance. Similarly, no attempt has been made to justify every departure from their interpretations, or those of other scholars, especially when such departures are based on new textual evidence. References to parallels in other texts provided in the introductory chapters are cross-referenced, but not repeated.

2. Cf. also LEr 6:4′ ke-e[n-gi-r]a i-bí ḫul ḫé-en-ši-bar gìr-bal-a ḫé-em-gul? "He (Enlil) looked disapprovingly at Sumer, and destroyed it overwhelmingly (?)"

3. Edzard, RAI 19 147f.

4. Grayson and Sollberger, RA 70 103ff. See Chap. II.

5. Hirsch, AfO 19 34, 37, 41, 44, 45, 50.

6. This despite the variant $esag_2$ for ama_5 noted by Krecher, ZA 60 202, in LU 130 urí[ki] ama_5 níg-diri-mu (spoken by Ningal). This should be compared to Hendursaga 256 ki-sikil-bi ama_5 níg-diri-ga dúr ki mu-un-gá-gá "That woman will make her home in an unusually large woman's quarters."

7. Cf. Maekawa, Mesopotamia 8/9, 77ff.

8. Alster Dumuzi p. 89 would translate lú bàn-da "skillful girl," based on bàn-da = *tašīmtu,* but in his passage lú bàn-da is parallel to um-ma "old woman," and a translation "young girl" presents no problem (translating "girl" because of the parallel "woman," as we translate dumu bàn-da here because of ama_5 "woman's quarters"). In the line from LW he cites there, lú bàn-da = "young boy," because it appears with ab-ba "old man."

9. See Cohen Enmerkar p. 193.

10. Uru bar(-ra) always means "suburb," contrasting with its frequent parallel uru šà(-ga) "inner city" (Krecher Kultlyrik 165). *wabartum* specifically means "foreign trading station" (outside the city walls), for which see Orlin, Assyrian Colonies 25; Larsen, Old Assyrian City-State 236. Cf. also l. 36 below.

11. var. gur-gur-.

12. var. -gi-gi.

13. The sign immediately before the gloss could be ki (collated).

14. Hinz, CAH I/2 648ff.

15. For a possible connection between this verb and the need for Enlil's permission to found the temple (see below), see the last paragraph of the comm. to 57.

16. Ferarra, St Po SM 2 5.

17. Compare uru ul here with Enlil's words in the Gudea passage just cited: uru-me-a níg-ul pa nam-è "Things eternal have appeared in our city" (for níg-ul pa-è, see AnOr 52 139 and 156).

18. Cf. Sollberger, RA 61 39ff.

19. Or is ki-gar to be connected with níg-ki-gar = iškinū ("additional payment"), No. Babylonian for níg-diri. The OIP passage would then mean "The one who makes things surpassing for the great gods."

20. My reading of V_2, read by Hallo, loc. cit., as ma-an-ù-um or ma-an-nin-um, is based on a new collation by Hallo himself.

21. Falkenstein, citing Güterbock, ZA 42 32 n. 1, and cf. Hallo, YNER 3 56.

22. E.g., Hallo, YNER 2 98; Jacobsen, AfO 26 11 and 14. The equation *mansû* = *šarru* cited by the latter is subsumed by both dictionaries under *massû* "leader."

23. The KAR 434 omen reads BÀ-*ut* MAN.SUM MAN *ša ki-ma*. . ., and the only reason to read the name man-sum there is the identification of that name with the line under discussion, an identification that is no longer necessary or even tenable.

24. See RLA s.v. Inthronisation.

25. Römer Königshymnen 223.

26. The verb in the variant duplicate CT 17 33:34f. is ḫu-mu-un-dar-r[e$^{?!}$] = *lil-ti-š*[*ú*] "May she split him."

27. Cf. Green Eridu 198.

28. Courtesy J. Klein (see now JCS 31 151 n. 10); cf. Castellino Shulgi 256 and 258.

29. For the ^{túg}íb-ba-RU there, cf. Krecher, ZA 63 214.

30. The 30-shekel garment also occurs in very difficult context in *Gilgamesh and Ḫuwawa* 86.

31. For the insertion of omitted lines, see Hallo, Essays Finklestein 101 ff.; An Or 52 118.

32. u_4-sar on Ni 4204 and 9910 (ISET 1 138 and 196). See Limet, Or 40 15.

33. TUM NF 4 13 ⌈ú$^{?}$⌉; 14 ⌈$u_4$$^{?}$⌉.

34. But cf. the metal mace with pointed knobs in E. Salonen Waffen pl. xxiv:2.

35. CAD Z 63.

36. Should the well-known si mú be read si sar?

37. Note that ^{d}Nin-sar is a gír-lá "knife bearer" and butcher (Deimel Pantheon s.v.).

38. Note Hh 12 69 (MSL 9 205) gír u_4-sar^{zabar} = (*paṭar*) [ ]. The missing word was restored [*askari*] by Landsberger, but perhaps the Akk. should read (*paṭru*) [*zaqtu*].

39. Alster Shuruppak 42.

40. Ibid. 11.

41. Cf. the *Dialogue of Pessimism* 52 (BWL 146) *sinništu paṭri parzilli šēlu* "Woman is a sharp iron dagger."

42. Sjöberg, loc. cit.; MSL 13 244:5′ff., 250f.:6ff.; CAD s.v. *karašû*. Of these, only ka garaš$_2$ = *pī karašîm* occurs in Akkadian contexts.

43. Falkenstein, *Das Sumerische* 29.

44. If the contraction sakar > sar actually occurred earlier than OB, or if both words (sakar and sar) are identical in meaning, one could etymologize u_4-SAR as "pointed luminous disc," i.e., "crescent, new moon."

45. Limet Métal 204 s.v. é-dim.

46. See Falkenstein, and Kutscher, YNER 6 110.

47. Falkenstein: "Mit der (Arbeits) kraft des Landes"; Gragg AOATS 5 48 "With the help of the people."

48. Cf. e.g. Falkenstein Gerichtsurkunden III s.v. šu.

49. See Chap. III.

50. Cf. Renger, ZA 58 131 n. 37.

51. Cf. Heimpel Tierbilder 14.5.

52. Cf. LU 67f. (Heimpel Tierbilder 14.6) for the city Ur compared to an ùz-zi.

53. Waetzoldt, RLA s.v. Hirte; cf. Butz, WZKM 65/66 49ff.

54. Alster Dumuzi 102f.

55. Strommenger, *5000 Years of the Art of Mesopotamia* 118; Moortgat, *The Art of Ancient Mesopotamia* 136; and cf. E. Gordon, Sumer 12 80ff.

56. Cited by Wilcke Kollationen; UET 6 130:4 collated by I. Finkel.

57. Cf. Stone, Bi Mes 7 267ff.

58. See Kienast, RLA s.v. Hungersnot.

59. Benito's line number; 439 in Kramer ed. See Wilcke Kollationen ad loc.

60. The interpretation of Durand, that 191 portrays homosexual liaisons, is highly unlikely. Reciprocal necrophilia is very difficult.

61. Either a standard expression for "many days," or reference to the actual duration of the ritual; cf. the seven-day Larsa ritual, in which gala and gala-maḫ are among the participating clergy, published by Kingsbury, HUCA 34 1ff.

62. Cf. Angim 74 ud-dam an-úr-ra dum-dam mu-ni-íb-za "He howled like a storm on the horizon."

63. Both Krecher and CAD were overlooked in YNER 6 79f., leading to serious misinterpretation and needless discussion.

64. The expression occurs elsewhere as a parallel to nir-da "punishment," garaš$_2$ "catastrophe," and nam-tag "sin" (see the comm. to 114).

65. Certainly homosexual, and possibly a eunuch, despite CAD s.v. *kurgarrû*. Cf. Bottéro, RLA 4 463ff. The association of the *kurgarra* with knives, music, and women's dress makes a comparison with the Galli of the Syrian goddess Atargatis inevitable. See *De Dea Syria* (SBL Texts and Translations 9) p. 55.

66. Römer Königshymnen 131 as corrected by Reisman, JCS 25 195.

67. See Greengus, JCS 20 70.

68. Pettinato, *Das altorientalische Menschenbild* 86ff.

69. The photo in Kramer, *Enmerkar and the Lord of Aratta* pl. 18 supports the emendation.

70. See S. Cohen, AOAT 25 109.

71. See Chap. III.

72. Given the parallel of example (4), S. Cohen's translation for this line must be changed to "he grew very afraid in the bedchamber, his holy abode."

73. SGL 1 15; Reisman Royal Hymns 50.

74. 7 mss.; 3 add ma; 1 adds UD.

75. RSO 32 96.

76. Var. ama$_5$.

77. TCS 3 28.

78. Ar Or 37 485.

79. See Green Eridu 188.

80. The evidence (see CAD s.v. *diktu, zaḫannu*) suggests that U.GA pronounced /zaḫan/ is Akk. *zaḫannu*, and pronounced /utu/ is *diktu*. The differentiation into U.GA.DUG$_4$ = zaḫan, and U.GA = utu$_2$ in Sb is probably secondary. All references, Sum. and Akk., listed under *diktu* in CAD suggest some sort of grain product; the *zaḫannu* soup or mash in MSL 11 89:101 is unhelpful in determining the nature of the substance. There is, however, no indication that either *diktu* or *zaḫannu* are dairy products (contra CAD).

81. CAD s.v. *dakšiu* translates "donkey saddle," arguing from the context of Hh 7A. But not all the items in the environment of lines 145f. there have to do with saddles or harnesses.

82. Cf. Salonen Hausgeräte I 175.

83. Gragg, TCS 3 168, reads ká for dag, according to the copy of his ms. A. The copies of C and S show dag, and collations of A BB and HH show ká in A and HH, dag in BB (K could not be located).

84. Hillers, *Lamentations* (The Anchor Bible).

85. Wilcke cites kir$_4$-ḪAR = *parāsu ša pilakki* "to pierce with a spindle." Did the equation derive originally from some notion of piercing the nose, or is it a late misinterpretation based on the association of KA.ḪAR and [giš]bala in the passage discussed there by Wilcke?

86. This is why the ceremony is performed for an ill or otherwise possessed, rather than a dead, person; cf. Van Dijk, Studien Falkenstein 240ff.; Hallo and Van Dijk, YNER 3 81ff; and now the comprehensive discussion of Tsukimoto, RAI 26 133ff.

87. See An Or 52 119.

88. Examples d (ši$_x$—gi$_4$-gi$_4$-gi$_4$), h (ki—ra-ra-ra; earthquake), i (ér-ra—zi-zi-zi).

89. LSU 455f., Steible Haja 5:9.

90. LSU 455f., LU 350, SGL 2 108:11.

91. Salonen Jagdtiere 260f. and St Or 43 3f. attempts unsuccessfully to support a definition "wild boar," based on a set of superficial phonetic and graphic similarities: The signs ŠUBUR and ŠAḪ, and the sounds šubur and šeg$_9$-bar/*šapparu*, šaḫ and šeg$_9$.

NOTE TO THE PLATES

Unless marked otherwise, photographs are laid out with a tablet's obverse above or to the left of the reverse.

I

C

II

D

N

G (CBS 7858) iii-iv

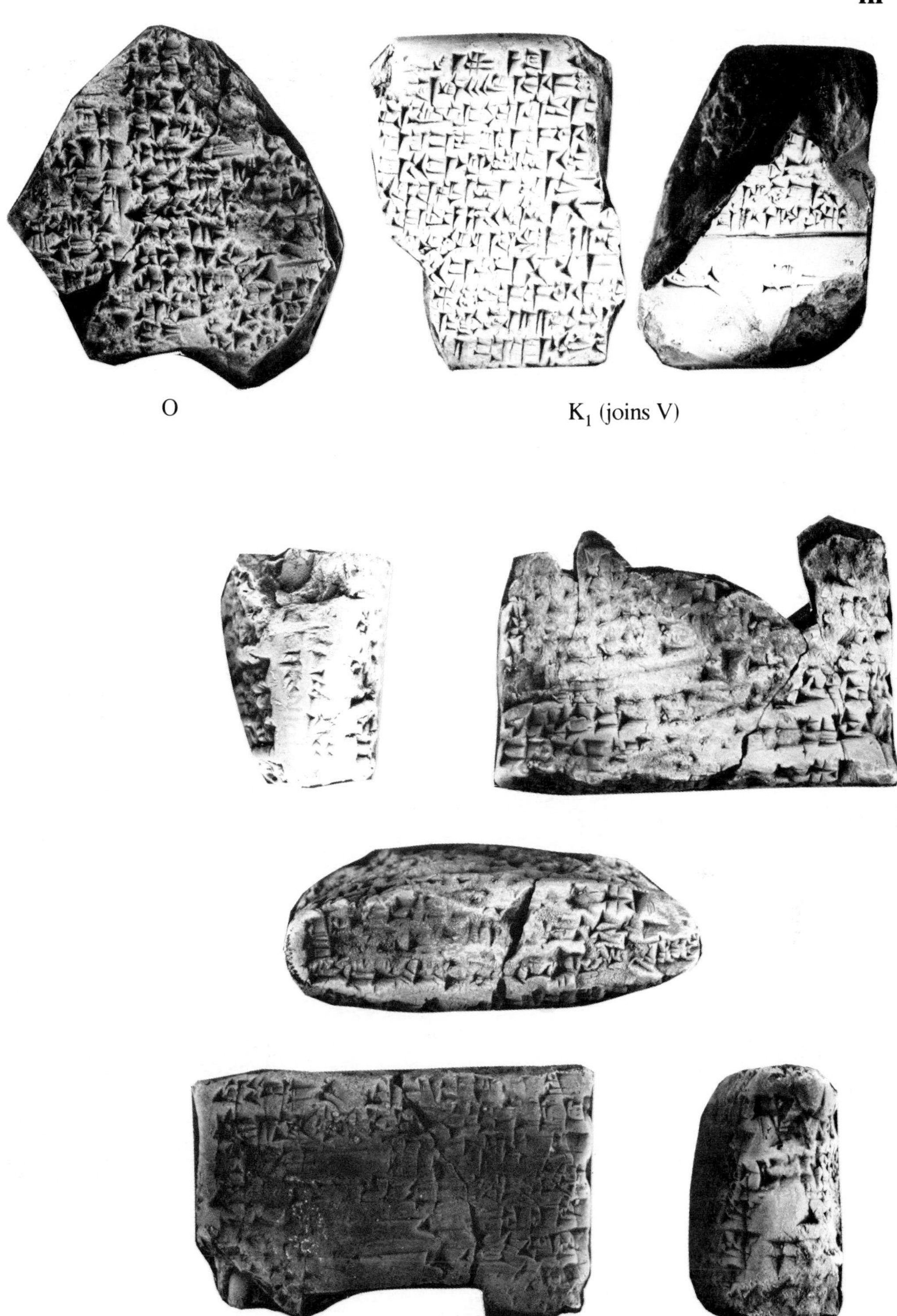

O

K$_1$ (joins V)

X

IV

Z (larger piece) (+) B_1

A_1

C_1 (rt.) + U_1

Y

D$_1$

F$_1$

E$_1$

G$_1$

VI

H_1

I_1

J_1

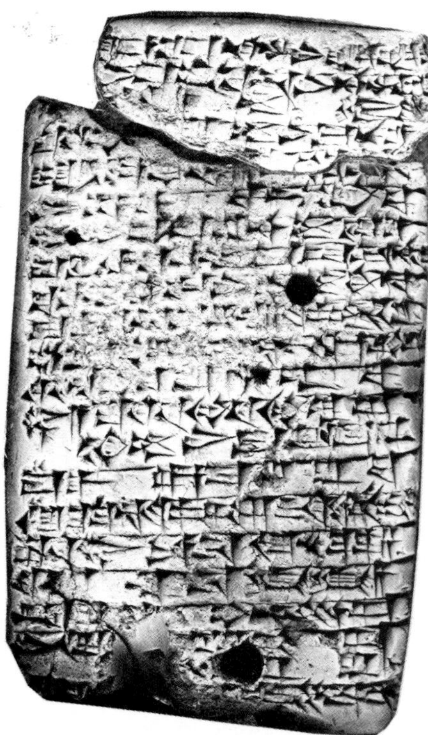

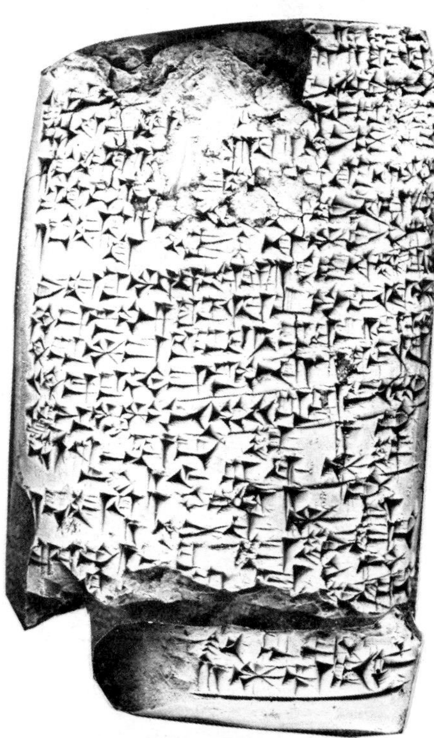

L_1 (smaller piece) + S_2

M_1

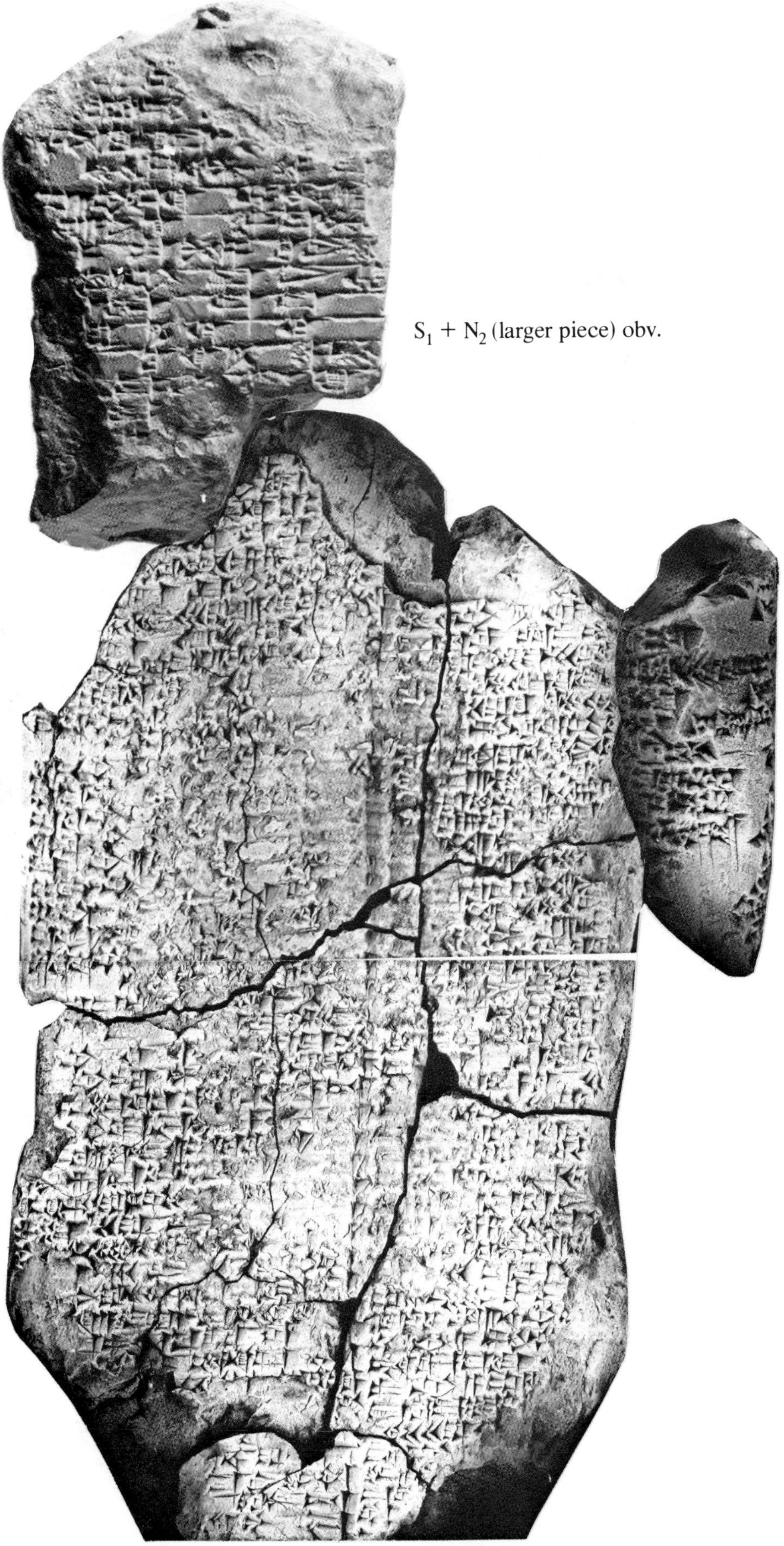

VII

$S_1 + N_2$ (larger piece) obv.

$S_1 + N_2$ rev.

X_1

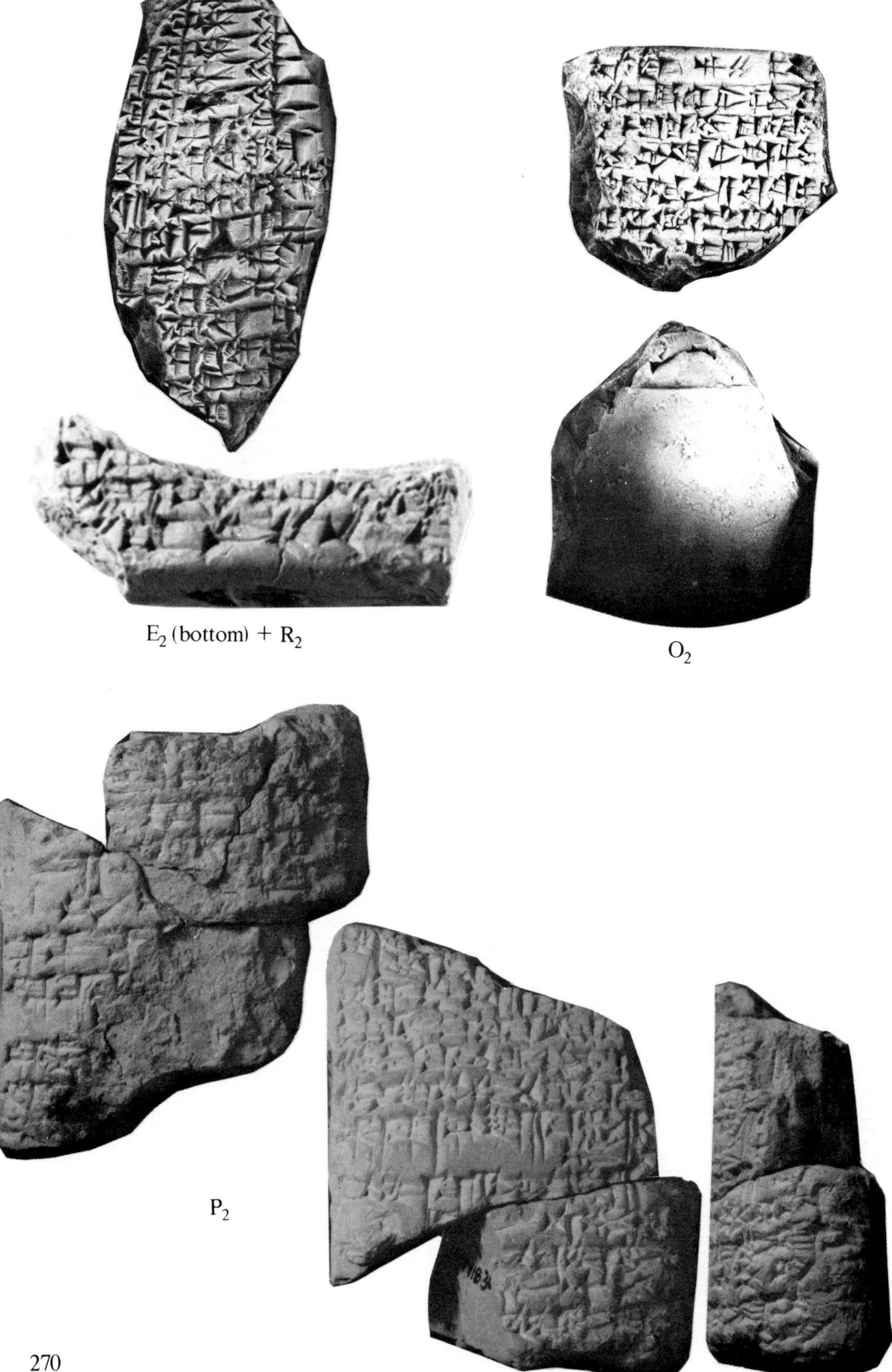

E_2 (bottom) + R_2

O_2

P_2

Q2

T2

V2

U_2 obv.

W_2

U_2 rev.

X_2

Y_2 + obv.

D_3

Y_2 + rev.

C_3

E3

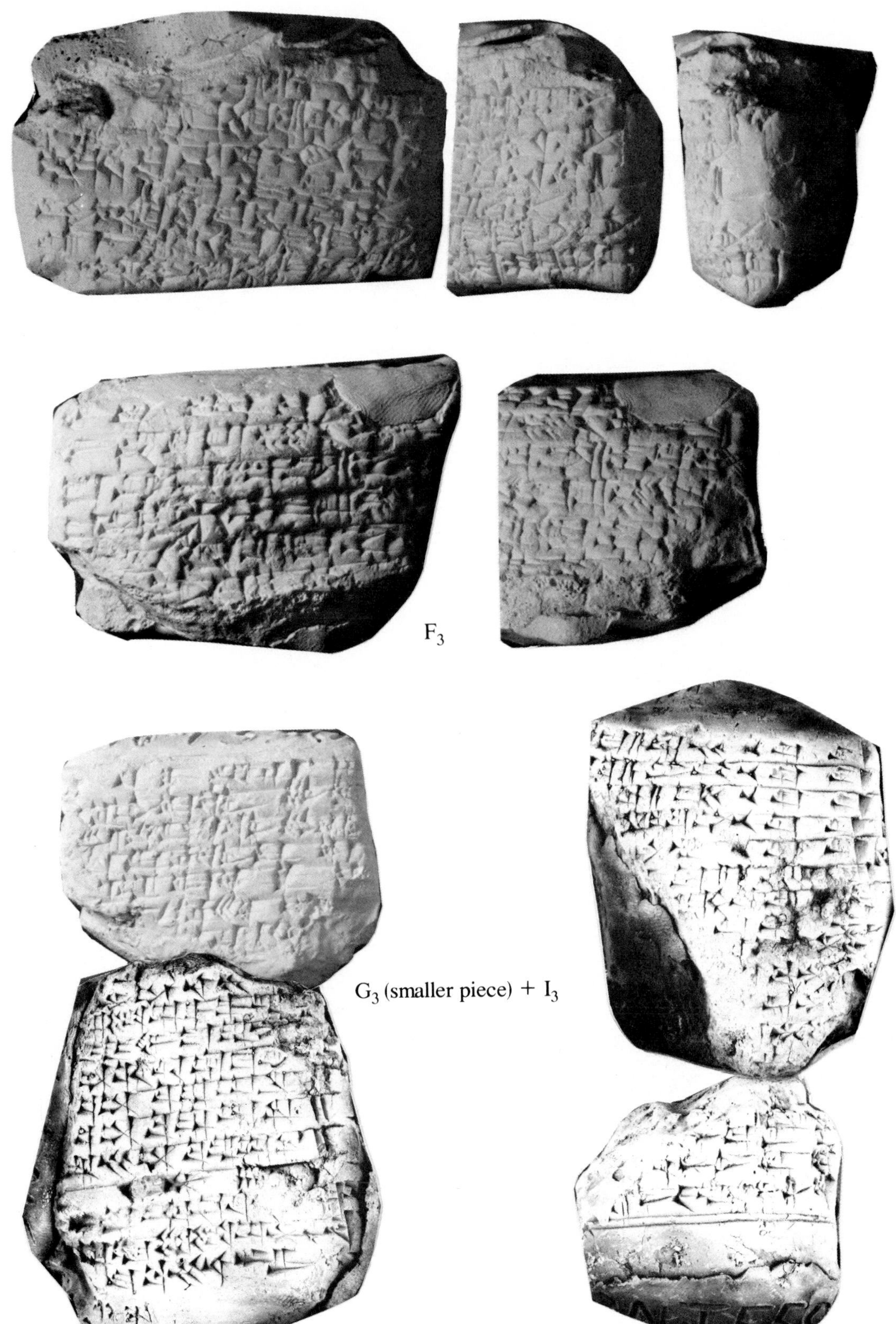

F$_3$

G$_3$ (smaller piece) + I$_3$

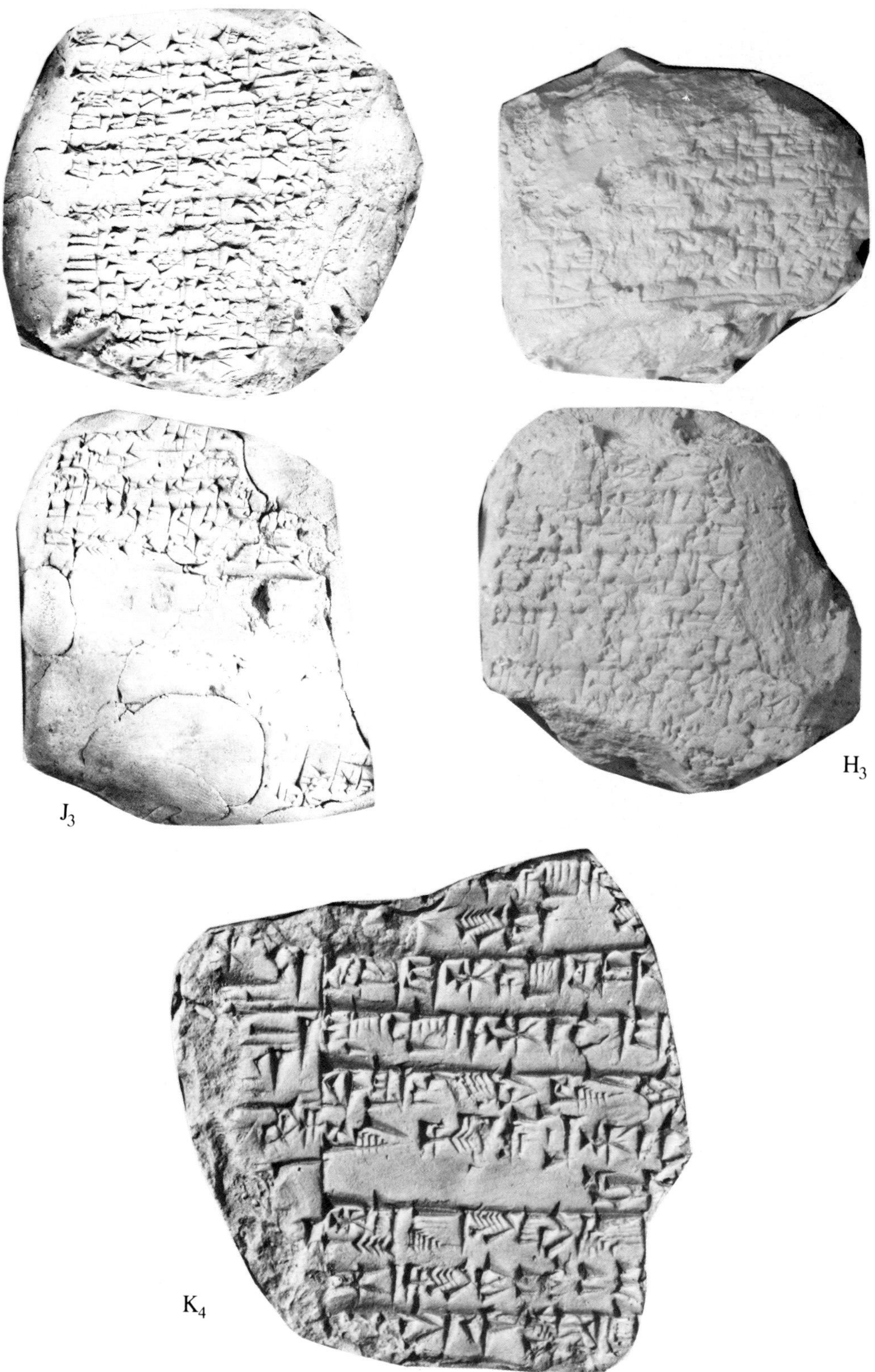

J3

H3

K4

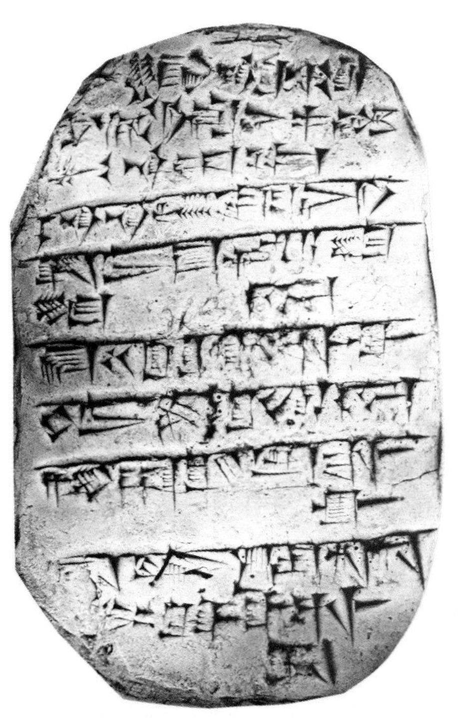

R_3

S_3

T_3

V_3

Y_3

A$_4$

W$_3$

U$_3$

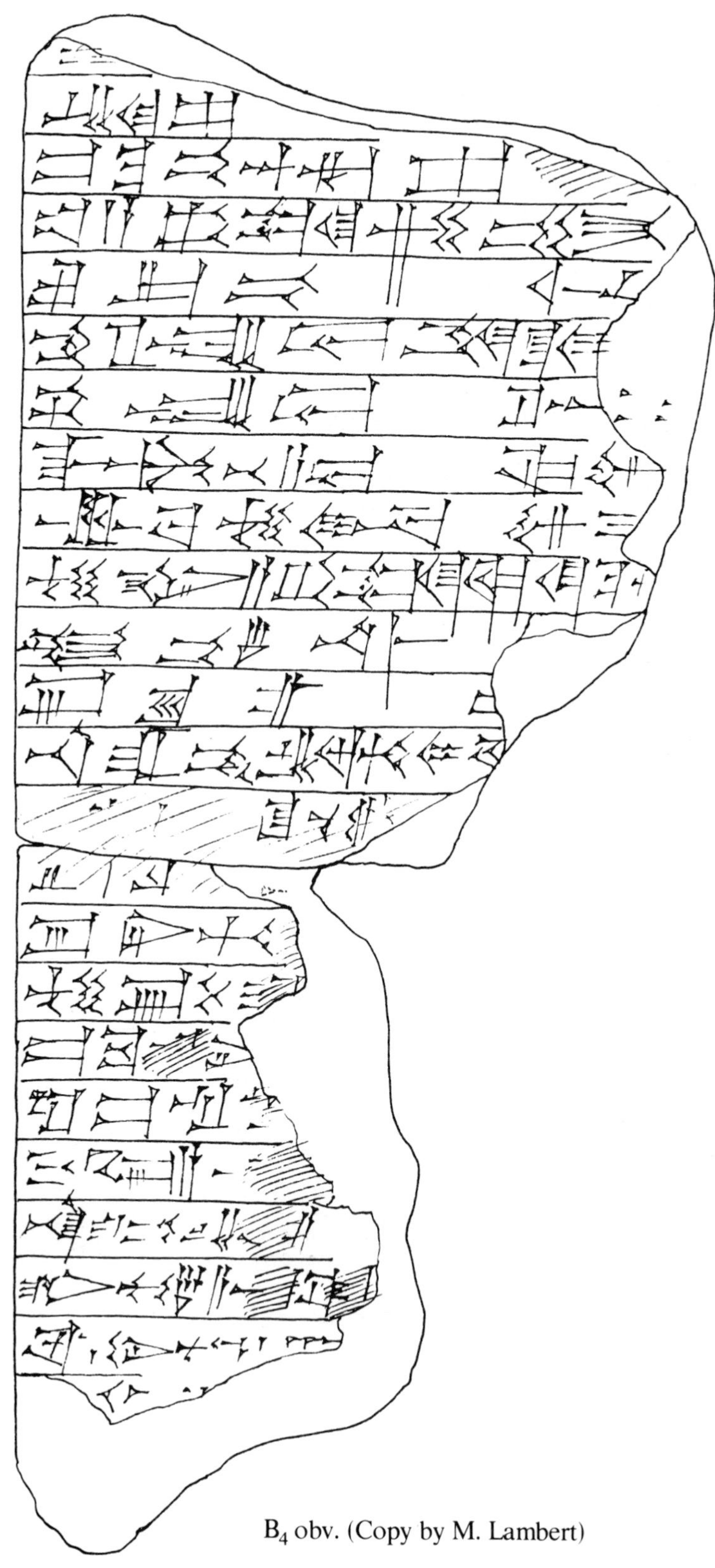

B_4 obv. (Copy by M. Lambert)

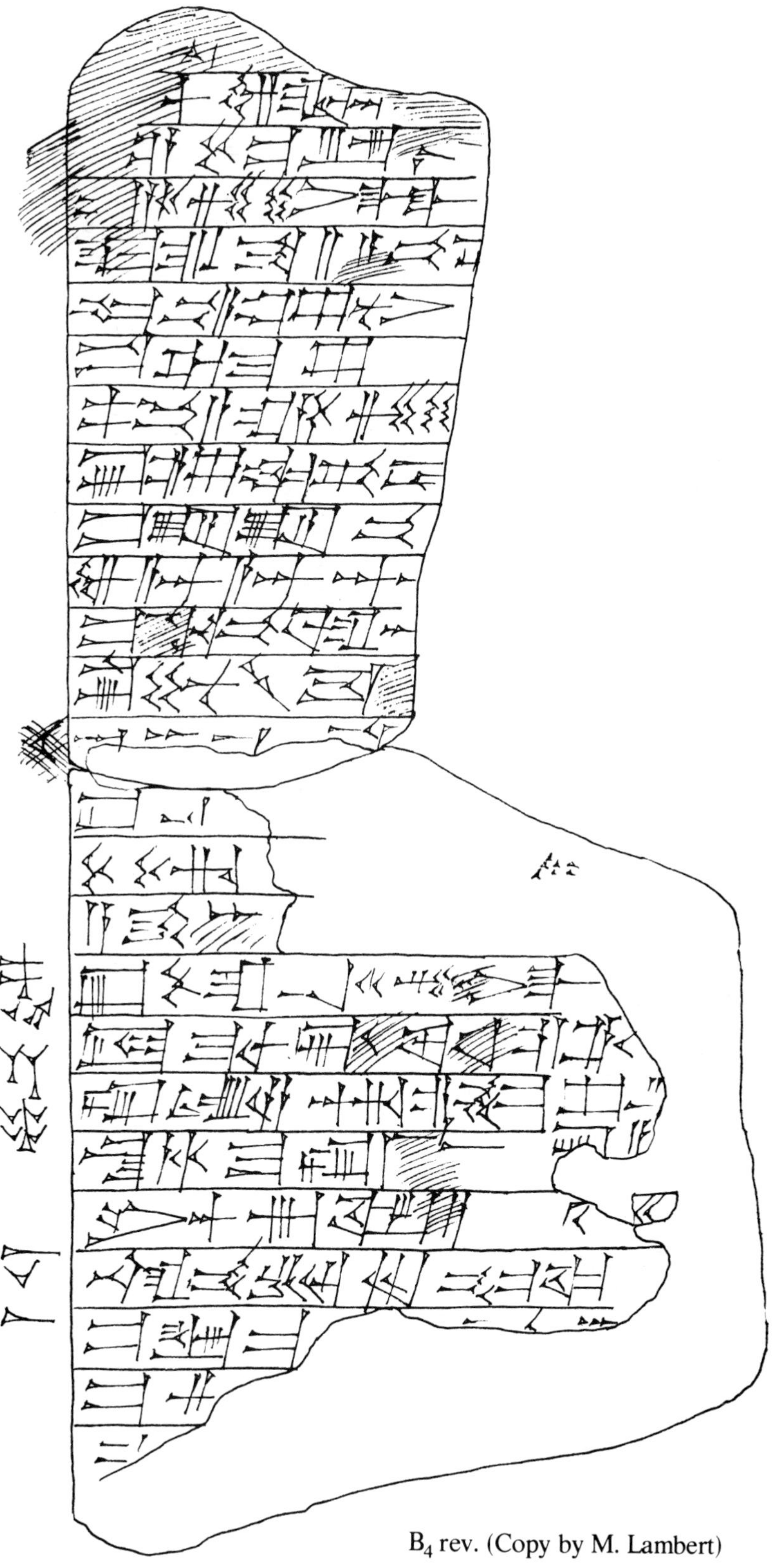

B_4 rev. (Copy by M. Lambert)

XXIV

E_4 F_4 G_4 I_4 J_4 L_4

INDEX OF SUMERIAN WORDS AND PROPER NAMES

Numbers refer to the line(s) in the text where each entry occurs (including variants). An asterisk indicates discussion in the commentary to that line or the citation of interesting references in Chap. III. Discussions of entries elsewhere in the volume are indicated by page numbers (preceded by p.*).*